Whillans's Tax Tables

Sixty-ninth edition

Edited by
Gina Antczak FCA CTA
Robert Wareham BSc (Econ) FCA

LexisNexis®
Tolley

Members of the LexisNexis Group worldwide

United Kingdom	LexisNexis UK, a Division of Reed Elsevier (UK) Ltd, Halsbury House, 35 Chancery Lane, LONDON, WC2A 1EL, and RSH, 1–3 Baxter's Place, Leith Walk, EDINBURGH EH1 3AF
Argentina	LexisNexis Argentina, BUENOS AIRES
Australia	LexisNexis Butterworths, CHATSWOOD, New South Wales
Austria	LexisNexis Verlag ARD Orac GmbH & Co KG, VIENNA
Canada	LexisNexis Butterworths, MARKHAM, Ontario
Chile	LexisNexis Chile Ltda, SANTIAGO DE CHILE
Czech Republic	Nakladatelství Orac sro, PRAGUE
France	Editions du Juris-Classeur SA, PARIS
Germany	LexisNexis Deutschland GmbH, FRANKFURT and MUNSTER
Hong Kong	LexisNexis Butterworths, HONG KONG
Hungary	HVG-Orac, BUDAPEST
India	LexisNexis Butterworths, NEW DELHI
Italy	Giuffrè Editore, MILAN
Malaysia	Malayan Law Journal Sdn Bhd, KUALA LUMPUR
New Zealand	LexisNexis Butterworths, WELLINGTON
Poland	Wydawnictwo Prawnicze LexisNexis, WARSAW
Singapore	LexisNexis Butterworths, SINGAPORE
South Africa	LexisNexis Butterworths, DURBAN
Switzerland	Stämpfli Verlag AG, BERNE
USA	LexisNexis, Dayton, OHIO

First published in 1948

© Reed Elsevier (UK) Ltd 2005

Published by LexisNexis Butterworths

A CIP Catalogue record for this book is available from the British Library.

ISBN 1 405 70741 0

Typeset by Phoenix Photosetting, Chatham, Kent
Printed and bound in Great Britain by Antony Rowe Ltd, Chippenham, Wiltshire

Visit LexisNexis Butterworths at www.lexisnexis.co.uk

Overseas

Average rates of exchange

Average for year ending	31.12.01	28.3.02	31.12.02	31.3.03	31.12.03	31.3.04
Algeria (Dinar)	110·1959	111·0258	119·1138	122·9761	125·8034	126·6578
Argentina (Peso)	1·4399	1·7986	4·7816	5·3381	4·8273	4·881
Australia ($A)	2·7864	2·7864	2·8049	2·7925	2·524	2·4488
Austria (Schilling)..........	22·134	1/4/0⁻–27/2/02 22·2856				
(Euro)		1/1/02–28/3/02 ⁻6264	1·5906	1·5573	1·4457	1·44
Bahrain (Dinar)	0·5433	0 5403	0·5671	0·5836	0·6154	0·6376
Bangladesh (Taka)........	80·4604	81·1787	86·7838	89·656	95·7319	99·4753
Barbados (BD$)	2·8675	2·8524	3·0091	3·0957	3·2483	3·3697
Belgium (Franc).............	64·8897	1/4/01–27/2/02 65·3356				
(Euro)		1/1/02–28/3/02 1·6264	⁻·5906	1·5573	1·4457	1·44
Bolivia (Boliviano)	9·5259	9·6567	10·8081	11·3623	12·5163	13·1051
Botswana (Pula)...........	8·5971	8·9924	9·4098	9·1141	8·0287	8·0961
Brazil (Real)	3·3991	3·5119	4·4345	4·9817	5·0623	4·9999
Brunei ($)	2·5864	2·5979	2·691	2·7364	2·8645	2·9419
Burma (Kyat)	9·6176	9·6342	9·8609	9·9464	10·1922	10·6399
Burundi (Franc)	1,184·7758	1,214·928	1,427·9542	1,541·758	1,739·2108	1,802·3
Canada (Can$)	2·23	2·2412	2·3585	2·3955	2·2881	2·2893
Cayman Islands (CI$)...	1·1805	1 1752	1·2372	1·272	1·3487	1·3987
Chile (Peso)	916·7394	945 912	1,039·465	1,095·468	1,125·31	1,102·876
China (Renminbi Yuan) ..	11·9157	11 8539	12·4779	12·8385	13·6132	14·0961
Colombia (Peso)	3,316·9487	3,307 4299	3,790·01	4,153·78	4,592·52	4,656·48
Congo Dem Rep (Zaire) (Congolese Franc).......	1/1/01–12/10/01 6·4914 19/10/01–31/12/01 458·7516	1/4/01–12/10/01 6·4617 19/10/01–28/3/02 466·494	525·7336	571·9449	702·3912	719·4719
Costa Rica (Colon)........	474·1405	481·⁻747	544·9313	574·9884	658·5835	699·2543
Cuba (Peso)..................	30·231	30·0972	31·6836	32·5763	34·5385	1/4/03–31/12/03 34·8824 1/1/04–31/3/04 1·8289
Cyprus (£)	0·9294	0·9347	0·9139	0·8945	0·8449	0·8467
Czech Republic (Koruna)	54·7895	53·8133	48·8242	47·7581	46·0249	46·464
Denmark (Krone)..........	11·9873	12·0585	11·8184	11·5705	10·7423	10·7070
Ecuador (Sucre)	1·4396	1·4322	1·5077	1·5513	1·6447	1·7031
Egypt (£)......................	5·8423	6·0799	6·9638	7·4503	9·5996	10·3236
El Salvador (Colon)	12·5911	12·5362	13·197	13·5688	14·3917	14·9044
Ethiopia (Birr)	12·0068	11·9931	12·6417	12·9708	13·9118	14·5257
European Union (Euro).	1·6085	1·6202	1·5906	1·5573	1·4457	1·44
Fiji (F$)........................	3·282	3·2756	3·2671	3·2512	3·0924	3·0813
Finland (Markka)...........	9·5635	1/4/01–27/2/02 9·6301				
(Euro)		1/1/02–28/3/02 1·6264	1·5906	1·5573	1·4457	1·44
France (Franc)	10·5516	1/4/01–27/2/02 10·6241				
(Euro)		1/1/02–28/3/02 1·6264	1·5906	1·5573	1·4457	1·44
French Cty/Africa (CFA franc)	1,058·6883	1,065·729	1,042·0842	1,017·883	947·6108	947·8783
French Pacific Is (CFP franc)	181·2759	182·5448	189·3468	184·3393	169·6251	169·7237
Gambia (Dalasi)	23·4964	24·2786	30·⁻816	33·5087	44·6984	48·429
Germany (Deutsche Mark)	3·1461	1/4/01–27/2/02 3·1677				
(Euro)		1/1/02–25/3/02 1·6264	1·5906	1·5573	1·4457	1·44
Ghana (Cedi)	10,522·25	10,566·23	12,006·85	12,669·67	14,076·0	14,825·84

3

Average rates of exchange — *continued*

Average for year ending	31.12.01	28.3.02	31.12.02	31.3.03	31.12.03	31.3.04
Greece (Drachma)	548·0827	1/4/01–27/2/02 551·8999				
(Euro)		1/1/02–28/3/02 1·6264	1·5906	1·5573	1·4457	1·44
Grenada/Wind. Isles (EC$)	3·8906	3·8596	4·0515	4·1764	4·3785	4·5399
Guyana (G$)	260·0487	258·6602	270·7951	278·0578	292·9325	303·5003
Honduras (Lempira)	22·288	22·4965	24·7993	25·8732	28·5611	29·9331
Hong Kong (HK$)	11·2318	11·1682	11·7178	12·4969	12·7301	13·1806
Hungary (Forint)	412·8118	406·5053	385·0885	376·5623	367·5425	372·2082
Iceland (Krona)	140·5823	145·2241	137·0658	132·2964	125·1424	125·943
India (Rupee)	67·9907	68·3407	73·0477	74·8503	76·1738	77·7583
Indonesia (Rupiah)	14,800·2838	14,876·8079	13,992·992	13,916·933	14,025·2	14,361·3
Iran (Rial)	2,520·331	2,507·895	5,888·04	8,472·51	13,411·2	14,059·8
Iraq (Dinar)	0·4473	0·4444	0·4679	0·4814	0·5082	1/4/03–20/2/04 0·5234 21/2/04–31/3/04 2187·62
Ireland (Rep. of) (Punt)		1/4/01–27/2/02 1·2669 1·2753				
(Euro)		1/1/02–28/3/02 1·6264	1·5906	1·5573	1·4457	1·44
Israel (Shekel)	6·0676	6·2059	7·1293	7·4159	7·4392	7·5603
Italy (Lira)	3,114·6298	1/4/01–27/2/02 3,136·0334				
(Euro)		1/1/02–28/3/02 1·6264	1·5906	1·5573	1·4457	1·44
Jamaica (J$)	65·8707	66·2455	72·6379	76·6837	93·5725	100·3891
Japan (Yen)	174·8889	179·0169	187·8315	188·3036	189·3354	190·9326
Jordan (Dinar)	1·0234	1·0174	1·0651	1·0964	1·1772	1·2188
Kenya (Shilling)	113·2002	112·628	118·4879	121·3613	124·3147	128·7432
Korea South (Won)	1,866·9225	1,869·044	1,875·2217	1,884·351	1,962·85	2,017·287
Kuwait (Dinar)	0·4418	0·4397	0·4569	0·4672	0·4875	0·5031
Laos (New Kip)	10,989·6667	10,941·25	11,466·425	11,789·48	12,582·15	13,154·55
Lebanon (£)	2,180·197	2,169·318	2,274·688	2,339·06	2,474·628	2,566·365
Libya (Dinar)	0·8506	1·1028	1·8923	1·9259	2·0808	2·1938
Luxembourg (Franc)	64·89	1/4/01–27/2/02 65·336				
(Euro)		1/1/02–28/3/02 1·6264	1·5906	1·5573	1·4457	1·44
Malawi (Kwacha)	104·1	100·0558	115·074	125·355	157·579	171·341
Malaysia (Ringgit)	5·4754	5·4464	5·7167	5·882	6·2175	6·4423
Malta (Lira)	0·6483	0·6498	0·6505	0·6451	0·616	0·6164
Mauritius (Rupee)	41·8852	42·4821	45·0819	45·412	45·8304	46·5149
Mexico (Peso)	13·4825	13·1936	14·5782	15·6552	17·6634	18·385
Morocco (Dirham)	16·3617	16·6136	16·5284	16·3463	15·6655	15·7817
Nepal (Rupee)	108·2814	108·8094	116·3692	119·1846	124·1903	126·7737
Netherlands (Guilder)	3·5408	1/4/01–27/2/02 3·5689				
(Euro)		1/1/02–28/3/02 1·6264	1·5906	1·5573	1·4457	1·44
N'nd Antilles (Guilder)	2·5625	2·5511	2·6856	2·7612	2·9276	3·036
New Zealand (NZ$)	3·4283	3·4237	3·2393	3·1306	2·8149	2·7677
Nicaragua (Gold Cordoba)	19·2644	19·5256	21·5082	22·4138	24·7196	25·9672
Nigeria (Naira)	165·943	165·6166	184·0362	194·3859	215·7939	226·7154
Norway (Krone)	12·8993	12·833	11·954	11·6072	11·5624	11·9099
Oman (Rial Omani)	0·561	0·5579	0·5792	0·596	0·63	0·6529
Pakistan (Rupee)	88·9265	88·6041	89·5939	91·3941	94·4568	97·6040
Papua New Guinea (Kina)	4·856	4·9971	5·9099	6·095	5·764	5·7436
Paraguay (Guarani)	5,922·722	6,318·8118	8,691·2127	9,756·686	10,568·0854	10,556·6188

4

Average for year ending	31.12.01	28 3.02	31.12.02	31.3.03	31.12.03	31.3.04
Peru (New Sol)	5·0538	5 0044	5·2931	5·4531	7·0487	7·2490
Philippines (Peso)	73·3236	73 7096	77·7051	81·0754	88·727	92·8336
Poland (Zloty)	5·8764	5 8728	6·1322	6·2282	6·0605	6·2744
Portugal (Escudo)	322·4898	1/4/01–27/2/02				
		324·7059				
		1/1/02–28/3/02				
(Euro)		1·6264	1·5906	1·5573	1·4457	1·44
Qatar (Riyal)	5·245	5·2156	5·4756	5·6355	5·9559	6·1714
Romania (Leu)	42,159·75	43,855·99	49,889·0667	51,638·82	54,460·65	56,162·18
Russia (Rouble–Market)	42·1512	42·763	47·4183	49·0329	50·3037	50·7326
Rwanda (R Franc)	611·8478	635·3418	708·029	748·4881	870·1093	922·732
Saudi Arabia (Riyal)	5·4034	5·3738	5·641	5·805	6·1359	6·3578
Seychelles (Rupee)	8·4104	8·0777	8·4761	8·7149	9·1568	9·4401
Sierra Leone (Leone)	2,786·703	2,878·362	3,094·516	3,173·768	3,794·318	4,046·3759
Singapore (S$)	2·5816	2·5972	2·6899	2·7354	2·8507	2·9295
Solomon Islands (SI$)	7·7128	7·9864	1C·4913	11·3636	12·3836	12·7742
Somali Republic						
(Schilling)	3,770·09	3,753 399	3,952·9042	4,064·276	4,309·0933	4,461·972
South Africa (Rand)	12·4064	13 661	15·7465	14·9793	12·3217	12·0949
Spain/Balearic Islands						
(Peseta)	267·6439	1/4/01–27/2/02				
		269·4832				
		1/1/02–28/3/02				
(Euro)		1·6264	1·5906	1·5573	1·4457	1·44
Sri Lanka (Rupee)	128·922	131·0694	143·9681	149·2486	157·8615	164·0631
Sudan (Dinar)	372·417	370·7689	390·3116	401·9422	428·0218	443·2834
Surinam (Guilder)	1/1/01–31/8/01	1/4/01–31/8/01				
	1,409·0588	1,400·426				
	1/9/01–31/12/01	1/9/01–28/3/02				
	3,150·1375	3,131·116	3,286·7917	3,467·533	4,090·3075	3,134·437
Swaziland (Lilangeli)	12·583	13·773	15·5637	14·788	11·3275	12·0136
Sweden (Krona)	14·8847	15·0502	14·5697	14·2735	13·1934	13·1427
Switzerland (Franc)	2·4295	2·4224	2·3336	2·2819	2·1973	2·2266
Syria (Pound)	74·5315	73·5174	74·7231	75·5653	77·6399	81·2087
Taiwan (New T$)	48·6974	49·3319	51·9757	53·3776	56·2877	57·7063
Tanzania (Schilling)	1,263·71	1,303·673	1,452·96	1,522·58	1,699·27	1,797·86
Thailand (Baht)	64·1079	63·9513	64·6788	66·2242	67·8966	68·7556
Tonga Islands (Pa 'Anga)	2·8083	2·7917	2·7637	2·7496	2·6096	2·84
Trinidad and Tobago						
(TT$)	8·8631	8·779	9·1895	9·4752	9·9007	10·2507
Tunisia (Dinar)	2·0695	2·0914	2·1331	2·1332	2·104	2·1393
Turkey (Lira)	1,778,556·77	1,966,915·2	2,287,542·21	2,464,005·116	2,456,924·17	2,405,776·37
Uganda (New Shilling)	2,530·906	2,509·444	2,704·318	2,840·852	3,210·6078	3,327·7742
United Arab Emirates						
(Dirham)	5·2927	5·2638	5·5247	5·6854	6·0083	6·2256
Uruguay						
(Peso Uruguayo)	19·1927	19·8333	32·3184	38·3931	114·6677	116·9099
USA (US$)	1·4401	1·432	1·5023	1·5466	1·6348	1·6939
Venezuela (Bolivar)	1,043·522	1,091·276	1,758·525	2,108·819	2,838·118	3,629·222
Vietnam (Dong)	21,329·6083	21,434·79	23,038·5083	23,813·17	25,528·0833	26,564·48
Yemen (Rial)	240·0541	243·6008	262·9526	272·0802	292·7023	306·0884
Zambia (Kwacha)	5,204·957	5,383·712	6,729·64	7,137·79	7,809·26	8,038·83
Zimbabwe (Dollar)	79·653	79·3536	83·4043	187·0132	1,141·414	2,499·284

Rates of exchange on year-end dates

	31.12.01	28.3.02	31.12.02	31.3.03	31.12.03	31.3.04
Australia ($A)	2·8432	2·6682	2·859	2·6157	2·376	2·4072
Austria (Schilling)	22·4919	27/2/02 22·5599				
(Euro)		28/3/02 1·6323	1·5342	1·4486	1·4192	1·4955
Belgium (Franc)	65·9375	27/2/02 66·1368				
(Euro)		28/3/02 1·6323	1·5342	1·4486	1·4192	1·4955
Canada (Can$)	2·3232	2·2719	2·5433	2·3251	2·3133	2·4154
Denmark (Krone)	12·1532	12·1341	11·3954	10·7573	10·5674	11·1342
European Union (Euro)	1·6346	1·6323	1·5342	1·4486	1·4192	1·4955
France (Franc)	10·7219	27/2/02 10·7544				
(Euro)		28/3/02 1·6323	1·5342	1·4486	1·4192	1·4955
Germany (Deutsche Mark)	3·1969	27/2/02 3·2066				
(Euro)		28/3/02 1·6323	1·5342	1·4486	1·4192	1·4955
Hong Kong (HK$)	11·349	11·1069	12·5546	12·3282	13·898	14·3188
Irish Republic (Punt)	1·2873	27/2/02 1·2912				
(Euro)		28/3/02 1·6323	1·5342	1·4486	1·4192	1·4955
Italy (Lira)	3,164·92	27/2/02 3,174·49				
(Euro)		28/3/02 1·6323	1·5342	1·4486	1·4192	1·4955
Japan (Yen)	190·745	188·73	191·047	187·433	191·85	191·201
Luxembourg (Franc)	65·9375	27/2/02 66·1368				
(Euro)		28/3/02 1·6323	1·5342	1·4486	1·4192	1·4955
Netherlands (Guilder)	3·6021	27/2/02 3·613				
(Euro)		28/3/02 1·6323	1·5342	1·4486	1·4192	1·4955
Norway (Krone)	13·0539	12·5763	11·153	11·4703	11·9095	12·6185
Portugal (Escudo)	327·697	27/2/02 328·688				
(Euro)		28/3/02 1·6323	1·5342	1·4486	1·4192	1·4955
South Africa (Rand)	17·4575	16·1838	13·8138	12·4413	11·9492	11·5831
Spain/Balearic Islands (Peseta)	271·966	27/2/02 272·788				
(Euro)		28/3/02 1·6323	1·5342	1·4486	1·4192	1·4955
Sweden (Krona)	15·2667	14·7501	14·0276	13·4023	12·8806	13·8598
Switzerland (Franc)	2·4164	2·3949	2·226	2·1362	2·214	2·3283
USA (US$)	1·4554	1·424	1·6099	1·5807	1·7901	1·8378

Note: The material on pages 3 to 6 is reproduced from information provided by the Inland Revenue and is Crown Copyright.

Double taxation agreements (including protocols and regulations)

Taxes on income and capital gains

Agreements terminated or superseded within the last six years are printed in italic. Amending protocols and exchanges of notes are printed in square brackets. Entry into force after 5.4.70 is indicated in the third column.

Country	SI/SR & O	Entry into force
Antigua & Barbuda	1947/2865	
	[1968/1096]	
Argentina	1997/1777	1.8.97
Armenia[2]	(1986/224	30.1.86)
Australia	1968/305	3.10.95
	[1980/707]	21.5.80
	2003/3199	17.12.03
Austria[1]	1970/1947	17.12.70
	[1979/117]	6.2.79
	[1994/768]	1.12.94
Azerbaijan	1995/762	3.10.95
Bahrain[9]	(talks 2003)	
Bangladesh	1980/708	8.7.80
Barbados	1970/952	26.6.70
	[1973/2096]	12.12.73
Belarus[3]	1986/224	30.1.86
	1995/2706	
Belgium[1]	1987/2053	21.10.89
Belize	1947/2866	
	[1968/573]	
	[1973/2097]	12.12.73
Bolivia	1995/2707	23.10.95
Bosnia Herzegovina[4]	1981/1815	16.9.82
Botswana[6]	1978/183	9.2.78
	(talks 1998)	
Brunei	1950/1977	
	[1968/306]	
	[1973/2098]	12.12.73
Bulgaria	1987/2054	28.12.87
Canada	1980/709	17.12.80
	[1980/1528]	18.12.80
	[1985/1996]	23.12.85
	1980/780 (dividend)	1.7.80
	[1987/2071]	1.1.88
	1996/1782	30.7.96
	[2003/2619]	4.5.04
Cayman Islands[9]	(talks 2004)	
Chile	2003/3200	
China[7]	1984/1826	23.12.84
	[1996/3164]	4.3.97
Croatia[4]	1981/1815	16.9.82
	(talks 2003)	
Cyprus	1975/425	18.3.75
	[1980/1529]	15.12.80
Czech Republic[5]	1991/2876	20.12.91
Denmark	1980/1960	17.12.80
	[1991/2877]	19.12.91
	[1996/3165]	20.6.97
Ecuador	(text agreed)	
Egypt	1980/1091	23.8.80
Estonia	1994/3207	19.12.94
European Economic Community	(Convention and Directives 90/434/EEC, 90/435/EEC, 90/436/EEC: see TA 1988 s 815B)	23.7.90
Falkland Islands	1997/2985	18.12.97
Fiji[1]	1976/1342	17.8.76
Finland	1970/153	
	[1980/710]	25.4.81
	[1985/1997]	20.2.87
	[1991/2878]	23.12.91
	[1996/3166]	8.8.97
France[1]	1968/1869	
	[1973/1328]	6.8.73
	[1987/466]	7.4.87
	[1987/2055]	23.12.87
	(new convention signed 28.1.2004)	
Gambia	1980/1963	5.7.82
Georgia[2]	2004/3325	
Germany[1]	1967/25	
	[1971/874]	1.6.71
Ghana	1993/1800	10.8.94
Greece[1,9]	1954/142	
	(talks 2003)	
Grenada	1949/361	
	[1968/1867]	
Guernsey*	1952/1215	
	[1994/3209]	3.1.95
Guyana	1992/3207	18.12.92
Hong Kong	(talks 2003)	
Hungary[10]	1978/1056	27.8.78
	(talks 2004)	
Iceland	1991/2879	19.12.91
India	1993/1801	25.10.93
Indonesia	1994/769	14.4.94
	(talks 2000)	
Iran[9]	(talks 2004)	
Irish Republic[1]	1976/2151	23.12.76
	[1976/2152]	23.12.76
	[1995/764]	21.9.95
	[1998/3151]	23.12.98
Isle of Man*	1955/1205	
	[1991/2880]	19.12.91
	[1994/3208]	3.1.95
Israel	1963/616	
	[1971/391]	25.3.71
Italy[9]	1990/2590	31.12.90
	(talks 2004)	
Ivory Coast	1987/169	10.2.87
Jamaica	1973/1329	31.12.73
Japan	1970/1948	25.12.70
	[1980/1530]	31.10.80
	(talks 2004)	
Jersey*	1952/1216	
	[1994/3210]	31.1.95
Jordan	2001/3924	24.3.02
Kazakhstan	1994/3211	15.7.96
	[1998/2567]	2.11.98
Kenya[1]	1977/1299	18.10.77
Kiribati	1950/750	
	[1968/309]	
	[1974/1271]	25.7.74
Korea	1996/3168	30.12.96
Kuwait	1999/2036	1.7.2000
Kyrgyzstan[2]	(1986/224	30.1.86)
Latvia	1996/3167	30.12.96
Lesotho	1997/2986	23.12.97
Lithuania[2]	(1986/224	30.1.86)
	2001/3925	28.11.02
	[2002/2847]	28.11.02
Luxembourg[1,9]	1968/1100	
	[1980/567]	21.5.80
	[1984/364]	19.3.84
	(talks 2003)	

Double taxation agreements – continued

Country	SI/SR & O	Entry into force
Macedonia[4,10]	1981/1815	16.9.82
Malawi	1956/619	
	[1964/1401]	
	[1968/1101]	
	[1979/302]	14.3.79
Malaysia	1997/2987	8.7.98
Malta	1995/763	27.3.95
Mauritius[1]	1981/1121	19.10.81
	[1987/467]	26.10.87
	[2003/2620]	22.10.03
Mexico	1994/3212	15.12.94
Moldova[2]	(1986/224	30.1.86)
Mongolia	1996/2598	4.12.96
Montserrat	1947/2869	
	[1968/576]	
Morocco	1991/2881	29.11.90
Myanmar (Burma)[1]	1952/751	
Namibia[1]	1962/2352	
	[1967/1490]	
	(agreement initialled)	
Netherlands[1,9]	1980/1961	6.4.81
	[1990/2152]	20.12.90
New Zealand	1984/365	16.3.84
	[2004/1274]	23.7.04
Nigeria	1987/2057	27.12.87
Norway[1]	1985/1998	20.12.85
	2000/3247	21.12.2000
Oman[8]	1998/2568	9.11.98
Pakistan	1987/2058	8.12.87
Papua New Guinea	1991/2882	20.12.91
Philippines	1978/184	9.2.78
Poland[6]	1978/282	25.2.78
	(talks 2004)	
Portugal[1]	1969/599	
Romania	1977/57	17.1.77
Russian Federation	1994/3213	18.4.97
St Christopher and Nevis	1947/2872	
Saudi Arabia	(talks 2003)	
Serbia and Montenegro[4,9]	1981/1815	16.9.82
Sierra Leone	1947/2873	
	[1968/1104]	
Singapore	1997/2988	19.12.97
Slovak Republic[5]	1991/2876	20.12.91

Country	SI/SR & O	Entry into force
Slovenia[4,6]	1981/1815	16.9.82
Solomon Islands	1950/748	
	[1968/574]	
	[1974/1270]	25.7.74
South Africa[1]	1969/864	
	2002/3138	17.12.02
Spain	1976/1919	25.11.76
	[1995/765]	26.5.95
Sri Lanka	1980/713	21.5.80
Sudan	1977/1719	25.10.77
Swaziland[1]	1969/380	
Sweden	1984/366	26.3.84
Switzerland[1]	1978/1408	7.10.78
	[1982/714]	18.5.82
	[1994/3215]	19.12.94
Taiwan	2002/3137	23.12.02
Tajikistan[3]	1986/224	30.1.86
Thailand[9]	1981/1546	20.11.81
	(talks 2004)	
Trinidad and Tobago	1983/1903	22.12.83
Tunisia	1984/133	8.2.84
Turkey	1988/932	26.10.88
Turkmenistan[3]	1986/224	30.1.86
Tuvalu	1950/750	
	[1968/309]	
	[1974/1271]	
Uganda	1993/1802	21.12.93
Ukraine	1993/1803	11.8.93
United Arab Emirates[9]	(text agreed)	
USA	1946/1331 (dividend)	
	[1955/499]	
	[1961/985]	
	[1980/779]	22.5.80
	1980/568	25.4.80
	[1994/1418] (dividend)	16.6.94
	[1996/1781] (dividend)	30.7.96
	2002/2848	31.3.03
Uzbekistan	1994/770	10.6.94
Venezuela	1996/2599	31.12.96
Vietnam	1994/3216	15.12.94
Zambia[1]	1972/1721	29.3.73
	[1981/1816]	14.1.83
Zimbabwe	1982/1842	11.2.83

[1] Individuals resident in these countries are entitled to personal reliefs, similar to the relief under TA 1988 s 278, under the provisions of double taxation treaties between these countries and the UK. Non-resident nationals of all EEA countries are entitled to personal allowances as from 6 April 1996: see FA 1996 s 145.

[2] SP 4/01: these countries do not consider themselves bound by the Convention with the former USSR, which the UK has applied as described in SP 3/92. In consequence, the UK will not apply the terms of the Convention to profits arising *after* 31 March 2002 (corporation tax) and to income and gains arising *after* 5 April 2002 (income tax and capital gains tax).

[3] SP 4/01: these countries and the UK will continue to operate the Convention with the former USSR in respect of their residents.

[4] SP 3/04: the treaty with former Yugoslavia is treated as remaining in force between the UK and, respectively, Croatia, Slovenia, Bosnia Herzegovina, Macedonia, Serbia and Montenegro pending new bilateral agreements. Discussions are to be held about a comprehensive double taxation convention between the UK and Croatia, Slovenia, Serbia and Montenegro. Negotiations are also planned with Macedonia.

[5] SP 5/93: the treaty with the former Czechoslovakia is treated as remaining in force between the UK and, respectively, the Czech Republic and the Slovak Republic.

[6] Completion of work on new treaties with these countries is planned before 31 March 2005 (IR Press Release of 15 July 2004).

[7] The 1984 Agreement does not apply to the Hong Kong Special Administrative Region.

[8] Certain provisions relating to profits, income and gains from ships and aircraft operated in international traffic take effect from 1 January 1979 (Article 29(2)).

[9] Negotiations with these countries are to be progressed before 31 March 2005 (IR Press Release of 15 July 2004 and IR Tax Bulletin August 2004).

[10] New or updated treaties with these countries are planned (IR Press Release of 15 July 2004).

* Negotiations have been opened with these countries and with the British Virgin Islands on Tax Information Exchange Agreements (IR Tax Bulletin August 2004).

Shipping and air transport profits

Country	SI or SR & O	Country	SI or SR & O
Algeria (air)	1984/362	Jordan	1979/300
Armenia (USSR air)*	1974/1269	Kuwait (air)**	1984/1825
Bahrain (air)	(text agreed)	Kyrgyzstan (USSR air)*	1974/1269
Belarus (USSR air)*	1974/1269	Lebanon	1964/278
Brazil	1968/572	Moldova (USSR air)*	1974/1269
Cameroon (air)	1982/1841	Qatar (air)	(text agreed)
China (air)	1981/1119	Russia (USSR air)*	1974/1269
Congo Democratic Republic	1977/1298	Saudi Arabia (air)	1994/767
Ethiopia (air)	1977/1297	Tajikistan (USSR air)*	1974/1269
Georgia (USSR air)*	1974/1269	Turkmenistan (USSR air)*	1974/1269
Hong Kong (air)	1998/2566	United Arab Emirates (air)	(text agreed)
(shipping)	2000/3248	USSR (air)*	1974/1269
Iran (air)	1960/2419		

* The Revenue has confirmed that this Arrangement will be treated in the same way as the Convention covering income and capital gains SI 1986/224. See notes 2 and 3 on p 8.

** Superseded by the comprehensive Agreement (SI 1999/2036, Art. 30) which entered into force on 1 July 2000, p 7 above.

Estates, inheritances and gifts

Country	SI	Country	SI
France*	1963/1319	Pakistan*	1957/1522
India*	1956/998	South Africa	1979/576
Ireland	1978/1107	Sweden	1981/840
Italy*	1968/304		1989/986
Netherlands	1980/706	Switzerland	1994/3214
	[1996/730]	USA	1979/1454

* Agreements pre-date UK inheritance tax/capital transfer tax.

Income arising abroad – Basis of assessment

	Securities	Professions, trades, etc	Pensions	Possessions
NON-RESIDENTS	Exempt	Exempt	Exempt	Exempt
RESIDENTS				
1) **Foreign domicile**	Remittance	Remittance	Remittance	Remittance
2) **UK domicile**				
(a) Non Commonwealth citizen[1]	Arising	Arising	90%[3] arising	Arising
(b) Commonwealth citizen[2]				
(i) ordinarily resident	Arising	Arising	90%[3] arising	Arising
(ii) not ordinarily resident	Remittance	Remittance	Remittance	Remittance

[1] But not citizen of the Republic of Ireland.

[2] Or citizen of the Republic of Ireland.

[3] Pensions paid by the governments of the Federal Republic of Germany or of Austria to victims of Nazi persecution are exempt.

It was announced in the Budget Speech on 17 April 2002 that the Government is reviewing the residence and domicile rules as they affect the tax liabilities of individuals (2002) SWTI 521.

Employment income liability of non-resident employees see p 85.

Tax-free (FOTRA) securities

Interest on all government stock is exempt from tax where the beneficial owner is not ordinarily resident in the UK (FA 1996 s 154; FA 1998 s 161). Except in the case of 3½% War Loan 1952 or after, the exemption does not apply where the securities are held for the purposes of a trade or business carried on in the UK.

General
Certificates of tax deposit

The Series 7 Prospectus came into operation on 1 October 1993.

From 1 October 1993, certificates are not available for purchase for use against corporation tax liabilities, although certificates purchased before that date can be used before 1 October 1999 and set against all liabilities listed in the schedule to the Series 6 Prospectus.

Certificates are available to individuals, trustees, companies or other persons or bodies for the payment of any taxes or other liabilities listed in the schedule to the Prospectus. Minimum first deposit £2,000; subsequent deposits not less than £500.

Interest is paid gross and is chargeable to tax. It will only be paid for the first 6 years of a deposit. Under the Series 7 Prospectus a deposit bears interest for the first year at the rate in force at the time of the deposit and for each subsequent year at the rate in force on the anniversary of the deposit. No bonus or interest supplement is payable.

Series 7
Deposits of £100,000 or over: rate varies according to number of months held for in relevant year:

A = under £100,000
B = £100,000 or over

From	Amount	Held for (mths in yr)	Pay't of tax %	Cashed %	From	Amount	Held for (mths in yr)	Pay't of tax %	Cashed %
Series 7 (1.10.93)					9.2.01	A	no limit	2.25	1.25
7.11.97	A	no limit	4	2		B	under 1	2.25	1.25
	B	under 1	4	2			1–under 3	4.75	2.5
		1–under 6	6.5	3.25			3–under 9	4.25	2.25
		6–12	6.25	3.25			9–12	4	2
5.6.98	A	no limit	4	2	6.4.01	A	no limit	2	1
	B	under 1	4	2		B	under 1	2	1
		1–under 3	6.5	3.25			1–under 3	4.25	2.25
		3–under 9	6.25	3.25			3–under 6	4	2
		9–12	6	3			6–under 9	3.75	2
9.10.98	A	no limit	3.75	2			9–12	3.5	1.75
	B	under 1	3.75	2	11.5.01	A	no limit	2	1
		1–under 3	6.25	3.25		B	under 1	2	1
		3–under 9	5.75	3			1–under 6	4	2
		6–under 9	5.5	2.75			6–12	3.75	2
		9–12	5.25	2.75	3.8.01	A	no limit	1.5	0.75
6.11.98	A	no limit	3.25	1.75		B	under 1	1.5	0.75
	B	under 1	3.25	1.75			1–under 3	4	2
		1–under 3	5.75	3			3–12	3.75	1.875
		3–under 6	5.25	2.75	19.9.01	A	no limit	1.25	0.75
		6–under 9	5	2.5		B	under 1	1.25	0.75
		9–12	4.75	2.5			1–under 3	3.5	1.75
11.12.98	A	no limit	3.25	1.75			3–under 9	3.25	1.75
	B	under 1	3	1.5			9–12	3	1.5
		1–under 3	5.25	2.75	5.10.01	A	no limit	1	0.5
		3–under 6	4.75	2.5		B	under 1	1	0.5
		6–under 9	4.5	2.25			1–under 3	3.25	1.75
		9–12	4.25	2.25			3–12	3	1.5
8.1.99	A	no limit	2.5	1.25	9.11.01	A	no limit	0.5	0.25
	B	under 1	2.5	1.25		B	under 1	0.5	0.25
		1–under 3	5	2.5			1–under 3	2.75	1.5
		3–under 6	4.5	2.25			3–under 6	2.5	1.25
		6–12	4	2			6–12	2.25	1.25
5.2.99	A	no limit	1.75	1	7.2.03	A	no limit	0.25	0
	B	under 1	1.75	1		B	under 1	0.25	0
		1–under 3	4.5	2.25			1–under 3	2.75	1.25
		3–under 6	4	2			3–under 9	2.25	1
		6–12	3.75	2			9–12	2	1
9.4.99	A	no limit	1.75	1	11.7.03	A	no limit	0	0
	B	under 1	1.75	1		B	under 1	0	0
		1–under 3	4.25	2.25			1–under 3	2.50	1.25
		3–under 6	4	2			3–under 6	2.25	1
		6–12	3.75	2			6–12	2	1
11.6.99	A	no limit	1.5	0.75	7.11.03	A	no limit	0.25	0
	B	under 1	1.5	0.75		B	under 1	0.25	0
		1–12	4	2			1–12	3	1.5
9.9.99	A	no limit	1.75	1	6.2.04	A	no limit	0.5	0.25
	B	under 1	1.75	1		B	under 1	0.5	0.25
		1–12	4.5	2.25			1–12	3	1.5
4.11.99	A	no limit	2	1	7.5.04	A	no limit	0.75	0.25
	B	under 1	2	1		B	under 1	0.75	0.25
		1–under 3	5	2.5			1–12	3.25	1.5
		3–under 12	4.75	2.5	11.6.04	A	no limit	1	0.5
14.1.00	A	no limit	2.25	1.25		B	under 1	1	0.5
	B	under 1	2.25	1.25			1–under 3	3.75	1.75
		1–under 9	5	2.5			3–under 6	3.5	1.75
		9–12	5.25	2.75			6–12	3.75	1.75
11.2.00	A	no limit	2.5	1.25	6.8.04	A	no limit	1.25	0.5
	B	under 1	2.5	1.25		B	under 1	1.25	0.5
		1–under 3	5.25	2.75			1–12	3.75	1.75
		3–under 6	5	2.5					
		6–12	5.25	2.75					

Due dates of tax

Capital gains tax

From 1996–97:
(TMA 1970 s 59B. There are no provisions for payment on account for capital gains tax.)
Normally 31 January following end of year of assessment.
(See also *Extended due dates* under **Income tax**, below.)

Corporation tax

Generally (accounting periods ending after 30 September 1993: pay and file and self assessment)
(TMA 1970 s 59D, substituted by FA 1998 Sch 18 para 29 for accounting periods ending after 30 June 1999.)
9 months and 1 day after end of accounting period.

Instalments for larger companies (TMA 1970 s 59E, SI 1998/3175)
(Large: profits exceeding upper relevant maximum amount in force at end of accounting period, subject to certain restrictions: reg 3.)
  1st instalment: 6 months and 13 days from start of accounting period (or date of final instalment if earlier);
  (2nd instalment: 3 months after 1st instalment if length of accounting period allows);
  (3rd instalment: 3 months after 2nd instalment, if length of accounting period allows);
  Final instalment: 3 months and 14 days from end of accounting period.

Transitional provisions (reg 4) percentage of total liability payable by instalments for accounting periods ending:
  after 30 June 1999 but before 1 July 2000: 60%
  after 30 June 2000 but before 1 July 2001: 72%
  after 30 June 2001 but before 1 July 2002: 88%
(balance due and payable in accordance with *Generally* above).

Advance corporation tax (abolished from 6 April 1999) (FA 1998 ss 31, 32, Sch 3)
Tax in respect of franked payments to be included in a return is due 14 days after a return period ends.
Return periods end on 31 March, 30 June, 30 September, 31 December and at the end of each accounting period, when not one of the above.

Close companies: tax on loans to participators
Loans etc made in accounting periods ending after 30 March 1996: 9 months and 1 day after the end of the accounting period. Previously 14 days after the end of the accounting period in which the loan was made. To be included in instalment payments for large companies in respect of accounting periods ending after 30 June 1999 (TMA 1970 s 59E(11), see above).

Income tax

From 1997–98:
(1) *Payment on account* (TMA 1970 s 59A)
A payment on account is required where a taxpayer was assessed to income tax in respect of the immediately preceding year in an amount exceeding the amount of tax deducted at source in respect of that year (subject to a de minimis limit, see below). This excess is known as the 'relevant amount'.
The payment on account is made in 2 equal instalments due on:
  (a) 31 January during the year of assessment, and
  (b) 31 July in the following year of assessment.
No payments on account are required where:
  (a) the aggregate of the relevant amount (see above) and the Class 4 NIC liability for the preceding year is less than £500; or
  (b) more than 80% of the taxpayer's income tax and Class 4 NIC liability for the immediately preceding year was met by tax deducted at source.

From 1996–97:
(2) *Payment of income tax* (TMA 1970 s 59B, Sch 3ZA)
Balance of income tax due for a year of assessment (after deducting payments on account, tax deducted at source and credits in respect of dividends, etc) is due on:
31 January following end of year of assessment (TMA 1970 s 59B(4)).

  Extended due dates:
  (a) If a taxpayer has given notice of liability within 6 months of the end of the year of assessment (as required by TMA 1970 s 7), but a notice to make a return is not given until after 31 October following the end of the year of assessment, the final payment is not due until 3 months after the notice is given (TMA 1970 s 59B(3)).
  (b) If tax is payable as a result of a taxpayer's notice of amendment, a Revenue notice of correction or a Revenue notice of closure following enquiry, in each case given less than 30 days before the due date (or the extended due date at (a) above), the additional tax is payable on or before the day following the end of a 30-day period beginning on the day on which the notice is given (TMA 1970 s 59B(5), Sch 3ZA as amended/inserted by FA 2001, Sch 29 paras 14–16).
  (c) If an assessment other than a self-assessment is made, tax payable under the assessment is due on the day following the end of a 30-day period beginning on the day on which notice of the assessment is given (TMA 1970 s 59B(6)).
The extensions under (b) and (c) do *not* alter the due date for *interest purposes* (see p 12).

Interest on overdue tax see p 12.   **Repayment supplement** see p 15.
Remission of tax see p 14.

Inheritance tax

Chargeable transfers other than on death, made between:
6 April and 30 September   –   30 April in next year.
1 October and 5 April   –   6 months after end of month in which chargeable transfer is made.
Chargeable events following conditional exemption for heritage etc property and charge on disposal of trees or underwood before the second death
                              –   6 months after end of month in which chargeable event occurs.
Transfers on death
Earlier of   (a) 6 months after end of month in which death occurs, and
               (b) delivery of account by personal representatives.
Tax or extra tax becoming payable on death:
(1) chargeable transfers and potentially exempt transfers within 7 years of death, or
(2) gifts in excess of £100,000 made to political parties before 15 March 1988 and within 1 year of death: due 6 months after end of month in which death takes place.

PAYE and national insurance

Employer's tax and Class 1 national insurance payable under PAYE	19 April following deduction year to date of payment (extended to 22 April where payments after 5 April 2004 are made by electronic means)
Class 1A national insurance	19 July following year in which contributions due to date of payment
PAYE settlement agreement and Class 1B national insurance	19 October following year to which agreement relates to date of payment
Class 4 national insurance	See under income tax on p 11

Stamp duties see page 98.

Interest on overdue tax

Interest on overdue income tax and capital gains tax

(NB: These rules apply with respect to liabilities for 1996–97 and subsequent years and to liabilities for 1995–96 and earlier years assessed after 5 April 1998. However, for partnerships with trades, etc set up and commenced before 6 April 1994, the previous rules continued to apply for the year 1996–97.)

For payments on account (under TMA 1970 s 59A(2)), tax not postponed pending an appeal (under TMA 1970 s 55) and balancing payments (under TMA 1970 s 59B), interest runs from the due date to the date of payment, on the amount outstanding. For the due date, see p 11. In respect of payments on account, interest is charged on the difference between the amount that ought to have been paid and the amount actually paid.

For tax resulting from amendments/corrections to returns and from discovery assessments (under TMA 1970 s 29), interest normally runs from the annual filing date for the relevant tax year.

Where a claim made under TMA 1970 s 59A(3) or (4) to reduce payments on account proves to be excessive, an underpayment may arise. In such a case, interest is charged on the difference between the amount actually paid and the amount that ought to have been paid if the claim had been made correctly.

Surcharge on unpaid income tax and capital gains tax (TMA 1970 s 59C, amended by FA 1995 s 109)

Applies from 1996–97, and for assessments for 1995–96 or an earlier year of assessment made after 5 April 1998 (FA 1995 s 109(2)). (Tax taken into account in determining certain other penalties (under TMA 1970 ss 7, 93(5), 95 and 95A) is ignored for the purposes of calculating the surcharge.)

28 days: Where income tax or capital gains tax becomes payable and all or part of it remains unpaid the day following 28 days after the due date, the taxpayer is liable to a surcharge of 5% of the unpaid tax.

6 months: The taxpayer is liable to a further surcharge of 5% on any of the tax remaining unpaid 6 months and 1 day from the due date.

Interest is payable on surcharge from the expiry of 30 days beginning on the day on which the surcharge is imposed until the date of payment. It is charged at the rate applying to overdue income tax and capital gains tax (see p 13).

Corporation tax (accounting periods ending after 30 September 1993)

Interest runs from the due date (see p 11) to the date of payment: TMA 1970 s 87A (wording amended by FA 1994 Sch 19 para 24 and SI 1998/3175 reg 7 for accounting periods ending after 30 June 1999) and ss 59D (substituted from the same date) and 59E (inserted from the same date).

For instalment payments by large companies for accounting periods ending after 30 June 1999, a special rate of interest runs from the due date to the earlier of the date of payment and nine months after the end of the accounting period (after which the normal rate applies): SI 1989/1297 regs 32A and 32B (inserted by SI 1998/3176 reg 6).

Inheritance tax

Interest runs from the due date (see above) to the date of payment.

Prescribed rate

	Rate	Period
Income tax, capital gains tax, Class 1, 1A, 4 and (from 6 April 1999) **1B national insurance contributions and** (from 1 October 1999) **stamp duty and stamp duty reserve tax:** (SI 1999/2538; SI 1999/2536)	7.5%	from 6 September 2004
	6.5%	6 December 2003–5 September 2004
	5.5%	6 August 2003–5 December 2003
	6.5%	6 November 2001–5 August 2003
	7.5%	6 May 2001–5 November 2001
	8.5%	6 February 2000–5 May 2001
	7.5%	6 March 1999–5 February 2000
	8.5%	6 January 1999–5 March 1999
	9.5%	6 August 1997–5 January 1999
	8.5%	31 January 1997–5 August 1997
	6.25%	6 February 1996–30 January 1997
Corporation tax self assessment: (accounting periods ending after 30 June 1999) (a) Instalment payments (except where tax still unpaid nine months after end of accounting period)	5.75%	from 16 August 2004
	5.5%	21 June 2004–15 August 2004
	5.25%	17 May 2004–20 June 2004
	5%	16 February 2004–16 May 2004
	4.75%	17 November 2003–15 February 2004
	4.5%	21 July 2003–16 November 2003
	4.75%	17 February 2003–20 July 2003
	5%	19 November 2001–16 February 2003
	5.5%	15 October 2001–18 November 2001
	5.75%	1 October 2001–14 October 2001
	6%	13 August 2001–30 September 2001
	6.25%	21 May 2001–12 August 2001
	6.5%	16 April 2001–20 May 2001
	6.75%	19 February 2001–15 April 2001
	7%	20 April 2000–18 February 2001
	8%	21 February 2000–19 April 2000
	7.75%	24 January 2000–20 February 2000
	7.5%	15 November 1999–23 January 2000
	7.25%	20 September 1999–14 November 1999
	7%	21 June 1999–19 September 1999
	7.25%	19 April 1999–20 June 1999
	7.5%	15 February 1999–18 April 1999
	8%	18 January 1999–14 February 1999
	8.25%	7 January 1999–17 January 1999
(b) Payments other than instalment payments (or for instalment payments still unpaid nine months after end of accounting period)	7.5%	from 6 September 2004
	6.5%	6 December 2003–5 September 2004
	5.5%	6 August 2003–5 December 2003
	6.5%	6 November 2001–5 August 2003
	7.5%	6 May 2001–5 November 2001
	8.5%	6 February 2000–5 May 2001
	7.5%	6 March 1999–5 February 2000
Corporation tax pay and file: (accounting periods ending after 30 September 1993)	6%	from 6 September 2004
	5%	6 December 2003–5 September 2004
	4.25%	6 August 2003–5 December 2003
	5%	6 November 2001–5 August 2003
	6%	6 May 2001–5 November 2001
	6.75%	6 February 2000–5 May 2001
	5.75%	6 March 1999–5 February 2000
	6.5%	6 January 1999–5 March 1999
	7.5%	6 August 1997–5 January 1999
	6.25%	6 February 1996–5 August 1997
	7%	6 March 1995–5 February 1996
	6·25%	6 October 1994–5 March 1995
	5·5%	6 January 1994–5 October 1994
	6·25%	1 October 1993–5 January 1994

Prescribed rate – continued

	Rate	Period
Income tax on company payments (due on or after 14 October 1999)	7.5%	from 6 September 2004
	6.5%	6 December 2003–5 September 2004
	5.5%	6 August 2003–5 December 2003
	6.5%	6 November 2001–5 August 2003
	7.5%	6 May 2001–5 November 2001
	8.5%	6 February 2000–5 May 2001
	7.5%	14 October 1999–5 February 2000
Income tax on company payments (due before 14 October 1999), **advance corporation tax, development land tax, petroleum revenue tax** (including **advance petroleum revenue tax**) and **stamp duty reserve tax** (before 13 October 1999)	5.75%	from 6 September 2004
	5%	6 December 2003–5 September 2004
	4.25%	6 August 2003–5 December 2003
	5%	6 November 2001–5 August 2003
	5.75%	6 May 2001–5 November 2001
	6.5%	6 February 2000–5 May 2001
	5.75%	6 March 1999–5 February 2000
	6.5%	6 January 1999–5 March 1999
	7.25%	6 August 1997–5 January 1999
	6.25%	6 February 1996–5 August 1997
	7%	6 March 1995–5 February 1996
Inheritance tax	4%	from 6 September 2004
	3%	6 December 2003–5 September 2004
	2%	6 August 2003–5 December 2003
	3%	6 November 2001–5 August 2003
	4%	6 May 2001–5 November 2001
	5%	6 February 2000–5 May 2001
	4%	6 March 1999–5 February 2000
	5%	6 October 1994–5 March 1999
	4%	6 January 1994–5 October 1994
	5%	6 December 1992–5 January 1994
	6%	6 November 1992–5 December 1992
	8%	6 July 1991–5 November 1992
	9%	6 May 1991–5 July 1991
	10%	6 March 1991–5 May 1991
	11%	6 July 1989–5 March 1991
	9%	6 October 1988–5 July 1989
	8%	6 August 1988–5 October 1988
	6%	6 June 1987–5 August 1988
	8%	16 December 1986–5 June 1987

Remission of tax

By concession, arrears of tax may be waived if they result from the Revenue's failure to make proper and timely use of information supplied by the taxpayer or, where it affects the taxpayer's coding, by his or her employer. The concession also applies to information supplied by the DSS affecting the taxpayer's entitlement to a retirement or widow's pension (see Concession A19). The concession only applies where the taxpayer could reasonably have believed that his or her affairs were in order and (unless the circumstances are exceptional) where the taxpayer is notified of the arrears more than 12 months after the end of the tax year in which the Revenue received the information indicating that more tax was due.

Repayment supplement

Income tax, capital gains tax, Class 1, 1A, 4 and (from 6 April 1999) **1B national insurance contributions and** (from 1 October 1999) **stamp duty and stamp duty reserve tax**

Calculated as simple interest on the amount of tax repaid. The supplement is tax free. (From 31 January 1997 the rate is determined under SI 1989/1297 as amended by SI 1996/3187, see below.)

See pages 16 and 17 for rates applicable to corporation tax and page 91 with respect to stamp duties.

Period to which supplement relates	Rate
from 6 September 2004	3·5%
6 December 2003–5 September 2004	2·5%
6 August 2003–5 December 2003	1·75%
6 November 2001–5 August 2003	2·5%
6 May 2001–5 November 2001	3·5%
6 February 2000–5 May 2001	4%
6 March 1999–5 February 2000	3%
6 January 1999–5 March 1999	4%
6 August 1997–5 January 1999	4·75%
6 February 1997–5 August 1997	4%
6 February 1996–5 February 1997	6·25%
6 March 1995–5 February 1996	7%
6 October 1994–5 March 1995	6·25%
6 January 1994–5 October 1994	5·5%
6 March 1993–5 January 1994	6·25%
6 December 1992–5 March 1993	7%
6 November 1992–5 December 1992	7·75%
6 October 1991–5 November 1992	9·25%
6 July 1991–5 October 1991	10%
6 May 1991–5 July 1991	10·75%
6 March 1991–5 May 1991	11·5%
6 November 1990–5 March 1991	12·25%
6 November 1989–5 November 1990	13%
6 July 1989–5 November 1989	12·25%
6 January 1989–5 July 1989	11·5%
6 October 1988–5 January 1989	10·75%
6 August 1988–5 October 1988	9·75%
6 May 1988–5 August 1988	7·75%
6 December 1987–5 May 1988	8·25%
6 September 1987–5 December 1987	9%
6 June 1987–5 September 1987	8·25%
6 April 1987–5 June 1987	9%

Income tax (TA 1988 s 824; FA 1997 s 92)

From 1996–97 (1997–98 for partnerships whose trade, profession or business commenced before 6 April 1994) repayment supplement applies to:
- (a) amounts paid on account of income tax
- (b) income tax paid by or on behalf of an individual
- (c) surcharges on late payments of tax
- (d) penalties incurred by an individual under any provision of TMA 1970

but excluding amounts paid in excess of the maximum the taxpayer is required to pay.

Except for tax deducted at source, the repayment supplement runs *from* the date on which the tax, penalty or surcharge was paid *to* the date on which the order for repayment is issued. For tax deducted at source, repayment supplement runs from 31 January after the end of the tax year for which the tax was deducted.

Capital gains tax (TCGA 1992 s 283; FA 1997 s 92)

From 1996–97 repayment supplement runs *from* the date on which the tax was paid *to* the date on which the order for repayment is issued.

Inheritance tax (IHTA 1984 s 235)

Repayments of inheritance tax or interest paid carries interest from the date of payment to the date on which the order for repayment is issued. The prescribed rates for unpaid tax apply equally to repayment supplements — see page 14.

Companies: interest on tax overpaid

Pay and file: accounting periods ending before 1 July 1999

Repayments of corporation tax, repayments of ACT in respect of foreign income dividends, repayments of income tax in respect of payments received, and payments of tax credits in respect of franked investment income received, made after the material date. Advance corporation tax is abolished from 6 April 1999 (FA 1998 ss 31, 32, SI 1999/358).

Calculated *from* the material date *to* the date the repayment order is issued.

For corporation tax, the material date is the later of

(a) the date on which the tax was paid and

(b) the date on which the tax became, or would have become, due and payable – generally, nine months and one day after the end of the accounting period.

For ACT, the material date is the date on which corporation tax for the accounting period in which the distribution was made became, or would have become, due and payable – generally, 9 months and 1 day after the end of the accounting period.

For repayments of income tax in respect of payments received and payments of tax credits in respect of franked investment income received, the material date is the date on which corporation tax for the accounting period in which the payments or the franked investment income were received became, or would have become, due and payable. Again, this is generally 9 months and 1 day after the end of the accounting period.

This rule is qualified in instances where there is a carry-back of surplus ACT or a carry-back of trading losses for more than 12 months.

Surplus ACT (s 826(7) repealed for accounting periods beginning on or after 6 April 1999 by FA 1998 Sch 3). Where there is in any accounting period ('the later period') an amount of surplus ACT and a claim is made under TA 1988 s 239(3) to carry this surplus ACT back to an earlier accounting period ('the earlier period'), then interest on any repayment of corporation tax for the earlier period (or of income tax on a payment received in the earlier period) resulting from the claim under s 239(3) begins to run only after the date on which the corporation tax for the *later* period (the period in which the surplus ACT arose) became due and payable.

This rule is in itself subject to modification where the surplus ACT arises because of a trading loss carried back (see below).

A similar rule (s 826(7C)) applies to the carry-back of a non-trading deficit on a company's loan relationships as applies to the carry-back of surplus ACT.

Trading losses carried back for more than 12 months (s 826(7A), (7B))

Where a claim is made under TA 1988 s 393A(1) to set off a loss incurred in a later period against the profits of an earlier period not falling within the 12 months immediately preceding the later period, and

(a) a repayment of corporation tax in respect of that earlier period or a repayment of income tax in respect of a payment received in the earlier period; or

(b) following a claim under TA 1988 s 242 to include surplus franked investment income in profits available for set-off, a payment of the whole or part of the tax credit comprised in franked investment income of the earlier period,

is made, interest in respect of that part of the repayment due to the claim under TA 1988 s 393A(1) or TA 1988 s 242 (so far as it relates to the claim under s 393A(1)) begins to run only after the date on which the corporation tax in respect of the later period (the lossmaking period) became, or would have become, due and payable.

Carry-back of trading loss giving rise to carry-back of surplus ACT (s 826(7AA) repealed for accounting periods beginning on or after 6 April 1999 by FA 1998 Sch 3). Where –

(a) a trading loss carried back under s 393A(1) from a later period ('the lossmaking period') gives rise to an amount of surplus ACT, and that surplus ACT is then carried back under s 239(3) to a still-earlier period and

(b) as a result a repayment of corporation tax for the still-earlier period (or of income tax on a payment received in the still-earlier period) falls to be made

then interest on those repayments begins to run only after the date on which the corporation tax for the *lossmaking period* became due and payable.

A similar rule (s 826(7CA)) applies to the carry-back of surplus ACT following the carry-back of a non-trading deficit on a company's loan relationships.

Rates	
from 6 September 2004	2.75%
6 December 2003–5 September 2004	2%
6 August 2003–5 December 2003	1.25%
6 November 2001–5 August 2003	2%
6 May 2001–5 November 2001	2.75%
6 February 2000–5 May 2001	3.5%
6 March 1999–5 February 2000	2.75%
6 January 1999–5 March 1999	3.25%
6 August 1997–5 January 1999	4%
6 February 1996–5 August 1997	3.25%

Accounting periods ending after 30 June 1999

SI 1989/1297 regs 3BA and 3BB (inserted by SI 1998/3176 reg 8)

For instalment payments by large companies and early payments by other companies, a special rate of interest runs from the date the excess arises (but not earlier than the due date of the first instalment) to the earlier of the date the repayment order is issued and 9 months after the end of the accounting period after which the normal rate of interest applies.

Rates on overpaid instalment payments and on corporation tax paid early (but not due by instalments):	
from 16 August 2004	4.5%
21 June 2004–15 August 2004	4.25%
17 May 2004–20 June 2004	4%
16 February 2004–16 May 2004	3.75%
17 November 2003–15 February 2004	3.5%
21 July 2003–16 November 2003	3.25%
17 February 2003–20 July 2003	3.5%
19 November 2001–16 February 2003	3.75%
15 October 2001–18 November 2001	4.25%
1 October 2001–14 October 2001	4.5%
13 August 2001–30 September 2001	4.75%
21 May 2001–12 August 2001	5%
16 April 2001–20 May 2001	5.25%
19 February 2000–15 April 2001	5.5%
21 February 2000–18 February 2001	5.75%
24 January 2000–20 February 2000	5.5%
15 November 1999–23 January 2000	5.25%
20 September 1999–14 November 1999	5%
21 June 1999–19 September 1999	4.75%
19 April 1999–20 June 1999	5%
15 February 1999–18 April 1999	5.25%
18 January 1999–14 February 1999	5.75%
7 January 1999–17 January 1999	6%

Rates on overpaid corporation tax in respect of periods after normal due date (SI 1989/1297 reg 3BB):

from 6 September 2004	4%
6 December 2003–5 September 2004	3%
6 August 2003–5 December 2003	2%
6 November 2001–5 August 2003	3%
6 May 2001–5 November 2001	4%
6 February 2000–5 May 2001	5%
6 March 1999–5 February 2000	4%

Penalties

A) Personal tax returns and information

Offence	Penalty
Failure to give notice of chargeability to income or capital gains tax within 6 months from end of year of assessment (TMA 1970 s 7).	Amount not exceeding tax assessed (either self-assessed under TMA 1970 s 9 or under a TMA 1970 s 29 'discovery' assessment) for that year and not paid before 1 February following that year.
Failure to comply with notice requiring return for income tax or capital gains tax (TMA 1970 s 93).	(a) Initial penalty of £100; and (b) upon direction by Commissioners, further penalty not exceeding £60 for each day on which failure continues after notification of direction; (c) if failure continues after six months following filing date, and no application for a direction under (b) has been made, a further penalty of £100. (d) In addition, if failure continues after first anniversary of filing date, and there would have been a liability to tax shown in the return, a penalty not exceeding the liability that would have been shown in the return. (e) If the taxpayer can prove that the liability to tax shown in the return would not have exceeded a particular amount, the sum of penalties under (a) and (c) above are not to exceed that amount.
Failure to comply with notice requiring partnership return (TMA 1970 s 93A).	(a) Initial penalty on each 'relevant partner' of £100; and (b) upon direction by Commissioners, further penalty on each relevant partner not exceeding £60 for each day on which failure continues after notification to representative partner of direction; (c) if failure continues after six months following filing date, and no application for a direction under (b) has been made, a further penalty on each relevant partner of £100. NB: A 'relevant partner' is any person who was a partner at any time during the period for which the return is required.
Fraudulently or negligently making an incorrect statement in connection with a claim to reduce payments on account (TMA 1970 s 59A).	Penalty not exceeding the difference between the amount paid on account and the amount that would have been paid had a correct statement been made.
Fraudulently or negligently delivering incorrect return or accounts or making an incorrect statement in connection with a claim for an allowance, deduction or relief (TMA 1970 s 95).	Penalty not exceeding the difference between the amount payable under the return etc and the amount which would have been payable if the return etc had been correct.
Fraudulently or negligently delivering incorrect partnership return or accounts or making an incorrect statement or declaration in connection with such a return (TMA 1970 s 95A).	Penalty on each relevant partner not exceeding the difference between the amount payable by him or her under the return, etc and the amount that would have been payable by him or her if the return, etc had been correct. For the meaning of 'relevant partner', see under TMA 1970 s 93A above.
(From 31.1.01) Failure to register as self-employed (and liable to Class 2 NIC) within three months after the month in which self-employment begins (SI 2001/1004 reg 87).	£100.

B) Corporation tax returns and information

Offence	Penalty
Pay and file (accounting periods ending before 1 July 1999)	
Failure to give notice of chargeability to corporation tax within 12 months after end of accounting period (TMA 1970 s 10).	Penalty not exceeding amount of tax unpaid 12 months after end of accounting period (after set-off of income tax credits).
Failure to comply with notice requiring return for corporation tax (TMA 1970 s 94).	(a) If return is delivered within 3 months of due date – £100 (£500 in respect of default for third consecutive period); (b) if return is delivered more than 3 months after due date – £200 (£1,000 in respect of default for third consecutive period); and (c) if return is delivered between 18 months and 2 years after end of return period – an additional penalty of 10% of tax unpaid at end of 18-month period; (d) if return is delivered more than 2 years after end of return period – an additional penalty of 20% of tax unpaid at end of 18-month period.

Offence	Penalty
Fraudulently or negligently delivering incorrect return or accounts or making an incorrect statement in connection with a claim for an allowance, deduction or relief (TMA 1970 s 96).	Penalty not exceeding the difference between the amount payable under the return etc and the amount which would have been payable if the return etc had been correct.
Self assessment (accounting periods ending on or after 1 July 1999)	*(For the restriction of penalties where multiple tax-related penalties are payable in respect of the same accounting period see FA 1998 Sch 18 para 90)*
Failure to give notice of when first accounting period begins and of when any subsequent accounting period begins that does not follow on immediately from the end of a previous accounting period within three months after the beginning of the accounting period in question. With effect for accounting periods beginning on or after 22 July 2004.	(a) An initial penalty not exceeding £300; and (b) a continuing penalty not exceeding £60 for each day on which the failure continues after imposition of initial penalty.
Fraudulently or negligently giving an incorrect notice. [FA 2004 s 55; TMA 1970 s 98].	Penalty not exceeding £3,000.
Failure to give notice of chargeability to corporation tax within 12 months after end of accounting period (FA 1998 Sch 18 para 2).	Penalty not exceeding amount of tax payable for that accounting period remaining unpaid 12 months after end of accounting period (taking no account of relief deferred under TA 1988 s 419(4A)).
Failure to deliver a company tax return by the filing date (FA 1998 Sch 18 paras 17, 18).	*Flat-rate penalties* (Unless FA 1998 Sch 18 para 19 (excuse for late delivery of returns) applies) (a) If return is delivered within 3 months of the filing date: £100 (£500 for third successive failure); (b) in any other case: £200 (£1,000 for third successive failure); (the increased penalties under (a) and (b) apply with modifications where the first or second period ends before 1 July 1999 (para 17(4)). *Tax-related penalties* (c) If return is delivered between 18 months (or the filing date, if later) and 2 years after the end of the return period: an additional penalty of 10% of the unpaid tax; (d) if return delivered more than 2 years after the end of the return period: an additional penalty of 20% of the unpaid tax.
Fraudulently or negligently delivering a company tax return which is incorrect (FA 1998 Sch 18 para 20).	An amount not exceeding the amount of tax understated (taking no account of relief deferred under TA 1988 s 419(4A)).
On discovering that a company tax return delivered by it (neither fraudulently nor negligently) is incorrect, a company does not remedy the error without reasonable delay (FA 1998 Sch 18 para 20).	An amount not exceeding the amount of tax understated (taking no account of relief deferred under TA 1988 s 419(4A)).
Fraudulently or negligently making an incorrect return, statement or declaration in connection with a claim for any tax allowance, deduction or relief, or submitting any incorrect accounts in connection with the ascertainment of the company's tax liability (FA 1998 Sch 18 para 89).	Penalty not exceeding the amount of tax understated (excluding relief deferred under TA 1988 s 419(4A)).

C) PAYE returns

Offence	Penalty
Failure to submit return P9D or P11D (benefits in kind) by due date (6 June following tax year 1995–96; 6 July following subsequent tax years) (TMA 1970 s 98(1)).	(a) An initial penalty not exceeding £300; and (b) a continuing penalty not exceeding £60 for each day on which the failure continues after imposition of the initial penalty.
Fraudulently or negligently submitting incorrect return P9D or P11D (TMA 1970 s 98(2)).	Penalty not exceeding £3,000.
Failure to submit returns P14 (individual end of year summary), P35 (annual return), P38 or P38A (supplementary returns for employees not on P35) by due date (19 May following tax year) (TMA 1970 s 98A).	(a) First 12 months: penalty of £100 for each 50 employees (or part thereof) for each month the failure continues; (b) failures exceeding 12 months: a penalty not exceeding the amount of PAYE or NIC due and unpaid after 19 April following year of assessment.
Fraudulently or negligently submitting incorrect form P14, P35, P38 or P38A (TMA 1970 s 98A).	Penalty not exceeding the difference between the amount payable under the return and the amount which would have been payable if the return had been correct.

C) PAYE returns — continued

Offence	Penalty
Failure to submit returns P11D(b) (Class 1A NIC returns) by due date (19 July following tax year, extended for 2000/01 only to 19 September 2001) (SI 2001/1004 reg 81).	(a) First 12 months: penalty of £100 for each 50 employees (or part thereof) for each month the failure continues (but total penalty not to exceed total Class 1A NIC due); (b) failures exceeding 12 months: a penalty not exceeding the amount of Class 1A NIC due and unpaid after 19 July following year of assessment.
Failure to submit information in connection with mandatory e-filing from year ending 5 April 2005 onwards (SI 1993/744 as amended by SI 2003/2494).	Penalty based on number of employees not exceeding £3,000 for 1,000 or more employees.

D) Inheritance tax returns and information

Offence	Penalty
Failure to deliver an account under IHTA 1984 s 216 or 217 (IHTA 1984 s 245). [1] The fixed penalty in (a) and (c) opposite (introduced by FA 2004 s 295(2)(a)) relates to failures where the account is due by 22 January 2005 (FA 2004 s 295(5)). [2] Where the account is due on or before 22 July 2004, the penalty in (d) opposite (introduced by FA 2004 s 295(2)(b)) relates to failures continuing after 21 July 2005 (FA 2004 s 295(6)).	(a) An initial penalty of [not exceeding][1] £100 (or the amount of tax payable if less); (b) further penalty not exceeding £60 (where penalty determined by court or Special Commissioners) for each day on which the failure continues after imposition of initial penalty; (c) if failure continues after six months following the date on which the account is due, and proceedings have not commenced, a further penalty of [not exceeding][1] £100 (or the amount of tax payable if less); and (d) if failure continues after the anniversary of the end of the period in which the account is due (where the account is due after 22 July 2004)[2], and IHT is payable, a penalty not exceeding £3,000.
Failure to make a return under IHTA 1984 s 218 or failure to comply with a notice under s 219 (IHTA 1984 s 245A(1)(2)).	(a) An initial penalty not exceeding £300; and (b) further penalty not exceeding £60 (where penalty determined by court or Special Commissioners) for each day on which the failure continues after imposition of initial penalty.
Failure to comply with the requirements of IHTA 1984 s 218A (IHTA 1984 s 245A(1A)(1B)). [3] Where the notification is due on or before 22 July 2004, the penalty in (c) opposite (introduced by FA 2004 s 295(3)(a)) relates to failures continuing after 21 July 2005 (FA 2004 s 295(7)).	(a) A penalty not exceeding £100; (b) further penalty not exceeding £60 (where penalty determined by court or Special Commissioners) for each day on which the failure continues after imposition of initial penalty; and (c) if failure continues after the anniversary of the end of the period in which the notification is due (where the notification is due after 22 July 2004)[3], and IHT is payable, a penalty not exceeding £3,000.
Failure to comply with a notice under IHTA 1984 s 219A(1) or (4) (IHTA 1984 s 245A(3)).	(a) An initial penalty not exceeding £50; and (b) further penalty not exceeding £30 (where penalty determined by court or Special Commissioners) for each day on which the failure continues after imposition of initial penalty.
The taxpayer fraudulently or negligently delivering, furnishing or producing incorrect accounts, information or documents (IHTA 1984 s 247(1); FA 2004 s 295(4)(9)).	For accounts, etc. delivered after 22 July 2004, a penalty not exceeding the difference noted in (b) below. For accounts, etc. delivered on or before 22 July 2004: (a) in the case of fraud, a penalty not exceeding the aggregate of £3,000 and the difference between the amount payable according to the information furnished and the amount that would have been payable if the accounts etc had been correct; and (b) in the case of negligence, a penalty not exceeding the aggregate of £1,500 and the difference between the amount payable according to the information furnished and the amount that would have been payable if the accounts etc had been correct.
A person other than the taxpayer fraudulently or negligently delivering, furnishing or producing incorrect accounts, information or documents (IHTA 1984 s 247(3); FA 2004 s 295(4)(9)).	For accounts, etc. delivered after 22 July 2004, a penalty not exceeding £3,000. For accounts, etc. delivered on or before 22 July 2004: (a) in the case of fraud, a penalty not exceeding £3,000; and (b) in the case of negligence, a penalty not exceeding £1,500.
Any person assisting in or inducing the delivery, furnishing or production of any account, information or document knowing it to be incorrect (IHTA 1984 s 247(4).)	A penalty not exceeding £3,000.

E) Special returns of information

Offence	Penalty
Failure to comply with a notice to deliver a return or other document, furnish particulars or make anything available for inspection under any of the provisions listed in column 1 of the table in TMA 1970 s 98. (FA 1999 s 89 extends this to corporation tax payment by instalments.)	(a) An initial penalty not exceeding £300 (£3,000 for failure to comply with TA 1988 s 765A(2)(a) or (b)); and (b) a continuing penalty not exceeding £60 (£600 for failure to comply with TA 1988 s 765A(2)(a) or (b)) for each day on which the failure continues after imposition of the initial penalty.
Failure to comply with requirement to furnish information, give certificates or produce documents or records under any of the provisions listed in column 2 of the table in TMA 1970 s 98. (FA 1999 s 86 extends this to advance pricing agreements.)	(a) An initial penalty not exceeding £300; and (b) a continuing penalty not exceeding £60 for each day on which the failure continues after imposition of the initial penalty.
Fraudulently or negligently delivering any incorrect document, information etc required under any of the provisions listed in column 1 or 2 of the table in TMA 1970 s 98.	Penalty not exceeding £3,000.
(Accounting periods ending after 30 June 1999.) Failure of a company to produce documents, etc, for the purposes of an enquiry (FA 1998 Sch 18 para 29).	(a) £50; (b) If failure continues after imposition of penalty under (a), an additional penalty for each day the failure continues, not exceeding £30 if determined by the Revenue under TMA 1970 s 100, and £150 if determined by the Commissioners under TMA 1970 s 100C.
Fraudulently or negligently making a false or misleading statement in the preparation of, or application to enter into, any advance pricing agreement (FA 1999 s 86).	Penalty not exceeding £10,000.

F) Other offences by taxpayers, agents etc

Offence	Penalty
Failure to retain records as required by TMA 1970 s 12B(1) (TMA 1970 s 12B(5)).	Penalty not exceeding £3,000.
Falsification of documents (TMA 1970 s 20BB).	On summary conviction, a fine not exceeding the statutory maximum (£5,000); on conviction on indictment, imprisonment for a term not exceeding 2 years or a fine or both.
Failure to produce documents required under TMA 1970 s 19A (power to enquire into self-assessment return, etc) (TMA 1970 s 97AA).	(a) Initial penalty of £50; and (b) further penalty not exceeding £30 (where penalty determined by officer of Board) or £150 (where penalty determined by Commissioners) for each day on which failure continues after imposition of initial penalty.
Offences in connection with the supply of information regarding European Economic Interest Groupings —	
(i) failure to supply information	An initial penalty not exceeding £300 per member of the Grouping at the time of failure and after direction by the Commissioners a continuing penalty not exceeding £60 per member of the Grouping at the end of the day for each day on which the failure continues after notification of the direction.
(ii) fraudulent or negligent delivery of an incorrect return, accounts or statement (TMA 1970 s 98B).	Not exceeding £3,000 for each member of the Grouping at the time of delivery.
Assisting in the delivery of incorrect returns, accounts or information (TMA 1970 s 99).	Not exceeding £3,000.
Fraudulently or negligently giving a certificate of non-liability to income tax for the purposes of receiving interest gross on a bank or building society account, or failing to comply with an undertaking given in such a certificate (TMA 1970 s 99A).	Not exceeding £3,000.
Refusal to allow a deduction of income tax authorised by the Taxes Acts (TMA 1970 s 106).	£50.
Obstruction of officer of the Board in inspection of property to ascertain its market value (TMA 1970 s 111).	Not exceeding level 1 on the standard scale.
Issue by a company of a certificate of approval for enterprise investment scheme relief fraudulently or negligently or without the authority of the inspector (TA 1988 s 306(6)).	Not exceeding £3,000.
False statement to obtain relief for payments to secure a retirement annuity, a purchased life annuity or under a personal pension scheme (TA 1988 ss 619(7), 653, 658(5)).	Not exceeding £3,000.

F) Other offences by taxpayers, agents etc — continued

Offence	Penalty
Creation or transfer of shares or debentures in a non-resident subsidiary company without the consent of HM Treasury (TA 1988 s 766).	On conviction on indictment— (a) imprisonment for not more than 2 years or a fine, or both; or (b) in the case of a UK company, a fine not exceeding the greater of £10,000, or three times the tax payable by the company attributable to income and gains arising in the previous 36 months.
Failure by a Lloyd's syndicate's managing agent to comply with notice requiring return of syndicate's profit or loss (FA 1993 Sch 19 para 2(3), (4)).	£60 for each 50 members of syndicate (or part thereof) for each day the failure continues.
Delivery by a Lloyd's syndicate's managing agent fraudulently or negligently of an incorrect return of syndicate profits (FA 1993 Sch 19 para 2(5)).	Not exceeding £3,000 for each member of the syndicate.
Obstructing, molesting or hindering an officer or other person employed in relation to Inland Revenue in the execution of his or her duty (Inland Revenue Regulation Act 1890 s 11).	Level 3 on the standard scale.
(Accounting periods ending after 30 June 1999). Deliberately or recklessly failing to pay corporation tax due in respect of total liability of company for accounting period, or fraudulently or negligently making claim for repayment (TMA 1970 s 59E(4); SI 1998/3175 reg 13).	Penalty not exceeding twice amount of interest charged under SI 1998/3175 reg 7.
(Accounting periods ending after 30 June 1999) Failure of a company to keep and preserve records (other than those only required for claims, etc, or dividend vouchers and certificates of income tax deducted where other evidence is available) (FA 1998 Sch 18 para 23).	Penalty not exceeding £3,000.
Failure to notify notifiable proposals or notifiable arrangements, or failure to notify the client of the relevant scheme reference number under the provisions of FA 2004 ss 308(1)(3), 309(1), 310 or s 312(1).	(a) An initial penalty not exceeding £5,000; (b) a continuing penalty not exceeding £600 for each day on which the failure continues after imposition of initial penalty.
Failure to notify scheme reference number etc. under FA 2004 s 313(1);	Penalty of £100 in respect of each scheme to which the failure relates;
for second failure, occurring within three years from the date on which the first failure began;	penalty of £500 in respect of each scheme to which the failure relates;
for subsequent failures, occurring within three years from the date on which the previous failure began. [TMA 1970 s 98C; FA 2004 s 315(1)].	penalty of £1,000 in respect of each scheme to which the failure relates.

G) Standard scale penalties under Criminal Justice Act[1]

Level	Amount	
	1.5.84–30.9.92 £	From 1.10.92 £
1	50	200
2	100	500
3	400	1,000
4	1,000	2,500
5 (statutory maximum)	2,000	5,000

[1] Criminal Justice Act 1982 s 37.

Mitigation of penalties

The Board has discretion to mitigate or entirely remit any penalty or to stay or compound any penalty proceedings (TMA 1970 s 102).

Interest on penalties

From 1996–97 penalties under TMA 1970 Parts II (ss 7–12B), IV (ss 28A–43B), VA (ss 59A–59D) and X (ss 93–107) carry interest at the prescribed rate (see p 14): TMA 1970 s 103A. Surcharges on unpaid income tax and capital gains tax carry interest under TMA 1970 s 59C (with effect from 9 March 1998, by virtue of SI 1998/310). As regards corporation tax, the provisions apply for accounting periods ending on or after 1 July 1999.

Stamp duties see p 98.

VAT see p 102.

Time limits for claims and elections

Whenever possible, a claim or election must be made on the tax return or by an amendment to the return (TMA 1970 s 42 and FA 1998 Sch 18 paras 9, 10, 67 and 79). Exceptions to this general rule are dealt with in TMA 1970 Sch 1A.

Except where another period is expressly prescribed, a claim for relief in respect of income tax and capital gains tax must be made within five years from the 31 January following the year of assessment to which it relates (TMA 1970 s 43(1) as amended). The time limit for claims by companies remains at six years from the end of the accounting period to which it relates (TMA 1970 s 43(1) (b) and, for accounting periods ending after 1 July 1999, FA 1998 Sch 18 para 55).

The tables below set out the main exceptions to the general limits.

Income tax only

Claim	Time limit
Farming and market gardening: Averaging relief to be available to a person carrying on a trade of farming or market gardening (TA 1988 s 96(8)).	1 year after 31 January next following end of second year which enters into the averaging calculation.
Post-cessation receipts: Post-cessation receipts to be charged as if received on the date of discontinuance or change of basis of computation (TA 1988 s 108).	1 year after 31 January following end of year of assessment in which sum received.
Post-cessation expenditure: Unrelieved qualifying post-cessation expenditure to be set against income (TA 1988 s 109A(1)).	1 year after 31 January following year of assessment in which payment made.
Loan benefits: Election by employee for alternative method to be applied in calculating the cash equivalent of the benefit obtained from a loan (ITEPA 2003 s 183).	1 year after 31 January next following year of assessment.
Election for treatment of all beneficial loans to a director by a close company, as a single loan (ITEPA 2003 s 187).	92 days after the end of the year of assessment.
Returns: Inspector to be required to issue a return to a person with PAYE income (ITEPA 2003 s 711).	5 years after 31 October next following year of assessment.
Jointly held property: Income from jointly owned property to be assessed on husband and wife in unequal shares (TA 1988 s 282B(2)).	60 days after date of declaration.
Enterprise investment scheme: Relief to be given for the enterprise investment scheme (TA 1988 s 306(1) as amended).	Not earlier than 4 months after the company commences its qualifying activity and no later than fifth anniversary of 31 January next following year of assessment in which shares issued.
Trading losses: Loss sustained in a trade, profession or vocation to be set against other income of the year or the last preceding year. Extended to certain pre-trading expenditure by TA 1988 s 401 (TA 1988 s 380) as substituted).	1 year after 31 January next following year of assessment in which loss arose.
Losses of new trade etc: Loss sustained in the first 4 years of a new trade, profession or vocation to be offset against other income arising in the 3 years immediately preceding the year of loss. Extended to certain pre-trading expenditure by TA 1988 s 401 (TA 1988 s 381(1)).	1 year after 31 January next following year of assessment in which loss sustained.
Schedule A losses: Claim for relief against total income (TA 1988 s 379A(3)).	1 year after 31 January next following year of assessment.
Copyright, assignment: *Certain sums received by an author in respect of the assignment of a copyright to be assessed as if received over a period of up to 3 years (repealed for payments receivable after 5 April 2001, see now TA 1988 Sch 4A below) (TA 1988 s 534(1), (5) as amended).*	*1 year after 31 January next following the latest year of assessment in which payment receivable.*
Copyright, assignment after 10 years: *Spreading claim made under TA 1988 s 535(1) in respect of sums received by author more than 10 years after first publication of the work to be recalculated on the death of the author or the discontinuance of his or her profession (repealed for payments receivable after 5 April 2001, see now TA 1988 Sch 4A below) (TA 1988 s 535(8A)).*	*1 year after 31 January next following year of assessment in which payment receivable.*
Design rights, assignment: *Sums received by a designer for the assignment of rights in a design to be assessed as if received over a period of up to 3 years (repealed for payments receivable after 5 April 2001, see now TA 1988 Sch 4A below) (TA 1988 s 537A(5), (5A) as amended).*	*1 year after 31 January next following the latest year of assessment in which payment receivable.*
Loss on disposal of unlisted shares: Loss on disposal by an individual of shares in a qualifying trading company to be offset against other income of the year of loss or the last preceding year (TA 1988 s 574(1) as substituted).	1 year after 31 January next following year of assessment in which loss incurred.

Claim	Time limit
Retirement annuity premiums: Relief to be given in respect of a qualifying premium paid under a retirement annuity contract entered into before 1 July 1988 and treated as paid in the immediately preceding year of assessment (or the year before that if no net relevant earnings in the immediately preceding year) (TA 1988 s 619(4) as amended).	31 January next following year of assessment in which premium paid.
Retirement annuity premiums, carry-forward of unused relief: Unused relief to be available against a qualifying premium paid under a retirement annuity contract entered into before 1 July 1988 where an assessment becomes final and conclusive more than 6 years after the year to which it relates (TA 1988 s 625(3)).	6 months after the date when the assessment becomes final.
Personal pension schemes, carry-back of relief: *Relief to be given in respect of a contribution paid under approved personal pension arrangements for the immediately preceding year of assessment (or the year before that if no net relevant earnings in the immediately preceding year) (repealed for contributions paid after 5 April 2001) (TA 1988 s 641(1), (4) as amended).*	*31 January next following year of assessment in which contributions paid.*
Personal pension schemes, contributions: Contributions paid before 1 February to be treated in whole or part as paid in preceding year of assessment (TA 1988 s 641A).	On or before date of payment of contribution.
Personal pension schemes, carry-forward of relief: *Unused relief to be available for relief against a contribution paid under approved personal pension arrangements where an assessment to tax for a year of assessment becomes final and conclusive more than 6 years after the end of that year (repealed from 2001–02) (TA 1988 s 642(4)).*	*6 months after the date when the assessment for the year in question becomes final and conclusive.*
Maintenance funds for historic buildings: Income arising to trustees of maintenance funds for historic buildings not to be treated as the income of the settlor (TA 1988 s 691(2), (4) as amended).	1 year from 31 January next following year of assessment to which it relates.
Completion of administration: Income of a beneficiary to be adjusted for past years on completion of the administration of a deceased's estate (TA 1988 s 700(1), (3) as amended).	3 years after 31 January next following year of assessment in which the administration is completed.
Creative artists, relief for fluctuation profits: Relevant profits of an individual in two consecutive years to be averaged (TA 1988 Sch 4A).	1 year after 31 January next following later tax year to which it relates (or in which adjustment for other reason is made).
Deduction of trading losses: Unrelieved trading losses to be set against capital gains (FA 1991 s 72, TA 1988 s 380(1)).	12 months from 31 January next following year of assessment in which loss sustained.
Rent a room relief: Relief not to be applied to an individual for a year of assessment (F(No 2)A 1992 Sch 10 para 10).	1 year after 31 January next following year of assessment or such later date as Board may allow.
Rent a room relief: Relief to be applied where the total of all relevant sums for a year exceed the individual's limit (F(No 2)A 1992 Sch 10 paras 11, 12).	1 year after 31 January next following year of assessment or such later date as Board may allow.
Enterprise Management Incentives: Notification of grant of options in shares under the Enterprise Management Incentives scheme to Inland Revenue (ITEPA 2003 Sch 5 para 44).	92 days from grant of option where option granted after 11 May 2001 (previously 30 days).
Gift aid: Election to treat donations to charity under gift aid made after 5 April 2003 as made in the previous year of assessment (FA 2002 s 98).	On or before the date on which the donor delivers his tax return for the previous year of assessment and not later than 31 January next following the end of that year.
Foster care receipts: Election to tax on the alternative method of calculating profits (FA 2003 s 176, Sch 36).	1 year after 31 January next following year of assessment (or such later date as the Board may allow).
Cash basis withdrawal for barristers and advocates: Election for increased adjustment under the transitional spreading provisions (FA 2002 Sch 22 para 12).	31 January following the tax year in question.

Corporation tax only

Claim	Time limit
Carry back of surplus ACT: *Surplus ACT paid to be carried back for offset against corporation tax liabilities for accounting periods beginning within six years prior to the period of payment (TA 1988 s 239(3)) (repealed for accounting periods beginning after 5 April 1999).*	*2 years.*
Trading losses: Loss sustained by a company in a trade in an accounting period to be offset against— (a) profits of that accounting period; (b) profits of the preceding year. Extended to certain pre-trading expenditure by TA 1988 s 401 (TA 1988 s 393A(1) (2A)(10)).	2 years or such further period as Board may allow.
Group relief: Group relief to be given for accounting periods ending after 30 September 1993 and before 1 July 1999. The surrendering company must consent to the claim (TA 1988 s 412, Sch 17A para 2).	2 years after the end of the surrendering company's accounting period or the date on which the relevant assessment becomes final, whichever is later.
Group relief: Group relief to be given for accounting periods ending after 30 June 1999. The surrendering company must consent to the claim (FA 1998 Sch 18 paras 66 to 77).	The last of: (a) 1 year from the filing date of the claimant company's return for the accounting period for which the claim is made; (b) 30 days after the end of an enquiry into the return; (c) if the Revenue amend the return after an enquiry, 30 days after issue of notice of amendment; (d) if an appeal is made against the amendment, 30 days after the determination of the appeal; (or such later time as the Revenue may allow).
Relief for investment companies: Loss on disposal by an investment company of shares in a qualifying trading company to be offset against other income of the period of loss or preceding accounting period (TA 1988 s 573(2)).	2 years.
Non-trading deficit on loan relationship: Claim for non-trading deficits on loan relationships (including non-trading debits on derivative contracts) in a company in an accounting period ending after 30 September 2002 to be: (a) offset against profits of the same period or carried back (FA 1996 s 83, Sch 8 paras 1, 3); (b) treated as a non-trading deficit of subsequent accounting period to be carried forward to succeeding accounting periods (FA 1996 s 83, Sch 8 para 4).	2 years after the end of the accounting period in which deficit arose (or such later time as the Revenue may allow). 2 years after the end of that subsequent accounting period.
Non-trading deficit on loan relationship: *Relief for non-trading deficits on loan relationships in a company in an accounting period ending after 31 March 1996 but before 1 October 2002 to be claimed by:* *(a) offset against profits of the same period;* *(b) group relief;* *(c) offset against post 31 March 1996 profits of earlier accounting periods (as for trading losses above); or* *(d) offset against non-trading profits for the next accounting period, and so on.* *(FA 1996 s 83, Sch 8)*	*2 years or such further period as Board may allow.*
Corporate Venturing Scheme: Relief to be given for losses on disposal of shares against income under Corporate Venturing Scheme (FA 2000 Sch 15 para 68).	2 years from end of accounting period in which loss is incurred.
Qualifying land remediation expenditure: Election for such expenditure of a capital nature to be allowed as a deduction from trade or Schedule A business profits (FA 2001 Sch 22 para 1(8)).	2 years after end of accounting period in which expenditure made.
Intangible assets: Election to replace accounts depreciation with fixed writing down allowance of 4% (FA 2002 Sch 29 para 10). Election to exclude from intangible assets provisions certain expenditure on computer software (FA 2002 Sch 29 para 83).	2 years after the end of the accounting period in which the asset was created or acquired. 2 years after the end of the accounting period in which the expenditure was incurred.
Controlled foreign companies: Claims for losses in pre-direction accounting periods to be taken into account in computing chargeable profits (TA 1988 Sch 24 para 9).	20 months after the end of the accounting period.
Research and development: Claim for tax credit to be made, amended or withdrawn in the company tax return (or amended return) (FA 1998 Sch 18 para 83E).	1 year from the filing date for the return or such later time as the Board may allow.

Income tax and corporation tax

Claim	Time limit
Gifts to educational establishments: Relief for gifts of plant and machinery to educational establishments (TA 1988 s 84(3), (3A)).	1 year after 31 January next following year of assessment in the basis period of which the gift was made (income tax); 2 years after end of accounting period in which the gift was made (corporation tax).
Herd basis: Herd basis to apply (TA 1988 s 97, Sch 5 para 2 as amended).	1 year after 31 January next following first year of assessment for which profits computed by reference to period in which herd was kept (income tax); 1 year after 31 January next following year of assessment in which fell the end of the first period of account in which herd was kept (partnerships); 2 years after end of first accounting period in which herd was kept (corporation tax).
Valuation of work in progress: Work in progress at date of discontinuance of profession or vocation to be valued at actual cost (TA 1988 s 101(2), (2A)).	1 year after 31 January next following year of assessment in which discontinuance occurred (income tax); 2 years after end of accounting period in which discontinuance occurred (corporation tax).
Furnished holiday lettings: Averaging treatment to be applied in determining the number of days on which holiday accommodation is let (TA 1988 s 504(6), (6A)).	1 year after 31 January next following year of assessment in which accommodation let (income tax); 2 years after end of accounting period in which accommodation let (corporation tax).
Patents (UK residents): UK resident in receipt of a capital sum from the sale of patent rights to be charged to tax for period of receipt (TA 1988 s 524(2), (2A)).	1 year after 31 January next following year of assessment in which sum received (income tax); 2 years after end of accounting period in which sum received (corporation tax).
Patents (non-residents): Non-resident in receipt of a capital sum on the sale of non-UK patent rights to be charged to tax as if the sum was received over a period of 6 years (TA 1988 s 524(4) as amended).	1 year after 31 January next following year of assessment in which sum is paid.
Know-how: Consideration for know-how sold together with a trade or part of a trade not to be treated as a payment for goodwill. Time limit runs from the date of the disposal. Both purchaser and vendor must elect (TA 1988 s 531(3)).	2 years from date of disposal.
Unremittable overseas income: Unremittable overseas income to be excluded from assessment (TA 1988 s 584(2), (6) (as substituted)).	1 year after 31 January next following year of assessment in which income arises (income tax); 2 years after end of accounting period in which income arises (corporation tax).
Appropriations to and from trading stock: Election for market value to be adjusted in certain cases where a chargeable gain or allowable loss would otherwise arise (TCGA 1992 s 161(3A)).	1 year after 31 January next following year of assessment in which assets are appropriated (income tax); 2 years after end of accounting period in which assets are appropriated (corporation tax—for accounting periods ending on or after 1 July 1999, otherwise 6 years after the end of the accounting period in question).
Directors' remuneration: Adjustment of employer's Schedule D calculation for emoluments paid subsequently, but within 9 months of the end of the employer's period of account (FA 1989 s 43(5); ITEPA 2003 Sch 6 para 157).	2 years from end of period of account.

Capital allowances

Claim	Time limit
Income tax claims: Claim for income tax capital allowances made in taxing the trade (CAA 2001 s 3(2), (3)(a)).	Claim to be made in return.
Disapply change in law made by CAA 2001: Election for a change in the law effected by CAA 2001 not to have effect for a period of account ending on 6 April 2001 or straddling that date and ending in 2001–02 (CAA 2001 s 577(1), Sch 3 para 8).	1 year after 31 January next following tax year in which relevant chargeable period ends (income tax). 2 years after end of relevant chargeable period (corporation tax).

Claim	Time limit
Corporation tax claims (accounting periods ending after 30 June 1999): Claims, amended claims and withdrawals of claims in respect of corporation tax capital allowances for accounting periods ending after 30 June 1999 (CAA 2001 s 3(2), (3)(b), FA 1998 Sch 18 para 82).	The last of: (a) 1 year after the filing date of the claimant company's return for the accounting period for which the claim is made; (b) 30 days after the end of an enquiry into the return; (c) if the Revenue amend the return after an enquiry, 30 days after issue of notice of amendment; (d) if an appeal is made against the amendment, 30 days after the determination of the appeal; (or such later time as the Revenue may allow).
Corporation tax claims (accounting periods ending before 1 July 1999): *Claims, amended claims and withdrawals of claims in respect of corporation tax capital allowances for accounting periods ending after 30 September 1993 and before 1 July 1999 (CAA 1990 s 145A, Sch A1 paras 2, 3). (New provisions apply for self-assessment by companies for accounting periods ending after 30 June 1999, see below.)*	*The latest of —* *(a) 2 years after the end of the accounting period;* *(b) the date on which the company's corporation tax assessment for the period becomes final; and* *(c) the date on which the determination of the company's losses or the amount available for group relief for the accounting period becomes final.*
Films: Expenditure on production or acquisition of films etc to be reallocated (F(No 2)A 1992 s 40B(6)).	1 year after 31 January next following year of assessment in which relevant period ends (income tax); 2 years after end of relevant period (corporation tax).[1]
Plant and machinery: Writing down allowance to be available where first year allowance not claimed (CAA 1990 s 25(3) as amended, (3A)). *The requirement for an election to pool expenditure is abolished for periods ending on or after 6 April 2001 (income tax) and 1 April 2001 (corporation tax).*	1 year after 31 January next following year of assessment in which ends chargeable period related to incurring of expenditure (income tax);[1] 2 years after end of chargeable period related to incurring of expenditure (corporation tax).
Short life assets: Plant or machinery to be treated as a short life asset (CAA 2001 s 85(2)).	1 year after 31 January next following year of assessment in which chargeable period in which qualifying expenditure occurred ends (income tax);[1] 2 years after end of chargeable period (corporation tax).
Short life asset transferred to connected person: Transfer of short life asset to a connected person to be treated as taking place at tax written down value (CAA 2001 s 89(6)).	2 years after end of chargeable period in which disposal occurred.
Ships: Single ship pool treatment not to apply to the whole or part of the expenditure (CAA 2001 s 129(2)).	1 year after 31 January next following year of assessment in which chargeable period ends (income tax);[1] 2 years after end of chargeable period (corporation tax).
Ships: Part or all of a first year allowance in respect of expenditure on a ship to be postponed to a later period (CAA 2001 s 130(4)).	1 year after 31 January next following year of assessment in which period of account ends (income tax);[1] 2 years after end of accounting period for which allowance made (corporation tax).
Oilfields: Oilfield abandonment expenditure to be deductible in relation to a ring fence trade (CAA 2001 s 164(2)).	2 years after end of chargeable period related to incurring of expenditure.
Equipment lessors: Plant or machinery which becomes a fixture and is subject to an equipment lease to be treated as belonging to equipment lessor. Election to be made by both lessor and lessee but not permitted if they are connected persons (CAA 2001 s 177(5)).	1 year after 31 January next following year of assessment in which chargeable period ends (income tax);[1] 2 years after end of chargeable period (corporation tax).
Lessee to be treated as owner of fixture: Plant or machinery which has become a fixture on land which is subsequently let to be treated as belonging to lessee. Election to be made by both lessor and lessee but not permitted if they are connected persons (CAA 2001 s 183(2)).	2 years after date on which lease takes effect.

Capital allowances — continued

Claim	Time limit
Excess corporation tax allowances: Excess of corporation tax capital allowances given by discharge or repayment of tax over the relevant class of income to be set against the profits of that period and the immediately preceding period (CAA 2001 s 260(6)).	2 years after the end of the accounting period for which allowances claimed.
Connected persons: Succession to a trade between connected persons to be ignored in computing capital allowances (CAA 2001 s 266).	2 years after the date of the succession.
Industrial buildings: Grant of a long lease of a building to be treated as a sale of the relevant interest by the lessor. Both lessor and lessee must elect (CAA 2001 ss 290, 291).	2 years after the date when the lease takes effect.
Agricultural buildings: Cessation of use, demolition or destruction of agricultural buildings or acquisition of relevant interest in capital expenditure on agricultural land and buildings to be treated as a balancing event (CAA 2001 ss 381, 382).	1 year after 31 January next following year of assessment in which chargeable period ends (income tax);[1] 2 years after end of chargeable period (corporation tax).
Connected persons: Disposal and acquisition of property between persons one of which controls the other or which are under common control to be treated as made at the lower of open market value and tax written down value (CAA 2001 s 570(5)).	2 years after the date of the disposal.

[1] For the purposes of income tax, applies from 1997–98 in respect of trades etc set up and commenced before 6 April 1994 and from 1996–97 for trades etc commenced after 5 April 1994: see FA 1996 s 135(3), Sch 21.

Capital gains

Claim	Time limit
Assets of negligible value: Loss to be allowed where the value of an asset has become negligible (TCGA 1992 s 24(2)).	Year for which loss to be allowed, or up to 2 years after the end of that year if the value is still negligible when claim made.
Assets held on 31 March 1982: Events occurring prior to 31 March 1982 to be ignored in computing gains arising after 5 April 1988 (TCGA 1992 s 35 (5), (6) as amended).	1 year after 31 January next following year of assessment in which disposal made (capital gains tax) or 2 years after end of accounting period in which disposal made (corporation tax).
Variation or disclaimer: Variation or disclaimer of the terms of a will or intestacy, made within two years of the death, to be treated as effected by the deceased (TCGA 1992 s 62(6), (7)).	6 months after instrument of variation or disclaimer effected or such longer time as the Board may allow.
Same-day acquisition of shares: Election to treat certain shares acquired after 5 April 2002 under employee share options as acquired separately from other shares under same-day rules (TCGA 1992 ss 105A, 105B).	1 year after 31 January following year of assessment in which disposal is made.
Pre-April 1982 share pools: Quoted ordinary (and participating preference) shares and units in certain unit trusts held (or deemed to have been held) at 6 April 1965 to be pooled at their 6 April 1965 values for disposals after 5 April 1985 (31 March 1985 for companies) or 19 March 1968, as the case may be (TCGA 1992 s 109(4), (5), Sch 2 paras 4(2), (11) as amended, 5).	1 year after 31 January next following year of assessment in which first relevant disposal made (capital gains tax); 2 years after end of accounting period in which first relevant disposal made (corporation tax); or such further time as the Board may allow.
Incorporation relief: Election to disapply incorporation relief under TCGA 1992 s 162 on a transfer of a business after 5 April 2002 (TCGA 1992 s 162A).	2 years after 31 January following year of assessment in which transfer takes place (reduced by 1 year where transferor disposes of all shares received in exchange by the end of the tax year following that in which transfer takes place).
Subsidiary company ceasing to be UK resident: Postponement of charge on deemed disposal of assets where a subsidiary company ceases to be resident in the UK (TCGA 1992 s 187(1)).	2 years after date of ceasing to be resident in UK.
Main residence: Determination of main residence for principal private residence exemption (TCGA 1992 s 222(5)(a)).	2 years from the beginning of the period for which a determination is required, ie the date of acquisition of a second or further residence, but provided that an initial notice has been given within the time limit it may subsequently be varied and the notice of variation may have effect for up to 2 years prior to the date on which it is made.

Claim	Time limit
Employee share ownership trusts: Rollover relief on disposal of shares to trustees of qualifying employee share ownership trust (TCGA 1992 s 229(1)).	2 years after date of acquisition of replacement assets.
Relief for loans to trades: Losses on certain loans to traders to be allowed as capital losses (TCGA 1992 s 253(3)).	The loss is treated as accruing on the date that the claim is made, or at an earlier date, which is: (a) no more than 2 years before the beginning of the year of assessment in which the claim is made (capital gains tax) or (b) no earlier than the first day of the earliest accounting period ending no more than 2 years before the date of the claim.
Relief for loans to traders (payments by guarantor): Losses arising from payments by guarantor o certain irrecoverable loans to traders to be allowed as capital losses at time of claim or 'earlier time' (TCGA 1992 s 253(4), (4A); FA 1996 s 135(2)).	5 years after 31 January next following year of assessment in which payment made (capital gains tax); 6 years after end of accounting period in which the payment was made (corporation tax accounting periods ending after 30 June 1999).
Deferred unascertainable consideration: Election for relevant loss to be treated as accruing in earlier year subject to certain conditions (TCGA 1992 ss 279A–279D; FA 2003 s 162).	1 year after 31 January next following the year of loss.
Tax paid by instalments: Tax to be paid by instalments where the consideration is payable over a period (TCGA 1992 s 280 as amended).	Date of payment of tax.
Election for valuation at 6 April 1965: Gain on a disposal of an asset held at 6 April 1965 to be computed as if the asset had been acquired on that date. An election once made is irrevocable (TCGA 1992 Sch 2 para 17).	1 year after 31 January next following year of assessment in which disposal made (capital gains tax); 2 years after end of accounting period in which disposal made (corporation tax); or such further time as the Board may by notice allow.
Assets held on 31 March 1982: Halving of postponed charges, or held over or rolled over gains, on disposals of assets acquired after 31 March 1982 (but before 6 April 1988) from a person who acquired (or is deemed to have acquired) them before 31 March 1982 (TCGA 1992 Sch 4 para 9).	1 year after 31 January next following year of assessment in which disposal (or other event) occurred (capital gains tax); 2 years after the end of the accounting period in which the disposal (or other event) occurred, or such longer time as the Board may allow (corporation tax).
Retirement relief: Retirement relief generally. (TCGA 1992 Sch 6 as amended paras 2, 5, 12, 16). (Phased out from 6 April 1999 and not available for disposals after 5 April 2003 (FA 1998 s 140).)	1 year after 31 January next following year of assessment.
Relief for trading losses: Election to base the calculation for relief for trading losses incurred in 2002–03 and 2003–04 against capital gains using pre-tapered gains (FA 2002 s 48).	1 year after 31 January following year of assessment in which loss is incurred.

Inheritance tax

Claim	Time limit
Maintenance funds for historic buildings: Transfer of property to a maintenance fund for historic buildings etc to be exempt (IHTA 1984 s 27 as amended).	2 years after the date of the transfer or such longer period as the Board may allow (transfers of value made after 16 March 1998).
Conditionally exempt transfers of qualifying heritage assets: Transfer of property of national, scientific, historic or artistic etc interest designated as such by the Treasury to be conditionally exempt (IHTA 1984 ss 30, 31 as amended).	2 years after the date of the transfer of value or death or such longer period as the Board may allow (transfers of value or death after 16 March 1998).
Conditional exemption for heritage property leaving discretionary trusts: Qualifying heritage assets leaving discretionary trusts to be conditionally exempt (IHTA 1984 s 78 as amended).	2 years after the date of transfer or other event or such longer period as the Board may allow (transfers of property made and other events occurring after 16 March 1998).
Woodlands: Tax in respect of trees or underwood forming part of the value of a person's estate immediately before death to be deferred (IHTA 1984 ss 125, 126).	2 years after death or such longer period as the Board may allow.
Variations of dispositions on death: Variations or disclaimers of dispositions taking effect on death to be treated as if effected by the deceased (IHTA 1984 s 142).	6 months after the date of the instrument.

Exchanges

Recognised stock exchanges

The following is a list of countries with exchanges which have been designated as recognised stock exchanges under TA 1988 s 841. Unless otherwise specified, any stock exchange (or options exchange) in a country listed below is a recognised stock exchange for the purposes of TA 1988 s 841, provided it is recognised under the law of the country concerned relating to stock exchanges.

The Revenue's interpretation of the phrase 'listed on a recognised stock exchange' and similar phrases is set out in its policy statement published on 27 November 2002.

Country	Date of recognition
Australia	
Australian Stock Exchange and its stock exchange subsidiaries	22 September 1988
Austria[3]	22 October 1970
Belgium[3]	22 October 1970
Brazil	
Rio De Janeiro Stock Exchange	17 August 1995
São Paulo Stock Exchange	11 December 1995
Canada	
Any stock exchange prescribed for the purposes of the Canadian Income Tax Act	22 October 1970
Cayman Islands	
Cayman Islands Stock Exchange	4 March 2004
China	
Hong Kong – Any stock exchange recognised under Section 2A(1) of the Hong Kong Companies Ordinance	26 February 1971
Denmark	
Copenhagen Stock Exchange	22 October 1970
Finland	
Helsinki Stock Exchange	22 October 1970
France[3]	22 October 1970
Germany[3]	5 August 1971
Greece	
Athens Stock Exchange	14 June 1993
Guernsey[3]	10 December 2002
Irish Republic[3]	22 October 1970
Italy[3]	3 May 1972
Japan[3]	22 October 1970
Korea	10 October 1994
Luxembourg[3]	21 February 1972
Malaysia	
Kuala Lumpur Stock Exchange	10 October 1994
Mexico	10 October 1994
Netherlands[3]	22 October 1970
New Zealand	22 September 1988
Norway[3]	22 October 1970
Portugal[3]	21 February 1972
Singapore	30 June 1977
South Africa	
Johannesburg Stock Exchange	22 October 1970
Spain[3]	5 August 1971
Sri Lanka	
Colombo Stock Exchange	21 February 1972
Sweden	
Stockholm Stock Exchange	16 July 1985
Switzerland	
Swiss Stock Exchange	12 May 1997
Thailand	10 October 1994
United Kingdom	6 April 1965
United States	
Any stock exchange registered with the Securities and Exchange Commission as a national securities exchange[1]	22 October 1970
Nasdaq Stock Market[2]	10 March 1992

[1] The term 'national securities exchange' does not include any local exchanges registered with the Securities and Exchange Commission.
[2] As maintained through the facilities of the National Association of Securities Dealers Inc and its subsidiaries.
[3] Any stock exchange which is a stock exchange within the meaning of the law of the country concerned relating to stock exchanges.

Recognised futures exchanges

The following is a list of exchanges which have been designated as recognised futures exchanges under TCGA 1992 s 288(6). By concession, those exchanges were recognised futures exchanges for the tax year of recognition onwards.

Recognised futures exchanges	Date of recognition
International Petroleum Exchange of London	6.8.85
London Metal Exchange	6.8.85
London Gold Market	12.12.85
London Silver Market	12.12.85
Chicago Mercantile Exchange	19.12.86
New York Mercantile Exchange	19.12.86
Philadelphia Board of Trade	19.12.86
Chicago Board of Trade	24.4.87
Mid America Commodity Exchange	29.7.87
Montreal Exchange	29.7.87
Hong Kong Futures Exchange	15.12.87
Commodity Exchange (Comex)	25.8.88
Sydney Futures Exchange	13.10.88
London International Financial Futures and Options Exchange (LIFFE)	18.3.92
OM Stockholm	18.3.92
OMLX	18.3.92
New York Board of Trade[1]	—[1]

[1] Formed by the merger of the New York Cotton Exchange (25.8.88) and the Coffee, Sugar and Cocoa Exchange (15.12.87) on 10.6.04.

Recognised investment exchanges and clearing houses

The following is a list of investment exchanges and clearing houses recognised as investment exchanges under the Financial Services and Markets Act 2000 and able to carry out investment business in the UK.

Recognised investment exchange	Date of recognition
London Stock Exchange	28 April 1988
International Petroleum Exchange	5 April 1988
London International Financial Futures Exchange	25 April 1988
London Metal Exchange	25 April 1988
OM London Securities and Derivatives Exchange	12 December 1989
Virt-x Exchange Ltd	20 June 2001
EDX London Ltd	27 June 2003

Recognised clearing house	Date of recognition
London Clearing House	1988
CRESTCo	15 July 1996

Recognised overseas investment exchanges and clearing houses

The following is a list of overseas investment exchanges and clearing houses recognised under the Financial Services and Markets Act 2000 and able to conduct investment business in the UK.

Recognised overseas investment exchange	Date of recognition
National Association of Securities Dealers Automated Quotations (NASDAQ)	19 April 1988
Sydney Futures Exchange	27 April 1988
Chicago Mercantile Exchange	19 August 1989
Chicago Board of Trade	31 July 1992
New York Mercantile Exchange	23 June 1993
Swiss Exchange	16 December 1998
Cantor Financial Futures Exchange	23 February 1999
Eurex Zurich	28 June 1999
Warenterminborse Hannover	23 December 1999
New Zealand Futures and Options Exchange	11 April 2000
Nasdaq LIFFE	22 August 2001

Recognised clearing house	Date of recognition
SIS x-clear AG	19 August 2004

Applications for clearances and approvals

Clearance application	Address
Transfer of long term insurance business (TCGA 1992 s 211, TA 1988 s 444A)	Both parties UK-resident: Robert Peel, Revenue Policy, Business Tax, 3rd Floor (3C/10), 1 Parliament Street, London SW1A 2BQ
	At least one party not UK-resident: Richard Thomas, Revenue Policy, Business Tax, Room 5W2, 5th Floor, 22 Kingsway, London WC2B 6NR
Demergers (TA 1988 s 215); Company purchase of own shares (TA 1988 s 225); Transactions in securities (TA 1988 s 707); Enterprise Investment Scheme – acquisition of shares by new company (TA 1988 s 304A(1)(f)); Share exchanges (TCGA 1992 ss 138, 139, 140B, 140D); and Intangible fixed assets (FA 2002 Sch 29 para 88)	Business Tax Clearance Team, 5th Floor, 22 Kingsway, London WC2B 6NR (Market sensitive applications to Margaret Draper; non-market sensitive applications to Mohini Sawhney — see note below)[1]
Company migration (FA 1988 s 130)	Mike Bowen, Revenue Policy International, 1 Parliament Street, London SW1A 2BQ
Advance pricing agreements (FA 1999 ss 85–87)	Ian Wood, Revenue Policy International, 1 Parliament Street, London SW1A 2BQ
	For APAs involving oil taxation: Nic Perks or Malcolm Phelps, Revenue Policy, International, Oil Taxation Office (APAs), Melbourne House, Aldwych, London WC2B 4LL
Controlled foreign companies (TA 1988 ss 747–756, Schs 24–26)	Stephen Hewitt or Mary Sharp, Revenue Policy International, 1 Parliament Street, London SW1A 2BQ
Corporate Venturing Schemes (FA 2000 Sch 15)	Small Company Enterprise Centre, Centre for Revenue Intelligence (CRI), Ty Glas, Llanishen, Cardiff CF14 5ZG

Approval application	Address
Pensions (TA 1988 ss 590, 591)	Inland Revenue, Pension Schemes Office, Yorke House, PO Box 62, Castle Meadow Road, Nottingham NG2 1BG
Employee share schemes (TA 1988 Sch 9)	Kevin Meehan, Revenue Policy, Capital and Savings, Employee Share Schemes, Second Floor, New Wing, Somerset House, London WC2R 1LB
Qualifying life assurance policies (TA 1988 Sch 15)	Claire Ritchie, Revenue Policy, Business Tax (Insurance), 1 Parliament Street, London SW1A 2BQ
Professional bodies (relief for subscriptions) (TA 1988 s 201)	A list of approved professional bodies and learned societies is available on the Revenue website (at www.inlandrevenue.gov.uk/list3/index.htm)

Application for treasury consent	Address
Transactions in shares or debentures (TA 1988 ss 765, 765A)	Andy Beazley, Doug Jones or Mary Sharp, Revenue Policy International, 1 Parliament Street, London SW1A 2BQ

Confirmation or pre-transaction advice	Address
Funding issues (TA 1988 ss 209, 703) Transactions in land (TA 1988 ss 35, 776)	Andy Beazley, Revenue Policy International, 1 Parliament Street, London SW1A 2BQ Applications for clearance should be sent to the Inspector of Taxes who deals with the returns

[1] Where clearance is sought under any one or more of TA 1988 ss 215, 225, 304A, 707; TCGA 1992 ss 138, 139, 140B, 140D; or FA 2002 Sch 29 para 88, clearance applications may be sent in a single letter to the above London address for clearances under those sections. The letter should make clear what clearance is required. Email applications can be sent to reconstructions@gtnet.gov.uk and fax applications to 020 7438 4409. For market sensitive information, call Margaret Draper on 020 7438 6585 before sending an email or fax. A reply by email should be requested if required. General enquiries can be made to Mohini Sawhney on 020 7438 8355.

Inland Revenue explanatory pamphlets

Tax Bulletin: published six times a year. Available on annual subscription or at the Revenue internet site (below): contact Mrs Sylvia Brown, Room G7, New Wing, Somerset House, London WC2R 1LB (020 7438 6373).

Copies of the pamphlets listed below are obtainable from Inland Revenue Enquiry Centres, Tax Offices and Inland Revenue National Insurance Contributions offices with the exception of:

Inheritance tax: IHT Customer Information Leaflet, IHT 4, IHT 11, IHT 13, IHT 14, available from Revenue Capital Taxes: (England and Wales) Ferrers House, PO Box 38, Castle Meadow Road, Nottingham NG2 1BB; (Scotland) Meldrum House, 15 Drumsheugh Gardens, Edinburgh EH3 7UG; (Northern Ireland) Dorchester House, 52–58 Great Victoria Street, Belfast BT2 7QL; (Stationery Orderline 0845 234 1000). IHT 15 is available only on the Internet. IHT 8, IHT 16–IHT 17 will only be available on the Internet once currect stocks run out.

Pension Schemes: IR76, IR12 and IR12 Supplement available only from the Revenue website from 30 November 2003.

Charities: IR2004 available from IR Charities, Meldrum House, 15 Drumsheugh Gardens, Edinburgh EH5 3LU (0845 302 0203).

Codes of Practice: COP4 is available from Inland Revenue APSS, St John's House, Merton Road, Bootle, Merseyside L69 9BB (0151 472 6218). COP8 and COP9 are available from Special Compliance Office, Angel Court, 199 Borough High Street, London SE1 1HZ (020 7234 3708). COP24 and COP25 are available from the SDLT Orderline 0845 302 1472.

Digest of DT agreements is available from Inland Revenue International, Centre for Non-Residents, Fitz Roy House, PO Box 46, Nottingham NG2 1BD (0845 070 0040).

Employers: leaflets 480, 490, CWG2 and other employer PAYE and NIC tables and guides are available from the Internet and from the Employer's Orderline 0845 7 643 646.

Shares Valuation: SV1 available as for Inheritance tax above.

Stamp duty land tax: series available from the Internet and from the SDLT Orderline 0845 302 1472.

Education Service Pack (The Red Box) (free): Helpline: 020 7401 4070, e-mail: requests@edcoms.co.uk. Education service pages are available at www.redbox gov.uk.

Internet: Most publications are available on the internet at: www.inlandrevenue.gov.uk

Welsh: Most leaflets are available in Welsh. Welsh call centre: 0845 302 1489.

*Available only on the internet.

Pamphlet	Date Supp	Title
Catalogue	2004	Catalogue of leaflets and booklets
IR 1*	2003	Extra-statutory concessions
IR 2	2003	Occupational pension schemes. A guide for members of tax-approved schemes
IR 3	2003	Personal pension schemes
IR 4	2003	Bankruptcy proceedings in England and Wales
IR 5	2002	Winding-up proceedings in England and Wales
IR 8*	2002	Solicitor's Office Enforcement Section, winding-up petitions
IR 10*	2004	Paying the right tax on your earnings and pension
IR 12*	2001 (2001)	Practice notes on approval of occupational pension schemes
IR 14/15 (C S)	2003	Construction industry scheme
IR 20	1999	Residents and non-residents. Liability to tax in the UK
IR 40 (CIS)	2003	Construction industry scheme. Conditions for getting a subcontractor's tax certificate
IR 45	2005	Contacting the Revenue when someone has died
IR 46*	2000	Clubs, societies and voluntary associations
IR 56	2004	Employed or self-employed? A guide for tax and national insurance
IR 59*	2003	Collection of student loans
IR 64	2004	Giving to charity by businesses
IR 65	2004	Giving to charity by individuals
IR 68*	2002	Accrued income scheme. Taxing securities on transfer
IR 69	2002	Expenses payments and benefits in kind. How to save yourself work
IR 76*	2001	Personal pension schemes. Guidance notes
IR 87	2004	Letting and your home
IR 97	1996	Approved SAYE share option schemes
IR 101	1996	Approved company share option plans. An outline for employees
IR 109	2002	Employer compliance reviews and negotiations
IR 110*	2003	Bank and Building Society interest. A guide for savers
IR 111	2004	Bank and Building Society interest. Are you paying tax when you don't need to?
IR 115	2005	Childcare provided by employers
IR 116 (CIS)	2003	Guide for subcontractors with tax certificates
IR 117 (CIS)	2003	Guide for subcontractors with Registration Cards
IR 121	2004	Moving into retirement
IR 122	2002	Volunteer drivers
IR 124	2002	Using your own vehicle for work
IR 131*	2004	Inland Revenue Statements of Practice
IR 134	2000	Income tax and national insurance contributions on relocation packages
IR 136	2001	Income tax and company vans
IR 137*	2003	The Enterprise Investment Scheme

Pamphlet	Date Supp	Title
IR 138	1995	Living or retiring abroad? A guide to UK tax on your UK income and pension
IR 139	1995	Income from abroad? A guide to UK tax on overseas income
IR 140	2002	Non-resident landlords, their agents and tenants
IR 143	2000	Income tax and redundancy
IR 145	2001	Low interest loans provided by employers
IR 148	2001	Are your workers employed or self-employed? A guide for tax and national insurance for contractors in the construction industry
IR 150	1999	Taxation of rents – a guide to property income
IR 155	2001	PAYE settlement agreements
IR 160	2004	Inland Revenue enquiries under self-assessment
IR 166*	2002	The euro
IR 169*	2002	Venture capital trusts (VCTs) – a brief guide
IR 170	2003	Blind person's allowance
IR 172	2003	Income tax and company cars
IR 175*	2001	Supplying services through a limited company or partnership
IR 177	2001	Share incentive plans and your entitlement to benefits
IR 178	2004	Giving shares and securities to charity
IR 180 (CIS)	2003	Construction Industry Scheme. A guide for non-residents
IR 2000*	2001	The corporate venturing scheme
IR 2001	2001	Trading by charities
IR 2002	2001	Share incentive plans. A guide for employees
IR 2003*	2001	Supplying services. How to calculate the deemed payment
IR 2004	2003	Setting up a charity in Scotland
IR 2005	2001	Share Incentive Plans. Guidance for employers and advisers
IR 2006	2001	Enterprise Management Incentives. A guide
IR 2007	2001	Capital Allowances for flats over shops
IR 2008	2005	ISAs, PEPs and TESSAs
IR 2009	2001	Why pay cash?
IR 2010	2004	Electronic payment methods
480	2004	Expenses and benefits. A tax guide
490	2003	Employee travel. A tax and NICs guide for employers
FEU50*	2000	A guide to paying foreign entertainers
DT Digest*	2004	Digest of double taxation treaties
PSO3*	2001	Occupational pension schemes – A guide for trustees of small self-administered schemes
CGT 1	2003	Capital gains tax. An introduction
CGT/FS1	2004	Capital gains tax. A quick guide
IHT 2*	2004	Inheritance tax on lifetime gifts
IHT 3	2004	Inheritance tax. An introduction
IHT 4	2003	Notes on informal calculations of inheritance tax
IHT 8*	2004	Alterations to an inheritance following a death
IHT 11	2004	Payment of inheritance tax from national savings or British Government Stock
IHT 12*	2003	When is an excepted estate grant appropriate?
IHT 13	2004	Inheritance tax and penalties
IHT 14	2004	Inheritance Tax. The personal representatives' responsibilities
IHT 15*	1996	How to calculate the liability
IHT 16*	2004	Inheritance Tax. Settled property
IHT 17*	2004	Businesses, farms and woodlands
IHT 18*	2004	Inheritance tax. Foreign aspects
IHT 19*	2003	Delivery of a reduced Inland Revenue account
SD 1	2003	Enquiries into land transaction returns
SD 2	2003	A quick guide to buying a property
SD 3	2003	A guide to leases
SD 4	2003	A brief guide for practitioners
SD 5	2003	A brief guide for practitioners in Scotland
SD 7	2004	Penalties for late land transaction returns
SD 8	2004	Enquiries under SDLT. How settlements are negotiated
Collection 1*	1995	Distraint
Collection 1(Sco)*	1994	Summary Warrant
Collection 1 (NI)*	2000	Distraint
Collection 2*	1994	Magistrates' Court proceedings
Collection 2 (Sco)*	1994	Sheriff Court proceedings
Collection 2 (NI)*	2000	Magistrates' Court proceedings
Collection 3*	1995	County Court proceedings
Collection 3 (Sco)*	1994	Court of Session proceedings
Collection 4 (Sco)*	2000	Sequestration and winding up
Collection 4 (NI)*	2000	Bankruptcy and winding up
COP 1	2003	Putting things right. How to complain
COP 3	2003	Reviews of employers' and contractors' records
COP 4	2002	Inspection of schemes operated by financial intermediaries
COP 8	2003	Special Compliance Office Investigations. Cases other than suspected serious fraud
COP 9	2003	Special Compliance Office Investigations. Cases of suspected serious fraud

Pamphlet	Date Supp	Title
COP 9 (Sco)	2004	Special Compliance Office Investigations in Scotland. Cases of suspected serious fraud
COP 9 (NI)	2004	Special Compliance Office Investigations in Northern Ireland. Cases of suspected serious fraud
COP 11	2004	Self Assessment. Local office enquiries
COP 14	2003	Enquiries into Company Tax Returns
COP 19	2004	National minimum wage. Information for employers. Enquiries by the Inland Revenue
COP 21	2003	Data protection
COP 22	2001	Orders for the delivery of documents
COP 24	2003	Stamp duty land tax enquiries
COP 25	2004	Stamp duty land tax. Enquiries into companies and partnerships
COP 26	2004	What happens if we have paid you too much tax credit?
COP 27*	2004	Child Tax Credit and Working Tax Credit. Local office enquiries
COP-AT*	2003	Anti-terrorism, Crime and Security Act: disclosure of information
—*	1999	Code of practice on consultation
AO1	2003	The Adjudicator's office for complaints about the Inland Revenue and the Valuation Office Agency
CTSA/BK3	2003	A modern system for corporation tax payments
CTSA/BK4	2003	A general guide to corporation tax self-assessment
E24	2005	Tips, gratuities, service charges and troncs
CH24A	2003	Child Benefit and Guardian's Allowance. If you think a decision is wrong
WTC1	2004	Child tax credit and working tax credit. An introduction
WTC2	2003	Child tax credit and working tax credit. A guide
WTC3	2004	Tax Credit Penalties. How tax credit examinations are settled
WTC4	2004	Tax Credit Penalties. How tax credit enquiries are settled
WTC5	2004	Help with the costs of childcare. Information for parents and childcare providers
WTC6	2004	Child tax credit and working tax credit. Other types of help you might be able to get
WTC7	2005	Tax Credit penalties – what happens at the end of a check
WTC/AP	2004	How to appeal against a tax credit decision or award
WTC/E6	2003	Working tax credit paid with wages
SA/BK4	2003	Self-assessment. A general guide to keeping records
SA/BK6	2003	Self-assessment. Penalties for late tax returns
SA/BK7	2003	Self-assessment. Surcharges for late payment of tax
SA/BK8	2004	Self-assessment. Your guide
SV 1	2004	Shares Valuation. An introduction
P/SE/1	2004	Thinking of working for yourself?
CWL 2*	2003	NI contributions for self-employed people. Class 2 and Class 4
CWL4	2001	Fund-raising events: exemption for charities and other qualifying bodies
CWL5	2002	The Voluntary Arrangements Service
CWG 2	2005	Employer's further guide to PAYE and NICs
—	2002	Red Box Education pack
—	2004	Tax Appeals. A guide to appealing against decisions of the Inland Revenue on tax and other matters (Department for Constitutional Affairs)
—	2004	Trusts. An introduction

National Insurance Contributions Leaflets see p 95.

Internal guidance booklets and manuals

Accounts Office Interest Review Unit (AORU) Manual
Applicant Compliance Guide
Assessed Taxes
Assessment Procedures Manual

Banking Manual
Business Income Manual

Capital Allowances Manual
Capital Gains Manual
Child Benefit Technical Manual
Collection Manual
Collection of Student Loans
Community Investment Tax Relief Manual
Company Taxation
Construction Industry Scheme
Corporate Finance Manual
Corporate Intangibles Research and Development
COTAX Manual

Decision Maker's Guide
Departmental Project Management Methodology
  Manual
Departmental Security Manual
Double Taxation Relief Manual

Employee Share Schemes Unit Manual
Employer Compliance Handbook
Employment Income Manual
Employment Procedures Manual
Employment Status Manual
Enforcement Manual
Enforcement Manual (Scotland)
Enquiry Manual
European Economic Interest Groupings

Finance Leasing Manual

General Insurance Manual

Income Tax Self Assessment: The Legal Framework
Independent Taxation Manual
Inheritance Tax Double Taxation Conventions and
  Agreements Manual
Insolvency Manual
Inspector's Manual

International Manual
International Tax Handbook

Life Assurance Manual
Lloyd's Manual

Manufactured Overseas Dividends Guidance Manual
Movements Manual (PAYE)

National Insurance Manual
New Tax Credits Claimant Compliance Manual

Oil Taxation Manual

PAYE Instructions (Collection)
Pension Schemes Manual
Pensioner Tax Back Manual
PEP and ISA Manual
Personal Contact Manual
Profit Related Pay Unit Manual
Property Income Manual
PSA Handbook
Purchasing Manual

Receivables Telephone Centre Manual
Recovery Manual
Redress Handbook
Regulation of Investigatory Powers Manual
Relief Instructions
Repayment Claims Manual
Residence Guide

SE Manual
Self Assessment Manual
Share Schemes Manual
Shares Valuation Division
Shares Valuation Manual
Stamp Duty Land Tax Manual
Stamp Office Manual

Tax Credits Office Manual
Tax Credits Technical Manual
Tonnage Tax Manual
Trusts, Settlements and Estates Manual

Venture Capital Schemes Manual

Copies of the manuals are available online and on CD-rom, with an updating service, as part of a database. Contact customer services at LexisNexis Butterworths, 2 Addiscombe Road, Croydon, Surrey CR9 5AF: telephone 020 8662 2000; fax 020 8662 2012. Extracts published in looseleaf format as *Simon's Direct Tax Service*, Binders 12 and 13: prices available on application to the publishers.

All internal guidance manuals are available for inspection free of charge in Inland Revenue Tax Enquiry Centres and on the Revenue internet site. The inheritance tax manuals may be inspected free of charge at certain Capital Taxes Offices.

Capital gains tax

Annual exemption

Individuals, personal representatives[1] and certain trusts[2]

Exempt amount of net gains	2000–01	2001–02	2002–03	2003–04	2004–05	2005–06
	£7,200	£7,500	£7,700	£7,900	£8,200	£8,500

[1] Year of death and following 2 years (maximum).
[2] Trusts for mentally disabled persons and those in receipt of attendance allowance or disability living allowance. Exemption divided by number of qualifying settlements created (after 9 March 1981) by one settlor, subject to a minimum of one-tenth.

Trusts generally

Exempt amount of net gains	2000–01	2001–02	2002–03	2003–04	2004–05	2005–06
	£3,600	£3,750	£3,850	£3,950	£4,100	£4,250

[1] Exemption divided by number of qualifying settlements created (after 6 June 1978) by one settlor, subject to a minimum of one-fifth.

Chattel exemption

	Disposals exemption	Marginal relief: Maximum chargeable gain
From 1989–90 onwards	£6,000	⅔ excess over £6,000

Rate of tax

2005–06	**Individuals:** gains taxed as top slice of income: 10% to starting rate limit, 20% to basic rate limit, 40% above basic rate limit, subject to taper relief in certain cases. **Trusts and personal representatives:** 40%, subject to taper relief in certain cases. **Trusts for vulnerable persons:** gains to be taxed as though they are those of the beneficiary (Budget 2005, Revenue Notice 10).
2004–05	**Individuals:** gains taxed as top slice of income*: 10% to starting rate limit, 20% to basic rate limit, 40% above, subject to taper relief in certain cases. **Trusts, personal representatives:** 40%, subject to taper relief in certain cases. **Trusts for vulnerable persons:** gains can be taxed (on election) (FA 2005 ss 23–45) as though they are those of the beneficiary (on the beneficiary if UK-resident or on the trustees if beneficiary is non-UK resident).
2000–01 to 2003–04	**Individuals:** gains taxed as top slice of income*: 10% to starting rate limit, 20% to basic rate limit, 40% above, subject to taper relief in certain cases. **Trusts, personal representatives:** 34%, subject to taper relief in certain cases
1999–2000	**Individuals:** gains taxed as top slice of income*: 20% to basic rate limit, 40% above, subject to taper relief in certain cases. **Trusts, personal representatives:** 34%, subject to taper relief in certain cases.

Settlements where settlor retains an interest: chargeable on settlor at own rates.
* Adjustment is necessary for savings income (including interest from banks and building societies, interest distributions from authorised unit trusts, interest from gilts and other securities including corporate bonds, purchased life annuities, and discounts). Adjustment is also necessary for dividends or other qualifying distributions from a UK-resident company.

Retirement relief (phased out from 6 April 1999)

Retirement relief is no longer available for disposals after 5 April 2003.

Disposals after	Minimum age	100% relief on gains up to	50% relief on gains between	Maximum relief
5 April 2002	50	£50,000	£50,000.01–£200,000	£125,000
5 April 2001	50	£100,000	£100,000.01–£400,000	£250,000
5 April 2000	50	£150,000	£150,000.01–£600,000	£375,000
5 April 1999	50	£200,000	£200,000.01–£800,000	£500,000
27 November 1995	50	£250,000	£250,000.01–£1,000,000	£625,000
29 November 1993	55	£250,000	£250,000.01–£1,000,000	£625,000

(% determined by qualifying period. Relief also available where early retirement occurs for reasons of ill-health. Relief given after indexation allowance but before tapering relief.)

Indexation allowance
(TCGA 1992 ss 53–57, 109)

For gains on disposals by individuals, trustees and personal representatives, an indexation allowance is given up to April 1998 and taper relief applies thereafter on disposals made after 5 April 1998 (see below). Indexation allowance is deducted before applying taper relief. The indexation allowance is calculated by multiplying each item of allowable expenditure by:

$$\frac{RD - RI}{RI}$$

where RD = Retail prices index figure for month of disposal
RI = Retail prices index for month of expenditure (or March 1982 if later)

See pages 44–57 for indexation allowances applicable for corporation tax and page 58 for RPI values.

For disposals after 31 March 1998 of assets acquired on or before that date the factors below can be used to calculate the indexation allowance available to April 1998 for acquisitions in the month shown.

	Jan	Feb	Mar	Apr	May	Jun	Jul	Aug	Sep	Oct	Nov	Dec
1982	–	–	1·047	1·006	0·992	0·987	0·986	0·985	0·987	0·977	0·967	0·971
1983	0·968	0·960	0·956	0·929	0·921	0·917	0·906	0·898	0·889	0·883	0·876	0·871
1984	0·872	0·865	0·859	0·834	0·828	0·823	0·825	0·808	0·804	0·793	0·788	0·789
1985	0·783	0·769	0·752	0·716	0·708	0·704	0·707	0·703	0·704	0·701	0·695	0·693
1986	0·689	0·683	0·681	0·665	0·662	0·663	0·667	0·662	0·654	0·652	0·638	0·632
1987	0·626	0·620	0·616	0·597	0·596	0·596	0·597	0·593	0·588	0·580	0·573	0·574
1988	0·574	0·568	0·562	0·537	0·531	0·525	0·524	0·507	0·500	0·485	0·478	0·474
1989	0·465	0·454	0·448	0·423	0·414	0·409	0·408	0·404	0·395	0·384	0·372	0·369
1990	0·361	0·353	0·339	0·300	0·288	0·283	0·282	0·269	0·258	0·248	0·251	0·252
1991	0·249	0·242	0·237	0·222	0·218	0·213	0·215	0·213	0·208	0·204	0·199	0·198
1992	0·199	0·193	0·189	0·171	0·167	0·167	0·171	0·171	0·166	0·162	0·164	0·168
1993	0·179	0·171	0·167	0·156	0·152	0·153	0·156	0·151	0·146	0·147	0·148	0·146
1994	0·151	0·144	0·141	0·128	0·124	0·124	0·129	0·124	0·121	0·120	0·119	0·114
1995	0·114	0·107	0·102	0·091	0·087	0·085	0·091	0·085	0·080	0·085	0·085	0·079
1996	0·083	0·078	0·073	0·066	0·063	0·063	0·067	0·062	0·057	0·057	0·057	0·053
1997	0·053	0·049	0·046	0·040	0·036	0·032	0·032	0·026	0·021	0·019	0·019	0·016
1998	0·019	0·014	0·011	–	–	–	–	–	–	–	–	–

Losses. For disposals after 30 November 1993, indexation allowance can only be used to reduce or extinguish a gain. It cannot be used to create or increase a capital loss.

Share identification rules
(TCGA 1992 ss 104, 105, 105A, 105B, 106A)

For acquisitions before 6 April 1998 and for acquisitions on or after that date, for corporation tax on capital gains purposes, shares and securities of the same class in the same company are pooled and treated as a single asset.

For acquisitions after 5 April 1998 for individuals, trustees and personal representatives, disposals are identified with acquisitions in the following order:
- same day acquisitions (subject to special rules distinguishing shares acquired after 5 April 2002 from approved employee share option schemes from other shares acquired on the same day);
- acquisitions within the following 30 days[1] (thus countering 'bed and breakfasting');
- previous acquisitions after 5 April 1998 on a last in/first out basis;
- shares acquired after 5 April 1982 in the pool at 5 April 1998 (the 'section 104 holding');
- shares acquired before 6 April 1982 (the '1982 holding');
- any shares acquired on or before 6 April 1965 on a last in/first out basis;
- if any shares disposed of are still not fully matched, shares acquired subsequent to the disposal (beyond the above mentioned 30-day period).

[1] The 30-day matching rule also applied (in priority to pooling and otherwise than for corporation tax purposes) to disposals and reacquisitions between 17 March 1998 and 5 April 1998 inclusive.

Taper relief

(TCGA 1992 s 2A, Sch A1; FA 2000 ss 66, 67; FA 2002 ss 46, 47, Sch 10; FA 2003 s 160)

Taper relief is available for disposals made after 5 April 1998 by individuals, trustees and personal representatives. The chargeable gain is reduced according to the number of complete years for which the asset has been held (counting from 6 April 1998). Non-business assets acquired before 17 March 1998 qualify for an addition of one year to the period for which they are held after 5 April 1998. Business assets acquired before 17 March 1998 also qualify for the one-year addition but only if disposed of before 6 April 2000.

Taper relief applies to gains after all deductions and before the annual exemption. Losses are set against pre-tapered gains in the most beneficial way possible. Where applicable, the combined period of holding by spouses is taken into account.

Business assets

Number of complete yrs after 5.4.98 for which asset held	% of gain chargeable	Equivalent tax rates.	
		Higher rate taxp'r	20% rate taxp'r
Disposals after 5 April 2002			
0	100	40	20
1	50	20	10
2 or more	25	10	5
Disposals after 5 April 2000 and before 6 April 2002			
0	100	40	20
1	87·5	35	17·5
2	75	30	15
3	50	20	10
4 or more	25	10	5
Disposals before 6 April 2000			
0	100	40	20
1	92·5	37	18·5
2	85	34	17
3	77·5	31	15·5

Non-business assets

Number of complete yrs after 5.4.98 for which asset held	% of gain chargeable	Equivalent tax rates:	
		Higher rate taxp'r	20% rate taxp'r
0	100	40	20
1	100	40	20
2	100	40	20
3	95	38	19
4	90	36	18
5	85	34	17
6	80	32	16
7	75	30	15
8	70	28	14
9	65	26	13
10 or more	60	24	12

Business assets A 'business asset' is one of the following:
- an asset used for the purposes of a trade carried on (alone or in partnership) by the taxpayer or, after 5 April 2004, any individual, trustee or personal representative; or
- an asset used for the purposes of a trade carried on by a 'qualifying company' (alone or, after 4 April 2004, in partnership); or
- shares or securities in a 'qualifying company'; or
- from 6 April 2000, an asset used for the purpose of any office or employment (full-time or part-time) held by the taxpayer with a person carrying on a trade; or
- before 6 April 2000, an asset used for the purpose of a qualifying office or employment to which the taxpayer is required to devote substantially the whole of his time.

Qualifying company From 6 April 2000, a 'qualifying company', by reference to an individual, is a trading company (or holding company of a trading group), where one or more of the following conditions is met:
- the company is unlisted (including an AIM company); or
- the taxpayer is an employee (full-time or part-time) of the company or a fellow group company (in which case the requirement that the company be a trading company etc. is dropped, provided the taxpayer's interest in the company, including connected person holdings, is no more than 10%); or
- the taxpayer can exercise at least 10% of the voting rights.

Before 6 April 2000, a 'qualifying company', by reference to an individual, is a trading company (or holding company of a trading group) where either:
- the taxpayer holds at least 5% of the voting rights and is a full-time employee of the company or a fellow group company; or
- the taxpayer holds at least 25% of the voting rights.

Leases

Depreciation table (TCGA 1992 Sch 8 para 1)

Yrs	%	Yrs	%	Yrs	%
50 (or more)	100	33	90·280	16	64·116
49	99·657	32	89·354	15	61·617
48	99·289	31	88·371	14	58·971
47	98·902	30	87·330	13	56·167
46	98·490	29	86·226	12	53·191
45	98·059	28	85·053	11	50·038
44	97·595	27	83·816	10	46.695
43	97·107	26	82·496	9	43·154
42	96·593	25	81·100	8	39·399
41	96·041	24	79·622	7	35·414
40	95·457	23	78·055	6	31·195
39	94·842	22	76·399	5	26·722
38	94·189	21	74·635	4	21·983
37	93·497	20	72·770	3	16·959
36	92·761	19	70·791	2	11·629
35	91·981	18	68·697	1	5·983
34	91·156	17	66·470	0	0

Formula: fraction of expenditure disallowed—

$$\frac{\left.\begin{array}{l}\text{Percentage for duration of lease}\\\text{at acquisition or expenditure}\end{array}\right\} \quad minus \quad \left\{\begin{array}{l}\text{Percentage for duration of}\\\text{lease at disposal}\end{array}\right.}{\text{Percentage for duration of lease at acquisition or expenditure}}$$

Fractions of years:

Add one-twelfth of the difference between the percentage for the whole year and the next higher percentage for each additional month. Odd days under 14 are not counted; 14 odd days or more count as a month.

Short leases: premiums treated as rent (TA 1988 s 34, TCGA 1992 Sch 8 para 5)

Part of premium for grant of a short lease which is chargeable to income tax as property income—

$P - (2\% \times (n - 1) \times P)$

Where P = amount of premium

n = number of complete years which lease has to run when granted

Length of Lease (complete years)	Amount chargeable to CGT %	Income tax charge %	Length of Lease (complete years)	Amount chargeable to CGT %	Income tax charge %	Length of Lease (complete years)	Amount chargeable to CGT %	Income tax charge %
Over 50	100	0	34	66	34	17	32	68
50	98	2	33	64	36	16	30	70
49	96	4	32	62	38	15	28	72
48	94	6	31	60	40	14	26	74
47	92	8	30	58	42	13	24	76
46	90	10	29	56	44	12	22	78
45	88	12	28	54	46	11	20	80
44	86	14	27	52	48	10	18	82
43	84	16	26	50	50	9	16	84
42	82	18	25	48	52	8	14	86
41	80	20	24	46	54	7	12	88
40	78	22	23	44	56	6	10	90
39	76	24	22	42	58	5	8	92
38	74	26	21	40	60	4	6	94
37	72	28	20	38	62	3	4	96
36	70	30	19	36	64	2	2	98
35	68	32	18	34	66	1 or less	0	100

Gilt-edged securities exempt from tax on chargeable gains

The following securities have been specified for the purposes of TCGA 1992 Sch 9 and are exempt from capital gains tax. A similar exemption exists for qualifying corporate bonds issued after 13 March 1984. The gain accruing on the disposal of an option or contract to acquire or dispose of gilt-edged securities or qualifying corporate bonds after 1 July 1986 is also exempt from capital gains tax. (Securities redeemed before 1 May 2005 do not appear on this list.) (See the Revenue website (www.inlandrevenue.gov.uk/cgt/gilts-list.htm) for a list of gilt-edged securities with a redemption date on or after 1 January 1992.)

Readers should note that under the loan relationship provisions of FA 1996 Part IV Chapter II, the definition of 'qualifying corporate bond' for the purposes of corporation tax only has been extended (see TCGA 1992 ss 117, 117A, 117B).

Stocks		Redemption dates	Dividend due dates	
10½%	Exchequer Stock 2005ᴿ	20 September 2005	20 March	20 September
8½%	Treasury Stock 2005	7 December 2005	7 June	7 December
2%	Index-Linked Treasury Stock 2006	19 July 2006	19 January	19 July
7¾%	Treasury Stock 2006	8 September 2006	8 March	8 September
9¾%	Conversion Stock 2006ᴿ	15 November 2006	15 May	15 November
7½%	Treasury Stock 2006	7 December 2006	7 June	7 December
4½%	Treasury Stock 2007	7 March 2007	7 March	7 September
7¼%	Treasury Stock 2007	7 June 2007	7 June	7 December
8½%	Treasury Loan 2007	16 July 2007	16 January	16 July
9%	Treasury Loan 2008ᴿ	13 October 2008	13 April	13 October
5%	Treasury Stock 2008	7 March 2008	7 March	7 September
2½%	Index-Linked Treasury Stock 2009	20 May 2009	20 May	20 November
4%	Treasury Stock 2009	7 March 2009	7 March	7 September
8%	Treasury Stock 2009ᴿ	25 September 2009	25 March	25 September
5¾%	Treasury Stock 2009	7 December 2009	7 June	7 December
4¾%	Treasury Stock 2010	7 June 2010	7 June	7 December
6¼%	Treasury Stock 2010	25 November 2010	25 May	25 November
9%	Conversion Loan 2011	12 July 2011	12 January	12 July
2½%	Index-Linked Treasury Stock 2011	23 August 2011	23 February	23 August
5%	Treasury Stock 2012	7 March 2012	7 March	7 September
9%	Treasury Stock 2012ᴿ	6 August 2012	6 February	6 August
5½%	Treasury Stock 2008–12*	10 September 2008/ 10 September 2012	10 March	10 September
2½%	Index-Linked Treasury Stock 2013	16 August 2013	16 February	16 August
8%	Treasury Stock 2013	27 September 2013	27 March	27 September
5%	Treasury Stock 2014	7 September 2014	7 March	7 September
7¾%	Treasury Loan 2012–15*	26 January 2012/26 January 2015	26 January	26 July
4¾%	Treasury Stock 2015	7 September 2015	7 March	7 September
8%	Treasury Stock 2015	7 December 2015	7 June	7 December
2½%	Index-Linked Treasury Stock 2016	26 July 2016	26 January	26 July
8¾%	Treasury Stock 2017	25 August 2017	25 February	25 August
12%	Exchequer Stock 2013–17*ᴿ	12 December 2013/ 12 December 2017	12 June	12 December
2½%	Index-Linked Treasury Stock 2020	16 April 2020	16 April	16 October
8%	Treasury Stock 2021	7 June 2021	7 June	7 December
2½%	Index-Linked Treasury Stock 2024	17 July 2024	17 January	17 July
5%	Treasury Stock 2025	7 March 2025	7 March	7 September
6%	Treasury Stock 2028	7 December 2028	7 June	7 December
4⅛%	Index-Linked Treasury Stock 2030	22 July 2030	22 January	22 July
4¼%	Treasury Stock 2032	7 June 2032	7 June	7 December
2%	Index-Linked Treasury Stock 2035	26 January 2035	26 January	26 July
4¼%	Treasury Stock 2036	7 March 2036	7 March	7 September
4¾%	Treasury Stock 2038	7 December 2038	7 June	7 December
4%	Consolidated Loanᴿ	1 February 1957 or after	1 February	1 August
3½%	War Loan	1 December 1952 or after	1 June	1 December
3½%	Conversion Loanᴿ	1 April 1961 or after	1 April	1 October
3%	Treasury Stockᴿ	5 April 1966 or after	5 April	5 October
2½%	Consolidated Stockᴿ	5 April 1923 or after	5 January 5 July	5 April, 5 October
2½%	Treasury Stockᴿ	1 April 1975 or after	1 April	1 October
2½%	Annuitiesᴿ	5 January 1905 or after	5 January 5 July	5 April, 5 October
2¾%	Annuitiesᴿ	5 January 1905 or after	5 January 5 July	5 April, 5 October

* Repaid at latest date shown unless the Treasury give notice of earlier repayment.
ᴿ Rump stocks (restricted market due to small number of stocks still in issue).

Reliefs

The following is a summary of the main reliefs and exemptions for the year 2005–06. The legislation should be referred to for conditions and exceptions.

Charities

Gains accruing to charities which are both applicable and applied for charitable purposes – extended from 6 April 2002 to donations to Community Amateur Sports Clubs (CASCs)	Exempt

Individuals

Annual exemption (see p 37 for earlier years)	£8,200
Chattel exemption (see p 37 for marginal relief)	£6,000
Compensation (injury to person, profession or vocation)	Exempt
Decorations for valour (acquired otherwise than for money or money's worth)	Gain exempt
Enterprise Investment Scheme (see p 73)	Gain on disposal after relevant three year period exempt to extent full relief given on shares
Foreign currency acquired for personal expenditure	Gain exempt
Gifts for public benefit, works of art, historic buildings etc	No chargeable gain/allowable loss
Gilt-edged stock (see p 41)	No chargeable gain/allowable loss
Married persons living together	No chargeable gain/allowable loss on disposals from one to the other
Motor vehicles	Gain exempt
Principal private residence	Gain exempt
If residence is partly let, exemption for the let part is limited to the smaller of—	(1) exemption on owner-occupied part and (2) £40,000
Qualifying corporate bonds	No chargeable gain (for loans made before 17 March 1998, allowable loss in certain cases if all or part of loss is irrecoverable)
Retirement relief (phased-out over 5 years beginning in 1999–2000: see p 37)	No relief in 2005–06
Hold-over relief for gifts	Restricted to: (1) gifts of business assets (including unquoted shares in trading companies and holding companies of trading groups). Relief is not available on the transfer of shares or securities to a company made after 8 November 1999: FA 2000 s 90 (2) gifts of heritage property (3) gifts to heritage maintenance funds (4) gifts to political parties, and (5) gifts which are chargeable transfers for inheritance tax. Where available, transferee's acquisition cost treated as reduced by held-over gain.
Venture capital trusts (see p 74)	Gain on disposal of shares by original investor exempt if company still a venture capital trust. Exemption applies only to shares acquired up to the permitted maximum of £200,000 per year of assessment (£100,000 for shares acquired before 6 April 2004). Deferral relief is available on gains on assets where the disposal proceeds are reinvested in VCT shares issued before 6 April 2004 and within one year before or after the disposal. This relief is withdrawn for shares issued after that date.

Businesses

Roll-over relief for replacement of business assets

Qualifying assets:
- Buildings and land both occupied and used for the purposes of the trade
- Fixed plant and machinery
- Ships, aircraft and hovercraft
- Satellites, space stations and spacecraft
- Goodwill*
- Milk and potato quotas*
- Ewe and suckler cow premium quotas*
- Fish quotas (from 29 March 1999)*
- UK oil licences (from 1 July 1999)

The 'replacement' assets must be acquired within 12 months before or 3 years after the disposal of the old asset. Both assets must be within any of the above classes. Holdover relief is available where the new asset is a depreciating asset (having a predictable useful life not exceeding 60 years).

*From 1 April 2002, subject to transitional rules, these items are removed from the list for companies only (as they fall within the intangible assets regime from that date (FA 2002 Sch 29 para 132(5))).

Personal representatives

Annual exemption

Year of death and following 2 years: (See p 37 for earlier years)	£8,200

Allowable expenses

Expenses allowable for the costs of establishing title in computing chargeable gains on disposal of assets in a deceased person's estate: deaths occurring after 5 April 1993 (SP 8/94). (The Revenue accepts computations based either on the scale or on the actual allowable expenditure incurred.)

Gross value of estate	Allowable expenditure
Up to £40,000	1.75% of the probate value of the assets sold by the personal representatives
Between £40,001 and £70,000	£700, to be divided between all the assets of the estate in proportion to the probate values and allowed in those proportions on assets sold by the personal representatives
Between £70,001 and £300,000	1% of the probate value of the assets sold
Between £300,001 and £400,000	£3,000, to be divided between all the assets of the estate in proportion to the probate values and allowed in those proportions on assets sold by the personal representatives
Between £400,001 and £750,000	0.75% of the probate value of the assets sold
Exceeding £750,000	Negotiable according to the facts of the particular case

Trustees

Annual exemption see p 37.

Allowable expenses

Expenses allowable in computing chargeable gains of corporate trustees in the administration of trusts and estates: acquisition, disposals and deemed disposals after 5 April 1993 (SP 8/94). (The Revenue accepts computations based either on the scale or on the actual allowable expenditure incurred.)

Transfers of assets to beneficiaries etc	
(a) Quoted stocks and shares (i) One beneficiary (ii) More than one beneficiary	 £20 per holding £20 per holding, divided equally between the beneficiaries
(b) Unquoted shares	As (a) above, plus any exceptional expenditure
(c) Other assets	As (a) above, plus any exceptional expenditure
Actual disposals and acquisitions	
(a) Quoted stocks and shares	Investment fee as charged by the trustee (where a comprehensive annual management fee is charged, the investment fee is taken to be £0.25 per £100 of the sale or purchase moneys)
(b) Unquoted shares	As (a) above, plus actual valuation costs
(c) Other assets	Investment fee (as (a) above), subject to a maximum of £60, plus actual valuation costs
Deemed disposals by trustees	
(a) Quoted stocks and shares	£6 per holding
(b) Unquoted shares	Actual valuation costs
(c) Other assets	Actual valuation costs

Indexation allowance

For corporation tax purposes, an indexation allowance is given as a deduction in calculating gains on disposals from the amount realised (or deemed to be realised) on disposal. The indexation allowance is calculated by multiplying each item of allowable expenditure by:

$$\frac{RD - RI}{RI}$$

where RD = Retail prices index figure for month of disposal

RI = Retail prices index for month of expenditure (or March 1982 if later)

See page 38 for indexation allowances up to April 1998 and taper relief which applies thereafter on disposals made after 5 April 1998 by individuals, trustees and personal representatives. See page 58 for RPI values.

The factors below can be used to calculate the indexation allowance—

Month of disposal

Base Month 1982	2000 Jan	Feb	Mar	Apr	May	June	July	Aug	Sept	Oct	Nov	Dec	2001 Jan	Feb	Mar	Apr	May	June	July	Aug	Sept	Oct	Nov	Dec
Mar	1·097	1·108	1·120	1·141	1·149	1·154	1·146	1·146	1·161	1·160	1·166	1·168	1·154	1·165	1·168	1·179	1·193	1·195	1·181	1·190	1·198	1·194	1·185	1·183
Apr	1·056	1·067	1·078	1·099	1·106	1·111	1·104	1·104	1·119	1·117	1·124	1·125	1·111	1·122	1·125	1·136	1·150	1·152	1·138	1·147	1·155	1·151	1·142	1·140
May	1·041	1·052	1·063	1·084	1·091	1·096	1·089	1·089	1·104	1·102	1·108	1·110	1·096	1·107	1·110	1·121	1·134	1·137	1·123	1·132	1·139	1·135	1·127	1·124
June	1·035	1·046	1·057	1·078	1·086	1·090	1·083	1·083	1·098	1·097	1·103	1·104	1·090	1·101	1·104	1·115	1·128	1·131	1·117	1·126	1·133	1·129	1·121	1·118
July	1·035	1·046	1·057	1·078	1·085	1·090	1·082	1·082	1·097	1·096	1·102	1·103	1·090	1·101	1·103	1·114	1·128	1·130	1·117	1·125	1·132	1·129	1·120	1·118
Aug	1·034	1·045	1·056	1·077	1·084	1·089	1·082	1·082	1·096	1·095	1·101	1·103	1·089	1·100	1·103	1·114	1·127	1·129	1·116	1·125	1·132	1·128	1·120	1·117
Sept	1·035	1·046	1·057	1·078	1·086	1·090	1·083	1·083	1·098	1·097	1·103	1·104	1·090	1·101	1·104	1·115	1·128	1·131	1·117	1·126	1·133	1·129	1·121	1·118
Oct	1·025	1·036	1·047	1·068	1·075	1·080	1·073	1·073	1·087	1·086	1·092	1·093	1·080	1·091	1·093	1·104	1·118	1·120	1·107	1·115	1·123	1·119	1·110	1·108
Nov	1·015	1·026	1·037	1·058	1·065	1·070	1·063	1·063	1·077	1·076	1·082	1·083	1·070	1·081	1·083	1·094	1·107	1·110	1·096	1·105	1·112	1·109	1·100	1·098
Dec	1·019	1·030	1·041	1·062	1·069	1·074	1·066	1·066	1·081	1·080	1·086	1·087	1·074	1·085	1·087	1·098	1·111	1·114	1·100	1·109	1·116	1·112	1·104	1·102
1983 Jan	1·017	1·028	1·038	1·059	1·066	1·071	1·064	1·064	1·078	1·077	1·083	1·084	1·071	1·082	1·084	1·095	1·109	1·111	1·098	1·106	1·114	1·110	1·101	1·099
Feb	1·008	1·019	1·030	1·050	1·057	1·062	1·055	1·055	1·070	1·068	1·074	1·076	1·062	1·073	1·076	1·086	1·100	1·102	1·089	1·097	1·104	1·101	1·092	1·090
Mar	1·004	1·015	1·026	1·046	1·054	1·059	1·051	1·051	1·066	1·065	1·071	1·072	1·059	1·069	1·072	1·083	1·096	1·098	1·085	1·093	1·101	1·097	1·089	1·086
Apr	·977	·987	·998	1·018	1·025	1·030	1·023	1·023	1·037	1·036	1·042	1·043	1·030	1·041	1·043	1·054	1·067	1·069	1·056	1·064	1·072	1·068	1·060	1·057
May	·968	·979	·990	1·010	1·017	1·022	1·014	1·014	1·029	1·027	1·033	1·035	1·022	1·032	1·035	1·045	1·058	1·061	1·048	1·056	1·063	1·059	1·051	1·049
June	·964	·974	·985	1·005	1·012	1·017	1·010	1·010	1·024	1·023	1·028	1·030	1·017	1·027	1·030	1·040	1·053	1·056	1·043	1·051	1·058	1·054	1·046	1·044
July	·953	·964	·974	·994	1·001	1·006	·999	·999	1·013	1·012	1·018	1·019	1·006	1·016	1·019	1·029	1·042	1·045	1·032	1·040	1·047	1·043	1·035	1·033
Aug	·944	·955	·965	·985	·992	·997	·990	·990	1·004	1·003	1·009	1·010	·997	1·008	1·010	1·020	1·033	1·036	1·023	1·031	1·038	1·034	1·026	1·024
Sept	·936	·946	·957	·977	·984	·988	·981	·981	·995	·994	1·000	1·001	·988	·999	1·001	1·011	1·024	1·027	1·014	1·022	1·029	1·025	1·017	1·015
Oct	·929	·939	·950	·970	·977	·981	·974	·974	·988	·987	·993	·994	·981	·992	·994	1·004	1·017	1·019	1·007	1·015	1·022	1·018	1·010	1·008
Nov	·922	·933	·943	·963	·970	·974	·967	·967	·981	·980	·986	·987	·974	·985	·987	·997	1·010	1·012	1·000	1·008	1·015	1·011	1·003	1·001
Dec	·917	·928	·938	·958	·964	·969	·962	·962	·976	·975	·981	·982	·969	·979	·982	·992	1·005	1·007	·994	1·002	1·009	1·006	·998	·996
1984 Jan	·918	·929	·939	·959	·966	·970	·963	·963	·977	·976	·982	·983	·970	·981	·983	·993	1·006	1·008	·996	1·004	1·010	1·007	·999	·997
Feb	·911	·921	·931	·951	·958	·962	·955	·955	·969	·968	·974	·975	·962	·973	·975	·985	·998	1·000	·987	·995	1·002	·999	·991	·989
Mar	·904	·915	·925	·944	·951	·956	·949	·949	·963	·962	·967	·968	·956	·966	·968	·979	·991	·994	·981	·989	·996	·993	·985	·982
Apr	·879	·890	·900	·919	·926	·930	·923	·923	·937	·936	·941	·943	·930	·940	·943	·953	·965	·967	·955	·963	·970	·966	·958	·956
May	·872	·883	·893	·912	·919	·923	·916	·916	·930	·929	·934	·935	·923	·933	·935	·946	·958	·960	·948	·956	·962	·959	·951	·949
June	·868	·878	·888	·907	·914	·918	·911	·911	·925	·924	·929	·930	·918	·928	·930	·941	·953	·955	·943	·951	·957	·954	·946	·944
July	·870	·880	·890	·909	·916	·920	·914	·914	·927	·926	·932	·933	·920	·930	·933	·943	·955	·957	·945	·953	·960	·956	·948	·946
Aug	·852	·862	·872	·891	·898	·902	·896	·896	·909	·908	·914	·915	·902	·912	·915	·925	·937	·939	·927	·935	·941	·938	·930	·928
Sept	·849	·859	·869	·888	·894	·899	·892	·892	·905	·904	·910	·911	·899	·909	·911	·921	·933	·935	·923	·931	·938	·934	·926	·924
Oct	·837	·847	·857	·876	·883	·887	·880	·880	·894	·893	·898	·899	·887	·897	·899	·909	·921	·923	·911	·919	·926	·922	·915	·912
Nov	·832	·842	·852	·870	·877	·881	·875	·875	·888	·887	·892	·893	·881	·891	·893	·903	·915	·918	·905	·913	·920	·916	·909	·907
Dec	·833	·843	·853	·872	·878	·883	·876	·876	·889	·888	·894	·895	·883	·893	·895	·905	·917	·919	·907	·915	·921	·918	·910	·908
1985 Jan	·827	·837	·846	·865	·872	·876	·869	·869	·883	·881	·887	·888	·876	·886	·888	·898	·910	·912	·900	·908	·914	·911	·903	·901
Feb	·812	·822	·832	·850	·857	·861	·854	·854	·868	·866	·872	·873	·861	·871	·873	·883	·895	·897	·885	·893	·899	·896	·888	·886
Mar	·795	·805	·815	·833	·839	·844	·837	·837	·850	·849	·855	·856	·844	·853	·856	·865	·877	·879	·867	·875	·881	·878	·871	·869
Apr	·758	·767	·777	·795	·801	·805	·799	·799	·812	·811	·816	·817	·805	·815	·817	·826	·838	·840	·828	·836	·842	·839	·832	·830
May	·750	·759	·769	·787	·793	·797	·791	·791	·803	·802	·808	·809	·797	·807	·809	·818	·830	·832	·820	·828	·834	·831	·823	·821
June	·746	·756	·765	·783	·789	·793	·787	·787	·800	·799	·804	·805	·793	·803	·805	·814	·826	·828	·816	·824	·830	·827	·819	·817
July	·749	·759	·768	·786	·792	·797	·790	·790	·803	·802	·807	·808	·797	·806	·808	·818	·829	·831	·820	·827	·833	·830	·823	·821
Aug	·745	·754	·764	·781	·788	·792	·786	·786	·798	·797	·802	·803	·792	·801	·803	·813	·824	·826	·815	·822	·829	·825	·818	·816
Sept	·746	·755	·765	·782	·789	·793	·787	·787	·799	·798	·803	·804	·793	·802	·804	·814	·825	·827	·816	·823	·829	·826	·819	·817
Oct	·743	·752	·762	·779	·786	·790	·784	·784	·796	·795	·800	·801	·790	·799	·801	·811	·822	·824	·813	·820	·827	·823	·816	·814
Nov	·737	·746	·756	·773	·780	·784	·778	·778	·790	·789	·794	·795	·784	·793	·795	·805	·816	·818	·807	·814	·820	·817	·810	·808
Dec	·735	·744	·753	·771	·777	·781	·775	·775	·788	·787	·792	·793	·781	·791	·793	·802	·814	·816	·804	·812	·818	·815	·807	·805

Base Month	2002												2003											
1982	Jan	Feb	Mar	Apr	May	June	July	Aug	Sept	Oct	Nov	Dec	Jan	Feb	Mar	Apr	May	June	July	Aug	Sept	Oct	Nov	Dec
Mar	1·181	1·188	1·197	1·212	1·218	1·218	1·214	1·220	1·236	1·239	1·243	1·247	1·246	1·257	1·265	1·281	1·285	1·282	1·282	1·286	1·297	1·299	1·300	1·310
Apr	1·138	1·145	1·153	1·168	1·174	1·174	1·171	1·177	1·192	1·195	1·199	1·203	1·201	1·213	1·220	1·236	1·240	1·237	1·237	1·241	1·252	1·253	1·254	1·264
May	1·123	1·129	1·138	1·153	1·159	1·159	1·155	1·161	1·176	1·180	1·183	1·187	1·186	1·197	1·204	1·220	1·224	1·221	1·221	1·225	1·236	1·237	1·238	1·248
June	1·117	1·123	1·132	1·147	1·153	1·153	1·149	1·155	1·170	1·173	1·177	1·181	1·180	1·191	1·198	1·214	1·217	1·215	1·215	1·219	1·230	1·231	1·232	1·242
July	1·117	1·123	1·131	1·146	1·152	1·152	1·148	1·154	1·169	1·173	1·176	1·180	1·179	1·190	1·197	1·213	1·217	1·214	1·214	1·218	1·229	1·230	1·231	1·241
Aug	1·116	1·122	1·131	1·145	1·151	1·151	1·148	1·154	1·168	1·172	1·176	1·179	1·178	1·189	1·197	1·212	1·216	1·214	1·214	1·217	1·228	1·230	1·231	1·241
Sept	1·117	1·123	1·132	1·147	1·153	1·153	1·149	1·155	1·170	1·173	1·177	1·181	1·180	1·191	1·198	1·214	1·217	1·215	1·215	1·219	1·230	1·231	1·232	1·242
Oct	1·107	1·113	1·121	1·136	1·142	1·142	1·138	1·145	1·159	1·163	1·166	1·170	1·169	1·180	1·187	1·203	1·207	1·204	1·204	1·208	1·219	1·220	1·221	1·231
Nov	1·096	1·103	1·111	1·126	1·132	1·132	1·128	1·134	1·149	1·152	1·156	1·159	1·158	1·169	1·176	1·192	1·196	1·193	1·193	1·197	1·208	1·209	1·210	1·220
Dec	1·100	1·106	1·115	1·129	1·136	1·136	1·132	1·138	1·152	1·156	1·160	1·163	1·162	1·173	1·180	1·196	1·200	1·197	1·197	1·201	1·212	1·213	1·214	1·224
1983																								
Jan	1·098	1·104	1·112	1·127	1·133	1·133	1·129	1·135	1·150	1·153	1·157	1·161	1·160	1·170	1·178	1·193	1·197	1·195	1·195	1·198	1·209	1·210	1·212	1·221
Feb	1·089	1·095	1·103	1·118	1·124	1·124	1·120	1·126	1·141	1·144	1·148	1·151	1·150	1·161	1·168	1·184	1·188	1·185	1·185	1·189	1·200	1·201	1·202	1·212
Mar	1·085	1·091	1·099	1·114	1·120	1·120	1·116	1·122	1·137	1·140	1·144	1·148	1·146	1·157	1·164	1·180	1·184	1·181	1·181	1·185	1·196	1·197	1·198	1·208
Apr	1·056	1·062	1·070	1·085	1·091	1·091	1·087	1·093	1·107	1·111	1·114	1·118	1·117	1·127	1·134	1·150	1·153	1·151	1·151	1·155	1·165	1·166	1·168	1·177
May	1·048	1·053	1·062	1·076	1·082	1·082	1·073	1·081	1·098	1·102	1·105	1·109	1·108	1·118	1·126	1·141	1·144	1·142	1·142	1·146	1·156	1·157	1·159	1·168
June	1·043	1·049	1·057	1·071	1·077	1·077	1·073	1·079	1·095	1·097	1·100	1·104	1·103	1·113	1·120	1·136	1·139	1·137	1·137	1·140	1·151	1·152	1·153	1·163
July	1·032	1·038	1·046	1·060	1·066	1·066	1·062	1·063	1·082	1·086	1·089	1·093	1·091	1·102	1·109	1·124	1·128	1·125	1·125	1·129	1·140	1·141	1·142	1·151
Aug	1·023	1·029	1·037	1·051	1·057	1·057	1·053	1·059	1·073	1·076	1·080	1·083	1·082	1·093	1·100	1·115	1·118	1·116	1·116	1·120	1·130	1·131	1·132	1·142
Sept	1·014	1·020	1·028	1·042	1·047	1·047	1·044	1·050	1·064	1·067	1·071	1·074	1·073	1·083	1·090	1·106	1·109	1·107	1·107	1·110	1·121	1·122	1·123	1·132
Oct	1·007	1·012	1·021	1·034	1·040	1·040	1·037	1·043	1·056	1·060	1·063	1·067	1·066	1·076	1·083	1·098	1·102	1·099	1·099	1·103	1·113	1·114	1·116	1·125
Nov	1·000	1·005	1·013	1·027	1·033	1·033	1·030	1·035	1·049	1·053	1·056	1·060	1·058	1·069	1·076	1·091	1·094	1·092	1·092	1·095	1·106	1·107	1·108	1·117
Dec	·994	1·000	1·008	1·022	1·028	1·028	1·024	1·030	1·044	1·047	1·051	1·054	1·053	1·063	1·070	1·085	1·089	1·086	1·086	1·090	1·100	1·101	1·103	1·112
1984																								
Jan	·996	1·001	1·009	1·023	1·029	1·029	1·025	1·031	1·045	1·048	1·052	1·055	1·054	1·065	1·072	1·086	1·090	1·088	1·088	1·091	1·101	1·103	1·104	1·113
Feb	·987	·993	1·001	1·015	1·021	1·021	1·017	1·023	1·037	1·040	1·044	1·047	1·046	1·056	1·063	1·078	1·081	1·079	1·079	1·083	1·093	1·094	1·095	1·104
Mar	·981	·987	·995	1·009	1·014	1·014	1·011	1·017	1·030	1·034	1·037	1·041	1·039	1·050	1·057	1·071	1·075	1·073	1·073	1·076	1·086	1·087	1·089	1·098
Apr	·955	·961	·969	·982	·988	·988	·984	·990	1·004	1·007	1·010	1·014	1·013	1·023	1·029	1·044	1·048	1·045	1·045	1·049	1·059	1·060	1·061	1·070
May	·948	·953	·961	·975	·980	·980	·977	·983	·996	·999	1·003	1·006	1·005	1·015	1·022	1·037	1·040	1·038	1·038	1·041	1·051	1·052	1·053	1·062
June	·943	·948	·956	·970	·975	·975	·972	·978	·991	·994	·998	1·001	1·000	1·010	1·017	1·031	1·035	1·032	1·032	1·036	1·046	1·047	1·048	1·057
July	·945	·951	·958	·972	·978	·978	·974	·980	·993	·997	1·000	1·003	1·002	1·012	1·019	1·034	1·037	1·035	1·035	1·038	1·048	1·049	1·051	1·059
Aug	·927	·932	·940	·954	·959	·959	·956	·961	·975	·978	·981	·985	·984	·994	1·000	1·015	1·018	1·016	1·016	1·019	1·029	1·030	1·031	1·040
Sept	·923	·929	·936	·950	·955	·955	·952	·958	·971	·974	·977	·981	·980	·990	·996	1·011	1·014	1·012	1·012	1·015	1·025	1·026	1·027	1·036
Oct	·911	·917	·925	·938	·943	·943	·940	·945	·959	·962	·965	·969	·968	·977	·984	·998	1·002	1·000	1·000	1·003	1·013	1·014	1·015	1·024
Nov	·905	·911	·919	·932	·937	·937	·934	·940	·953	·956	·959	·963	·962	·971	·978	·992	·996	·993	·993	·997	1·007	1·008	1·009	1·018
Dec	·907	·913	·920	·933	·939	·939	·936	·941	·954	·958	·961	·964	·963	·973	·980	·994	·997	·995	·995	·998	1·008	1·009	1·010	1·019
1985																								
Jan	·900	·906	·913	·926	·932	·932	·929	·934	·947	·951	·954	·957	·956	·966	·973	·987	·990	·988	·988	·991	1·001	1·002	1·003	1·012
Feb	·885	·890	·898	·911	·916	·916	·913	·919	·932	·935	·938	·942	·940	·950	·957	·971	·974	·972	·972	·975	·985	·986	·987	·996
Mar	·867	·873	·880	·893	·899	·899	·895	·901	·914	·917	·920	·923	·922	·932	·939	·953	·956	·954	·954	·957	·967	·968	·969	·977
Apr	·828	·834	·841	·854	·859	·859	·856	·861	·874	·877	·880	·883	·882	·892	·898	·912	·915	·913	·913	·916	·926	·927	·928	·936
May	·820	·825	·833	·845	·851	·851	·848	·853	·865	·869	·872	·875	·874	·883	·890	·903	·906	·904	·904	·907	·917	·918	·919	·927
June	·816	·822	·829	·841	·847	·847	·844	·849	·861	·865	·868	·871	·870	·879	·886	·899	·902	·900	·900	·903	·913	·914	·915	·923
July	·820	·825	·832	·845	·850	·850	·847	·852	·865	·868	·871	·874	·873	·883	·889	·903	·906	·904	·904	·907	·916	·917	·918	·927
Aug	·815	·820	·827	·840	·845	·845	·842	·847	·860	·863	·866	·869	·868	·878	·884	·898	·901	·899	·899	·902	·911	·912	·913	·922
Sept	·816	·821	·828	·841	·846	·846	·843	·848	·861	·864	·867	·870	·869	·879	·885	·899	·902	·900	·900	·903	·912	·913	·914	·923
Oct	·813	·818	·826	·838	·843	·843	·840	·845	·858	·861	·864	·867	·866	·876	·882	·896	·899	·897	·897	·900	·909	·910	·911	·920
Nov	·807	·812	·819	·832	·837	·837	·834	·839	·852	·855	·858	·861	·860	·869	·876	·889	·892	·890	·890	·893	·903	·904	·905	·913
Dec	·804	·810	·817	·829	·835	·835	·831	·837	·849	·852	·855	·858	·857	·867	·873	·887	·890	·888	·888	·891	·900	·901	·902	·911

Indexation allowance — continued

Month of disposal

Base Month	2004												2005	
1982	Jan	Feb	Mar	Apr	May	June	July	Aug	Sept	Oct	Nov	Dec	Jan	Feb
Mar	1·305	1·314	1·324	1·338	1·348	1·351	1.351	1.359	1.368	1.374	1.379	1.390	1.378	
Apr	1·259	1·268	1·278	1·291	1·301	1·305	1.305	1.312	1.321	1.327	1.332	1.343	1.331	
May	1·243	1·252	1·262	1·275	1·285	1·289	1.289	1.296	1.305	1.311	1.316	1.327	1.314	
June	1·237	1·246	1·255	1·269	1·279	1·282	1.282	1.290	1.298	1.304	1.309	1.320	1.308	
July	1·236	1·245	1·255	1·268	1·278	1·282	1.282	1.289	1.297	1.303	1.308	1.319	1.307	
Aug	1·236	1·244	1·254	1·267	1·277	1·281	1.281	1.288	1.297	1.303	1.308	1.319	1.306	
Sept	1·237	1·246	1·255	1·269	1·279	1·282	1.282	1.290	1.298	1.304	1.309	1.320	1.308	
Oct	1·226	1·234	1·244	1·258	1·267	1·271	1.271	1.278	1.287	1.293	1.298	1.309	1.296	
Nov	1·215	1·224	1·233	1·247	1·256	1·260	1.260	1.267	1.276	1.282	1.286	1.297	1.285	
Dec	1·219	1·228	1·237	1·251	1·260	1·264	1.264	1.271	1.280	1.286	1.291	1.302	1.289	
1983														
Jan	1·216	1·225	1·235	1·248	1·258	1·261	1.261	1.268	1.277	1.283	1.288	1.299	1.287	
Feb	1·207	1·215	1·225	1·238	1·248	1·252	1.252	1.259	1.267	1.273	1.278	1.289	1.277	
Mar	1·203	1·211	1·221	1·234	1·244	1·247	1.247	1.255	1.263	1.269	1.274	1.285	1.273	
Apr	1·172	1·181	1·190	1·203	1·213	1·216	1.216	1.223	1.232	1.238	1.242	1.253	1.241	
May	1·163	1·172	1·181	1·194	1·203	1·207	1.207	1.214	1.222	1.228	1.233	1.244	1.232	
June	1·158	1·166	1·176	1·189	1·198	1·202	1.202	1.209	1.217	1.223	1.228	1.238	1.227	
July	1·147	1·155	1·164	1·177	1·186	1·190	1.190	1.197	1.205	1.211	1.216	1.226	1.215	
Aug	1·137	1·145	1·155	1·167	1·177	1·180	1.180	1.187	1.195	1.201	1.206	1.216	1.205	
Sept	1·128	1·136	1·145	1·158	1·167	1·171	1.171	1.178	1.186	1.192	1.196	1.207	1.195	
Oct	1·120	1·128	1·138	1·150	1·160	1·163	1.163	1.170	1.178	1.184	1.188	1.199	1.187	
Nov	1·113	1·121	1·130	1·143	1·152	1·155	1.155	1.162	1.170	1.176	1.181	1.191	1.180	
Dec	1·107	1·115	1·124	1·137	1·146	1·150	1.150	1.157	1.165	1.170	1.175	1.185	1.174	
1984														
Jan	1·108	1·116	1·126	1·138	1·148	1·151	1.151	1.158	1.166	1.172	1.176	1.187	1.175	
Feb	1·100	1·108	1·117	1·130	1·139	1·142	1.142	1.149	1.157	1.163	1.167	1.178	1.166	
Mar	1·093	1·101	1·110	1·123	1·132	1·135	1.135	1.142	1.150	1.156	1.161	1.171	1.159	
Apr	1·066	1·073	1·082	1·095	1·104	1·107	1.107	1.114	1.122	1.128	1.132	1.142	1.131	
May	1·058	1·060	1·075	1·087	1·096	1·100	1.100	1.106	1.114	1.120	1.124	1.134	1.123	
June	1·053	1·061	1·069	1·082	1·091	1·094	1.094	1.101	1.109	1.114	1.119	1.129	1.118	
July	1·055	1·063	1·072	1·084	1·093	1·097	1.097	1.103	1.111	1.117	1.121	1.131	1.120	
Aug	1·036	1·044	1·053	1·065	1·074	1·077	1.077	1.084	1.091	1.097	1.101	1.111	1.100	
Sept	1·032	1·040	1·049	1·061	1·070	1·073	1.073	1.080	1.087	1.093	1.097	1.107	1.096	
Oct	1·019	1·027	1·036	1·048	1·057	1·060	1.060	1.067	1.075	1.080	1.084	1.094	1.083	
Nov	1·013	1·021	1·030	1·042	1·051	1·054	1.054	1.060	1.068	1.074	1.078	1.088	1.077	
Dec	1·015	1·023	1·031	1·043	1·052	1·056	1.056	1.062	1.070	1.075	1.080	1.090	1.079	
1985														
Jan	1·008	1·015	1·024	1·036	1·045	1·048	1.048	1.055	1.062	1.068	1.072	1.082	1.071	
Feb	·992	·999	1·008	1·020	1·029	1·032	1.032	1.038	1.046	1.051	1.056	1.065	1.055	
Mar	·973	·981	·989	1·001	1·010	1·013	1.013	1.019	1.027	1.032	1.037	1.046	1.036	
Apr	·932	·939	·948	·959	·968	·971	.971	.977	.985	.990	.994	1.004	.993	
May	·923	·930	·939	·950	·959	·962	.962	.968	.976	.981	.985	.995	.984	
June	·919	·926	·935	·946	·955	·958	.958	.964	.971	.977	.981	.990	.980	
July	·923	·930	·938	·950	·958	·961	.961	.968	.975	.980	.985	.994	.984	
Aug	·918	·925	·933	·945	·953	·956	.956	.963	.970	.975	.979	.989	.978	
Sept	·919	·926	·934	·946	·954	·957	.957	.964	.971	.976	.980	.990	.979	
Oct	·915	·923	·931	·943	·951	·954	.954	.960	.968	.973	.977	.987	.976	
Nov	·909	·916	·925	·936	·944	·947	.947	.954	.961	.966	.970	.980	.969	
Dec	·906	·914	·922	·933	·942	·945	.945	.951	.958	.964	.968	.977	.967	

Month of disposal

Base Month	2000												2001											
	Jan	Feb	Mar	Apr	May	June	July	Aug	Sept	Oct	Nov	Dec	Jan	Feb	Mar	Apr	May	June	July	Aug	Sept	Oct	Nov	Dec
1986																								
Jan	·731	·740	·750	·767	·774	·778	·771	·771	·784	·783	·788	·789	·778	·787	·789	·798	·810	·812	·801	·808	·814	·811	·804	·802
Feb	·725	·734	·743	·761	·767	·771	·765	·765	·777	·776	·782	·783	·771	·780	·783	·792	·803	·805	·794	·801	·807	·804	·797	·795
Mar	·722	·732	·741	·759	·765	·769	·763	·763	·775	·774	·779	·780	·769	·778	·780	·790	·801	·803	·792	·799	·805	·802	·795	·793
Apr	·706	·715	·724	·742	·748	·752	·746	·746	·758	·757	·762	·763	·752	·761	·763	·772	·784	·786	·774	·782	·788	·785	·777	·775
May	·703	·712	·721	·738	·745	·749	·743	·743	·755	·754	·759	·760	·749	·758	·760	·769	·780	·782	·771	·778	·784	·781	·774	·772
June	·704	·713	·722	·739	·745	·750	·743	·743	·756	·755	·760	·761	·750	·759	·761	·770	·781	·783	·772	·779	·785	·782	·775	·773
July	·708	·718	·727	·744	·750	·755	·748	·748	·761	·760	·765	·766	·755	·764	·766	·775	·786	·788	·777	·784	·790	·787	·780	·778
Aug	·703	·712	·722	·739	·745	·749	·743	·743	·755	·754	·759	·760	·749	·758	·760	·770	·781	·783	·772	·779	·785	·782	·775	·773
Sept	·695	·704	·713	·730	·736	·741	·734	·734	·747	·746	·751	·752	·741	·750	·752	·761	·772	·774	·763	·770	·776	·773	·766	·764
Oct	·692	·701	·710	·728	·734	·738	·732	·732	·744	·743	·748	·749	·738	·747	·749	·758	·769	·771	·760	·767	·773	·770	·763	·761
Nov	·678	·687	·696	·713	·719	·723	·717	·717	·729	·728	·733	·734	·723	·732	·734	·743	·754	·756	·745	·752	·758	·755	·748	·746
Dec	·672	·681	·690	·707	·714	·718	·712	·712	·724	·723	·728	·729	·718	·727	·729	·738	·749	·751	·740	·747	·753	·750	·743	·741
1987																								
Jan	·666	·675	·684	·701	·707	·711	·705	·705	·717	·716	·721	·722	·711	·720	·722	·731	·742	·744	·733	·740	·746	·743	·736	·734
Feb	·659	·668	·677	·694	·700	·704	·698	·698	·710	·709	·714	·715	·704	·713	·715	·724	·735	·737	·726	·733	·739	·736	·729	·727
Mar	·656	·665	·674	·691	·697	·701	·695	·695	·707	·706	·711	·712	·701	·710	·712	·721	·732	·734	·723	·730	·736	·733	·726	·724
Apr	·637	·645	·654	·671	·677	·681	·675	·675	·687	·686	·691	·692	·681	·690	·692	·700	·711	·713	·702	·709	·715	·712	·705	·703
May	·635	·644	·653	·669	·675	·679	·673	·673	·685	·684	·689	·690	·679	·688	·690	·699	·710	·711	·701	·708	·713	·711	·704	·702
June	·635	·644	·653	·669	·675	·679	·673	·673	·685	·684	·689	·690	·679	·688	·690	·699	·710	·711	·701	·708	·713	·711	·704	·702
July	·637	·645	·654	·671	·677	·681	·675	·675	·687	·686	·691	·692	·681	·690	·692	·700	·711	·713	·702	·709	·715	·712	·705	·703
Aug	·632	·641	·649	·666	·672	·676	·670	·670	·682	·681	·686	·687	·676	·685	·687	·695	·706	·708	·697	·704	·710	·707	·700	·698
Sept	·627	·636	·645	·661	·667	·671	·665	·665	·677	·676	·681	·682	·671	·680	·682	·690	·701	·703	·692	·699	·705	·702	·695	·693
Oct	·619	·628	·637	·653	·659	·663	·657	·657	·669	·668	·672	·673	·663	·672	·673	·682	·693	·695	·684	·691	·697	·694	·687	·685
Nov	·611	·620	·629	·645	·651	·655	·649	·649	·661	·660	·664	·665	·655	·663	·665	·674	·685	·687	·676	·683	·689	·686	·679	·677
Dec	·613	·621	·630	·647	·652	·656	·651	·651	·662	·661	·666	·667	·656	·665	·667	·676	·686	·688	·678	·684	·690	·687	·681	·679
1988																								
Jan	·613	·621	·630	·647	·652	·656	·651	·651	·662	·661	·666	·667	·656	·665	·667	·676	·686	·688	·678	·684	·690	·687	·681	·679
Feb	·607	·615	·624	·640	·646	·650	·644	·644	·656	·655	·660	·661	·650	·659	·661	·669	·680	·682	·671	·678	·684	·681	·674	·672
Mar	·600	·609	·618	·634	·640	·644	·638	·638	·649	·648	·653	·654	·644	·652	·654	·663	·673	·675	·665	·671	·677	·674	·668	·666
Apr	·575	·583	·592	·608	·613	·617	·612	·612	·623	·622	·627	·628	·617	·626	·628	·636	·647	·648	·638	·645	·650	·647	·641	·639
May	·569	·577	·586	·602	·607	·611	·605	·605	·617	·616	·621	·621	·611	·620	·621	·630	·640	·642	·632	·638	·644	·641	·635	·633
June	·563	·571	·580	·596	·601	·605	·599	·599	·611	·610	·615	·615	·605	·614	·615	·624	·634	·636	·626	·632	·638	·635	·629	·627
July	·561	·570	·578	·594	·600	·604	·598	·598	·609	·608	·613	·614	·604	·612	·614	·622	·633	·634	·624	·631	·636	·634	·627	·625
Aug	·544	·552	·561	·576	·582	·586	·580	·580	·591	·590	·595	·596	·586	·594	·596	·604	·614	·616	·606	·613	·618	·615	·609	·607
Sept	·537	·545	·554	·569	·575	·578	·573	·573	·584	·583	·588	·589	·578	·587	·589	·597	·607	·609	·599	·605	·611	·608	·601	·600
Oct	·521	·530	·538	·553	·559	·563	·557	·557	·568	·567	·572	·573	·563	·571	·573	·581	·591	·593	·583	·589	·595	·592	·585	·584
Nov	·515	·523	·531	·546	·552	·555	·550	·550	·561	·560	·565	·565	·555	·564	·565	·574	·584	·585	·575	·582	·587	·585	·578	·576
Dec	·510	·519	·527	·542	·548	·551	·546	·546	·557	·556	·560	·561	·551	·559	·561	·569	·579	·581	·571	·578	·583	·580	·574	·572
1989																								
Jan	·501	·509	·517	·532	·538	·541	·536	·536	·547	·546	·550	·551	·541	·550	·551	·559	·569	·571	·561	·568	·573	·570	·564	·562
Feb	·490	498	·506	·521	·527	·530	·525	·525	·536	·535	·539	·540	·530	·538	·540	·548	·558	·560	·550	·556	·562	·559	·553	·551
Mar	·484	·492	·500	·515	·520	·524	·518	·518	·529	·528	·533	·533	·524	·532	·533	·541	·551	·553	·543	·549	·555	·552	·546	·544
Apr	·458	·465	·473	·488	·493	·497	·492	·492	·502	·501	·506	·507	·497	·505	·507	·514	·524	·526	·516	·522	·528	·525	·519	·517
May	·449	·457	·464	·479	·484	·488	·483	·483	·493	·492	·497	·497	·488	·496	·497	·505	·515	·517	·507	·513	·518	·516	·510	·508
June	·444	·451	·459	·474	·479	·483	·477	·477	·488	·487	·491	·492	·483	·490	·492	·500	·510	·511	·502	·508	·513	·510	·504	·503
July	·442	·450	·458	·473	·478	·481	·476	·476	·487	·486	·490	·491	·481	·489	·491	·499	·508	·510	·500	·506	·512	·509	·503	·501
Aug	·439	·446	·454	·469	·474	·478	·472	·472	·483	·482	·486	·487	·478	·485	·487	·495	·504	·506	·497	·503	·508	·505	·499	·497
Sept	·429	·437	·444	·459	·464	·467	·462	·462	·473	·472	·476	·477	·467	·475	·477	·485	·494	·496	·486	·492	·497	·495	·489	·487
Oct	·418	·426	·433	·448	·453	·456	·451	·451	·461	·460	·465	·466	·456	·464	·466	·473	·483	·484	·475	·481	·486	·483	·477	·476
Nov	·406	·414	·421	·435	·441	·444	·439	·439	·449	·448	·452	453	·444	·451	·453	·461	·470	·472	·462	·468	·473	·471	·465	·463
Dec	·402	·410	·418	·432	·437	·440	·435	·435	·445	·444	·449	449	·440	·448	·449	·457	·466	·468	·459	·465	·470	·467	·461	·460
1990																								
Jan	·394	·402	·409	·423	·428	·432	·427	·427	·437	·436	·440	·441	·432	·439	·441	·449	·458	·459	·450	·456	·461	·459	·453	·451
Feb	·386	·394	·401	·415	·420	·423	·418	·418	·428	·428	·432	·433	·423	·431	·433	·440	·449	·451	·442	·448	·453	·450	·444	·443
Mar	·372	·380	·387	·401	·406	·409	·404	·404	·414	·414	·418	·418	·409	·417	·418	·426	·435	·437	·428	·433	·438	·436	·430	·428
Apr	·332	·339	·346	·360	·365	·368	·363	·363	·373	·372	·376	·376	·368	·375	·376	·384	·392	·394	·385	·391	·396	·393	·388	·386
May	·320	·327	·334	·348	·353	·356	·351	·351	·361	·360	·364	·365	·356	·363	·365	·372	·380	·382	·373	·379	·384	·381	·376	·374
June	·315	·322	·329	·343	·347	·350	·346	·346	·355	·354	·358	·359	·350	·358	·359	·366	·375	·376	·368	·373	·378	·376	·370	·369
July	·314	·321	·328	·341	·346	·349	·345	·345	·354	·353	·357	·358	·349	·356	·358	·365	·374	·375	·367	·372	·377	·375	·369	·368
Aug	·301	·308	·315	·329	·333	·336	·331	·331	·340	·340	·343	·344	·336	·343	·344	·351	·360	·361	·353	·358	·363	·361	·355	·354
Sept	·288	·295	·302	·316	·320	·323	·319	·319	·328	·327	·331	·332	·323	·330	·332	·339	·347	·349	·340	·346	·350	·348	·343	·341
Oct	·279	·285	·292	·305	·310	·313	·309	·309	·318	·317	·321	·322	·313	·320	·322	·328	·337	·338	·330	·335	·340	·338	·332	·331
Nov	·282	·288	·295	·308	·313	·316	·312	·312	·321	·320	·324	·325	·316	·323	·325	·332	·340	·342	·333	·338	·343	·341	·335	·334
Dec	·283	·289	·296	·309	·314	·317	·313	·313	·322	·321	·325	·326	·317	·324	·326	·333	·341	·343	·334	·339	·344	·342	·336	·335

47

Indexation allowance — continued

Month of disposal

Base Month ↓

1986	2002 Jan	Feb	Mar	Apr	May	June	July	Aug	Sept	Oct	Nov	Dec	2003 Jan	Feb	Mar	Apr	May	June	July	Aug	Sept	Oct	Nov	Dec
Jan	·801	·806	·813	·825	·831	·831	·828	·833	·845	·848	·851	·855	·854	·863	·869	·883	·886	·884	·884	·887	·896	·897	·898	·907
Feb	·794	·799	·806	·819	·824	·824	·821	·826	·838	·842	·845	·848	·847	·856	·862	·876	·879	·877	·877	·880	·889	·890	·891	·900
Mar	·792	·797	·804	·816	·822	·822	·818	·824	·836	·839	·842	·845	·844	·854	·860	·873	·876	·874	·874	·877	·887	·888	·889	·897
Apr	·774	·779	·787	·799	·804	·804	·801	·806	·818	·821	·825	·828	·827	·836	·842	·855	·858	·856	·856	·859	·869	·870	·871	·879
May	·771	·776	·783	·796	·801	·801	·798	·803	·815	·818	·821	·824	·823	·832	·839	·852	·855	·853	·853	·856	·865	·866	·867	·875
June	·772	·777	·784	·797	·802	·802	·799	·804	·816	·819	·822	·825	·824	·833	·840	·853	·856	·854	·854	·857	·866	·867	·868	·876
July	·777	·782	·789	·802	·807	·807	·804	·809	·821	·824	·827	·830	·829	·839	·845	·858	·861	·859	·859	·862	·871	·873	·874	·882
Aug	·772	·777	·784	·796	·801	·801	·798	·803	·816	·819	·822	·825	·824	·833	·839	·852	·855	·853	·853	·856	·866	·867	·868	·876
Sept	·763	·768	·775	·787	·792	·792	·789	·794	·807	·810	·813	·816	·815	·824	·830	·843	·846	·844	·844	·847	·857	·858	·859	·867
Oct	·760	·765	·772	·785	·790	·790	·787	·792	·804	·807	·810	·813	·812	·821	·827	·840	·844	·841	·841	·845	·854	·855	·856	·864
Nov	·745	·750	·757	·770	·775	·775	·772	·777	·789	·792	·795	·798	·797	·806	·812	·825	·828	·826	·826	·829	·838	·839	·840	·848
Dec	·740	·745	·752	·764	·769	·769	·766	·771	·783	·786	·789	·792	·791	·800	·806	·819	·822	·820	·820	·823	·832	·833	·834	·842
1987																								
Jan	·733	·738	·745	·757	·762	·762	·759	·764	·776	·779	·782	·785	·784	·793	·799	·812	·815	·813	·813	·816	·825	·826	·827	·835
Feb	·726	·731	·738	·750	·755	·755	·752	·757	·769	·772	·775	·778	·777	·786	·792	·805	·808	·806	·806	·809	·818	·819	·820	·828
Mar	·723	·728	·735	·747	·751	·751	·749	·753	·765	·768	·771	·774	·773	·782	·788	·801	·804	·802	·802	·805	·814	·815	·816	·824
Apr	·702	·707	·714	·726	·731	·731	·728	·733	·745	·748	·750	·753	·752	·761	·767	·780	·783	·781	·781	·784	·793	·794	·795	·803
May	·701	·706	·712	·724	·729	·729	·726	·731	·743	·746	·749	·752	·751	·760	·765	·778	·781	·779	·779	·782	·791	·792	·793	·801
June	·701	·706	·712	·724	·729	·729	·726	·731	·743	·746	·749	·752	·751	·760	·765	·778	·781	·779	·779	·782	·791	·792	·793	·801
July	·702	·707	·714	·726	·731	·731	·728	·733	·745	·748	·750	·753	·752	·761	·767	·780	·783	·781	·781	·784	·793	·794	·795	·803
Aug	·697	·702	·709	·721	·726	·726	·723	·728	·739	·742	·745	·748	·747	·756	·762	·775	·778	·776	·776	·779	·787	·788	·789	·797
Sept	·692	·697	·704	·716	·721	·721	·718	·723	·734	·737	·740	·743	·742	·751	·757	·770	·772	·771	·771	·773	·782	·783	·784	·792
Oct	·684	·689	·696	·707	·712	·712	·709	·714	·726	·729	·732	·735	·734	·742	·748	·761	·764	·762	·762	·765	·774	·775	·776	·783
Nov	·676	·681	·688	·699	·704	·704	·701	·706	·718	·721	·723	·726	·725	·734	·740	·752	·755	·753	·753	·756	·765	·766	·767	·775
Dec	·678	·682	·689	·701	·706	·706	·703	·708	·719	·722	·725	·728	·727	·736	·742	·754	·757	·755	·755	·758	·767	·768	·769	·776
1988																								
Jan	·678	·682	·689	·701	·706	·706	·703	·708	·719	·722	·725	·728	·727	·736	·742	·754	·757	·755	·755	·758	·767	·768	·769	·776
Feb	·671	·676	·683	·694	·699	·699	·696	·701	·713	·716	·718	·721	·720	·729	·735	·747	·750	·748	·748	·751	·760	·761	·762	·770
Mar	·665	·670	·676	·688	·693	·693	·690	·695	·706	·709	·712	·715	·714	·722	·728	·741	·744	·742	·742	·744	·753	·754	·755	·763
Apr	·638	·643	·649	·661	·665	·665	·663	·667	·679	·681	·684	·687	·686	·695	·700	·713	·716	·714	·714	·716	·725	·726	·727	·734
May	·632	·637	·643	·654	·659	·659	·656	·661	·672	·675	·678	·681	·680	·688	·694	·706	·709	·707	·707	·710	·718	·719	·720	·728
June	·626	·630	·637	·648	·653	·653	·650	·655	·666	·669	·672	·674	·674	·682	·688	·700	·703	·701	·701	·704	·712	·713	·714	·721
July	·624	·629	·635	·647	·651	·651	·649	·653	·664	·667	·670	·673	·672	·680	·686	·698	·701	·699	·699	·702	·710	·711	·712	·720
Aug	·606	·611	·617	·628	·633	·633	·630	·635	·646	·649	·652	·654	·653	·662	·667	·679	·682	·680	·680	·683	·691	·692	·693	·701
Sept	·599	·603	·610	·621	·625	·625	·623	·627	·638	·641	·644	·647	·646	·654	·660	·672	·674	·673	·673	·675	·684	·685	·685	·693
Oct	·583	·587	·594	·605	·609	·609	·606	·611	·622	·625	·627	·630	·629	·637	·643	·655	·658	·656	·656	·658	·667	·668	·668	·676
Nov	·575	·580	·586	·597	·602	·602	·599	·604	·615	·617	·620	·623	·622	·630	·635	·647	·650	·648	·648	·651	·659	·660	·661	·668
Dec	·571	·576	·582	·593	·597	·597	·595	·599	·610	·613	·616	·618	·617	·626	·631	·643	·646	·644	·644	·646	·655	·655	·656	·664
1989																								
Jan	·561	·566	·572	·583	·587	·587	·585	·589	·600	·603	·605	·608	·607	·615	·621	·632	·635	·633	·633	·636	·644	·645	·646	·653
Feb	·550	·555	·561	·572	·576	·576	·573	·578	·589	·591	·594	·597	·596	·604	·609	·621	·623	·622	·622	·624	·632	·633	·634	·641
Mar	·543	·548	·554	·565	·569	·569	·566	·571	·581	·584	·587	·589	·589	·597	·602	·614	·616	·614	·614	·617	·625	·626	·627	·634
Apr	·516	·521	·527	·537	·542	·542	·539	·543	·554	·556	·559	·562	·561	·569	·574	·585	·588	·586	·586	·589	·597	·598	·598	·605
May	·507	·511	·517	·528	·532	·532	·530	·534	·544	·547	·550	·552	·551	·559	·564	·576	·578	·577	·577	·579	·587	·588	·589	·596
June	·502	·506	·512	·523	·527	·527	·524	·529	·539	·542	·544	·547	·546	·554	·559	·570	·573	·571	·571	·574	·581	·582	·583	·590
July	·500	·505	·511	·521	·526	·526	·523	·527	·538	·540	·543	·545	·545	·552	·558	·569	·571	·570	·570	·572	·580	·581	·582	·589
Aug	·497	·501	·507	·517	·522	·522	·519	·523	·534	·536	·539	·541	·541	·548	·554	·565	·567	·566	·566	·568	·576	·577	·578	·585
Sept	·486	·491	·497	·507	·511	·511	·509	·513	·523	·526	·528	·531	·530	·538	·543	·554	·557	·555	·555	·557	·565	·566	·567	·574
Oct	·475	·479	·485	·495	·500	·500	·497	·501	·511	·514	·517	·519	·518	·526	·531	·542	·545	·543	·543	·546	·553	·554	·555	·562
Nov	·462	·467	·473	·483	·487	·487	·484	·489	·499	·501	·504	·506	·505	·513	·518	·529	·532	·530	·530	·532	·540	·541	·542	·549
Dec	·459	·463	·469	·479	·483	·483	·481	·485	·495	·497	·500	·503	·502	·509	·514	·525	·528	·526	·526	·529	·536	·537	·538	·545
1990																								
Jan	·450	·454	·460	·470	·474	·474	·472	·476	·486	·489	·491	·494	·493	·500	·505	·516	·519	·517	·517	·520	·527	·528	·529	·536
Feb	·442	·446	·452	·462	·466	·466	·463	·468	·478	·480	·483	·485	·484	·492	·497	·507	·510	·508	·508	·511	·518	·519	·520	·527
Mar	·428	·432	·437	·447	·451	·451	·449	·453	·463	·465	·468	·470	·470	·477	·482	·493	·495	·493	·493	·496	·503	·504	·505	·512
Apr	·385	·389	·395	·404	·408	·408	·406	·410	·420	·422	·424	·427	·426	·433	·438	·448	·451	·449	·449	·452	·459	·460	·460	·467
May	·373	·377	·383	·392	·396	·396	·394	·398	·407	·410	·412	·414	·414	·421	·426	·436	·438	·437	·437	·439	·446	·447	·448	·454
June	·368	·372	·377	·387	·391	·391	·388	·392	·402	·404	·406	·409	·408	·415	·420	·430	·433	·431	·431	·433	·440	·441	·442	·448
July	·367	·371	·376	·386	·390	·390	·387	·391	·401	·403	·405	·408	·407	·414	·419	·429	·431	·430	·430	·432	·439	·440	·441	·447
Aug	·353	·357	·362	·372	·375	·375	·373	·377	·386	·389	·391	·393	·393	·400	·404	·415	·417	·415	·415	·418	·425	·425	·426	·432
Sept	·340	·344	·350	·359	·363	·363	·360	·364	·374	·376	·378	·381	·380	·387	·391	·401	·404	·402	·402	·404	·411	·412	·413	·419
Oct	·330	·334	·339	·348	·352	·352	·350	·354	·363	·365	·368	·370	·369	·376	·381	·391	·393	·391	·391	·394	·401	·401	·402	·408
Nov	·333	·337	·342	·352	·355	·355	·353	·357	·366	·368	·371	·373	·372	·379	·384	·394	·396	·395	·395	·397	·404	·405	·405	·412
Dec	·334	·338	·343	·353	·356	·356	·354	·358	·367	·370	·372	·374	·373	·380	·385	·395	·397	·396	·396	·398	·405	·406	·406	·413

B a s e M o n t h	1986	2004 Jan	Feb	Mar	Apr	May	June	July	Aug	Sept	Oct	Nov	Dec	2005 Jan	Feb
	Jan	·902	·910	·918	·929	·938	·941	.941	.947	.954	.963	.964	.973	.963	
	Feb	·895	·903	·911	·922	·931	·934	.934	.940	.947	.952	.956	.966	.955	
	Mar	·893	·900	·908	·920	·928	·931	.931	.937	.945	.951	.954	.963	.953	
	Apr	·875	·882	·890	·901	·910	·913	.913	.919	.926	.931	.935	.944	.934	
	May	·871	·878	·887	·898	·906	·909	.909	.915	.922	.923	.932	.941	.931	
	June	·872	·879	·888	·899	·907	·910	.910	.916	.923	.929	.933	.942	.932	
	July	·878	·885	·893	·904	·913	·916	.916	.922	.929	.934	.938	.947	.937	
	Aug	·872	·879	·887	·898	·907	·910	.910	.916	.923	.928	.932	.941	.931	
	Sept	863	·870	·878	·889	·897	·900	.900	.906	.913	.919	.923	.932	.922	
	Oct	860	·867	·875	·886	·894	·897	.897	.903	.911	.916	.920	.929	.919	
	Nov	·844	·851	·859	·870	·878	·881	.881	.887	.894	.899	.904	.913	.903	
	Dec	·838	·845	·853	·864	·872	·875	.875	.881	.888	.893	.897	.906	.896	
	1987														
	Jan	·831	·838	·846	·857	·865	·868	.868	.874	.881	.886	.890	.899	.889	
	Feb	·824	·831	·839	·850	·858	·861	.861	.867	.874	.878	.882	.891	.881	
	Mar	·820	·827	·835	·846	·854	·857	.857	.863	.870	.875	.879	.888	.878	
	Apr	·799	·806	·813	·824	·832	·835	.835	.841	.848	.853	.857	.865	.856	
	May	·797	·804	·812	·822	·830	·833	.833	.839	.846	.851	.855	.864	.854	
	June	·797	·804	·812	·822	·830	·833	.833	.839	.846	.851	.855	.864	.854	
	July	·799	·806	·813	·824	·832	·835	.835	.841	.848	.853	.857	.865	.856	
	Aug	·793	·800	·808	·819	·827	·830	.830	.835	.842	.847	.851	.860	.850	
	Sept	·788	·795	·803	·813	·821	·824	.824	.830	.837	.842	.846	.854	.845	
	Oct	·779	·786	·794	·805	·812	·815	.815	.821	.828	.833	.837	.845	.836	
	Nov	·771	·778	·785	·796	·804	·807	.807	.812	.819	.824	.828	.837	.827	
	Dec	·773	·779	·787	·798	·805	·808	.808	.814	.821	.826	.830	.838	.829	
	1988														
	Jan	·773	·779	·787	·798	·805	·808	.808	.814	.821	.826	.830	.838	.829	
	Feb	·766	·772	·780	·791	·798	·801	.801	.807	.814	.819	.823	.831	.822	
	Mar	·759	·766	·773	·784	·792	·794	.794	.800	.807	.812	.816	.824	.815	
	Apr	·731	·737	·745	·755	·763	·766	.766	.771	.778	.783	.786	.795	.785	
	May	·724	·731	·738	·749	·756	·759	.759	.765	.771	.776	.780	.788	.779	
	June	·718	·724	·732	·742	·750	·752	.752	.758	.765	.769	.773	.781	.772	
	July	·716	·723	·730	·740	·748	·751	.751	.756	.763	.768	.771	.780	.770	
	Aug	·697	·703	·711	·721	·728	·731	.731	.737	.743	.748	.752	.760	.751	
	Sept	·689	·696	·703	·713	·720	·723	.723	.729	.735	.740	.744	.752	.743	
	Oct	·672	·679	·686	·696	·703	·706	.706	.711	.718	.722	.726	.734	.725	
	Nov	·665	·671	·678	·688	·695	·698	.698	.704	.710	.715	.718	.726	.717	
	Dec	·660	·666	·674	·684	·691	·694	.694	.699	.705	.710	.714	.722	.713	
	1989														
	Jan	·650	·656	·663	·673	·680	·683	.683	.688	.695	.699	.703	.711	.702	
	Feb	·638	·644	·651	·661	·668	·671	.671	.676	.682	.687	.691	.699	.690	
	Mar	·630	·637	·644	·654	·661	·663	.663	.669	.675	.679	.683	.691	.682	
	Apr	·602	·608	·615	·625	·632	·634	.634	.640	.646	.650	.654	.661	.653	
	May	·592	·598	·605	·615	·622	·624	.624	.630	.636	.640	.643	.651	.643	
	June	·587	·593	·600	·609	·616	·619	.619	.624	.630	.634	638	.646	.637	
	July	·585	·591	·598	·608	·615	·617	.617	.623	.629	.633	636	.644	.635	
	Aug	·581	·587	·594	·604	·611	·613	.613	.618	.624	.629	632	.640	.631	
	Sept	·570	·576	·583	·593	·599	·602	.602	.607	.613	.617	621	.629	.620	
	Oct	·558	·564	·571	·580	·587	·590	.590	.595	.601	.605	609	.616	.608	
	Nov	·545	·551	·558	·567	·574	·576	.576	.581	.587	.592	595	.603	.594	
	Dec	·541	·547	·554	·563	·570	·572	.572	.577	.583	.588	591	.598	.590	
	1990														
	Jan	·532	·538	·545	·554	·561	·563	.563	.568	.574	.578	582	.589	.581	
	Feb	·523	·529	·536	·545	·552	·554	.554	.559	.565	.569	572	.580	.572	
	Mar	·508	·514	·521	·530	·536	·539	.539	.544	.549	.554	557	.564	.556	
	Apr	·464	·469	·476	·484	·491	·493	.493	.498	.504	.508	511	.518	.510	
	May	·451	·456	·463	·471	·478	·480	.480	.485	.490	.494	498	.505	.497	
	June	·445	·451	·457	·466	·472	·474	.474	.479	.485	.489	492	.499	.491	
	July	·444	·450	·456	·465	·471	·473	.473	.478	.483	.487	491	.498	.490	
	Aug	·429	·435	·441	·450	·456	·458	.458	.463	.468	.472	475	.482	.475	
	Sept	·416	·422	·428	·436	·442	·445	.445	.449	.455	.459	462	.469	.461	
	Oct	·405	·411	·417	·425	·431	·434	.434	.438	.444	.447	450	.457	.450	
	Nov	·408	·414	·420	·428	·435	·437	.437	.442	.447	.451	454	.461	.453	
	Dec	·410	·415	·421	·430	·436	·438	.438	.443	.448	.452	455	.462	.454	

49

Indexation allowance — continued

Month of disposal

Base Month	2000												2001											
1991	Jan	Feb	Mar	Apr	May	June	July	Aug	Sept	Oct	Nov	Dec	Jan	Feb	Mar	Apr	May	June	July	Aug	Sept	Oct	Nov	Dec
Jan	·280	·286	·293	·306	·311	·314	·310	·310	·319	·318	·322	·323	·314	·321	·323	·329	·338	·339	·331	·336	·341	·339	·333	·332
Feb	·273	·280	·286	·299	·304	·307	·303	·303	·312	·311	·315	·316	·307	·314	·316	·322	·331	·332	·324	·329	·334	·332	·326	·325
Mar	·268	·275	·282	·295	·299	·302	·298	·298	·307	·306	·310	·311	·302	·309	·311	·317	·326	·327	·319	·324	·329	·326	·321	·320
Apr	·252	·258	·265	·278	·282	·285	·281	·281	·290	·289	·293	·294	·285	·292	·294	·301	·309	·310	·302	·307	·312	·310	·304	·303
May	·248	·255	·261	·274	·279	·282	·277	·277	·286	·285	·289	·290	·282	·288	·290	·297	·305	·306	·298	·303	·308	·306	·300	·299
June	·242	·249	·256	·268	·273	·276	·271	·271	·280	·280	·283	·284	·276	·283	·284	·291	·299	·301	·292	·298	·302	·300	·295	·293
July	·245	·252	·259	·271	·276	·279	·274	·274	·283	·283	·286	·287	·279	·286	·287	·294	·302	·303	·295	·300	·305	·303	·297	·296
Aug	·242	·249	·256	·268	·273	·276	·271	·271	·280	·280	·283	·284	·276	·283	·284	·291	·299	·301	·292	·298	·302	·300	·295	·29
Sept	·238	·244	·251	·264	·268	·271	·267	·267	·276	·275	·279	·279	·271	·278	·279	·286	·294	·296	·288	·293	·297	·295	·290	·288
Oct	·233	·240	·246	·259	·264	·266	·262	·262	·271	·270	·274	·275	·266	·273	·275	·281	·289	·291	·283	·288	·292	·290	·285	·283
Nov	·229	·235	·242	·254	·259	·262	·257	·257	·266	·265	·269	·270	·262	·268	·270	·277	·285	·286	·278	·283	·288	·285	·280	·279
Dec	·228	·234	·241	·254	·258	·261	·256	·256	·265	·265	·268	·269	·261	·268	·269	·276	·284	·285	·277	·282	·287	·284	·279	·278
1992																								
Jan	·229	·235	·242	·254	·259	·262	·257	·257	·266	·265	·269	·270	·262	·268	·270	·277	·285	·286	·278	·283	·288	·285	·280	·279
Feb	·222	·229	·236	·248	·252	·255	·251	·251	·260	·259	·263	·263	·255	·262	·263	·270	·278	·280	·271	·277	·281	·279	·274	·272
Mar	·219	·225	·232	·244	·249	·252	·247	·247	·256	·255	·259	·260	·252	·258	·260	·266	·274	·276	·268	·273	·277	·275	·270	·268
Apr	·200	·207	·213	·226	·230	·233	·228	·228	·237	·236	·240	·241	·233	·239	·241	·247	·255	·256	·249	·254	·258	·256	·251	·249
May	·196	·202	·209	·221	·225	·228	·224	·224	·233	·232	·235	·236	·228	·235	·236	·243	·251	·252	·244	·249	·253	·251	·246	·245
June	·196	·202	·209	·221	·225	·228	·224	·224	·233	·232	·235	·236	·228	·235	·236	·243	·251	·252	·244	·249	·253	·251	·246	·245
July	·200	·207	·213	·226	·230	·233	·228	·228	·237	·236	·240	·241	·233	·239	·241	·247	·255	·256	·249	·254	·258	·256	·251	·249
Aug	·199	·206	·212	·225	·229	·232	·228	·228	·236	·235	·239	·240	·232	·238	·240	·246	·254	·256	·248	·253	·257	·255	·250	·248
Sept	·195	·202	·208	·220	·225	·227	·223	·223	·232	·231	·235	·235	·227	·234	·235	·242	·250	·251	·243	·248	·253	·250	·245	·244
Oct	·191	·197	·204	·216	·220	·223	·219	·219	·227	·227	·230	·231	·223	·229	·231	·237	·245	·247	·239	·244	·248	·246	·241	·239
Nov	·193	·199	·205	·218	·222	·225	·220	·220	·229	·228	·232	·233	·225	·231	·233	·239	·247	·248	·241	·246	·250	·248	·243	·241
Dec	·197	·203	·210	·222	·226	·229	·225	·225	·233	·233	·236	·237	·229	·236	·237	·244	·251	·253	·245	·250	·254	·252	·247	·246
1993																								
Jan	·208	·215	·221	·234	·238	·241	·236	·236	·245	·244	·248	·249	·241	·247	·249	·255	·263	·265	·257	·262	·266	·264	·259	·257
Feb	·200	·207	·213	·226	·230	·233	·228	·228	·237	·236	·240	·241	·233	·239	·241	·247	·255	·256	·249	·254	·258	·256	·251	·249
Mar	·196	·202	·209	·221	·225	·228	·224	·224	·233	·232	·235	·236	·228	·235	·236	·243	·251	·252	·244	·249	·253	·251	·246	·245
Apr	·185	·191	·198	·210	·214	·217	·213	·213	·221	·220	·224	·225	·217	·223	·225	·231	·239	·240	·233	·238	·242	·240	·235	·233
May	·181	·187	·193	·206	·210	·213	·208	·208	·217	·216	·220	·220	·213	·219	·220	·227	·235	·236	·228	·233	·237	·235	·230	·229
June	·182	·188	·194	·206	·211	·213	·209	·209	·218	·217	·221	·221	·213	·220	·221	·228	·235	·237	·229	·234	·238	·236	·231	·230
July	·184	·190	·197	·209	·213	·216	·212	·212	·220	·220	·223	·224	·216	·222	·224	·230	·238	·240	·232	·237	·241	·239	·234	·232
Aug	·179	·185	·192	·204	·208	·211	·207	·207	·215	·214	·218	·219	·211	·217	·219	·225	·233	·234	·226	·231	·236	·234	·229	·227
Sept	·174	·180	·187	·199	·203	·206	·202	·202	·210	·209	·213	·214	·206	·212	·214	·220	·228	·229	·221	·226	·230	·228	·223	·222
Oct	·175	·181	·188	·200	·204	·207	·202	·202	·211	·210	·214	·214	·207	·213	·214	·221	·228	·230	·222	·227	·231	·229	·224	·223
Nov	·177	·183	·189	·201	·206	·208	·204	·204	·213	·212	·215	·216	·208	·215	·216	·222	·230	·232	·224	·229	·233	·231	·226	·225
Dec	·174	·180	·187	·199	·203	·206	·202	·202	·210	·209	·213	·214	·206	·212	·214	·220	·228	·229	·221	·226	·230	·228	·223	·222
1994																								
Jan	·179	·185	·192	·204	·208	·211	·207	·207	·215	·214	·218	·219	·211	·217	·219	·225	·233	·234	·226	·231	·236	·234	·229	·227
Feb	·172	·179	·185	·197	·201	·204	·200	·200	·208	·208	·211	·212	·204	·210	·212	·218	·226	·227	·220	·224	·229	·227	·222	·220
Mar	·169	·175	·182	·194	·198	·201	·196	·196	·205	·204	·208	·208	·201	·207	·208	·215	·222	·224	·216	·221	·225	·223	·218	·217
Apr	·155	·162	·168	·180	·184	·187	·182	·182	·191	·190	·193	·194	·187	·193	·194	·200	·208	·209	·202	·207	·211	·209	·204	·202
May	·151	·158	·164	·176	·180	·182	·178	·178	·187	·186	·189	·190	·182	·189	·190	·196	·204	·205	·198	·202	·207	·205	·200	·198
June	·151	·158	·164	·176	·180	·182	·178	·178	·187	·186	·189	·190	·182	·189	·190	·196	·204	·205	·198	·202	·207	·205	·200	·198
July	·157	·163	·169	·181	·185	·188	·184	·184	·192	·192	·195	·196	·188	·194	·196	·202	·210	·211	·203	·208	·213	·210	·206	·204
Aug	·151	·158	·164	·176	·180	·182	·178	·178	·187	·186	·189	·190	·182	·189	·190	·196	·204	·205	·198	·202	·207	·205	·200	·198
Sept	·149	·155	·161	·173	·177	·180	·176	·176	·184	·183	·187	·188	·180	·186	·188	·194	·201	·203	·195	·200	·204	·202	·197	·196
Oct	·147	·154	·160	·171	·176	·178	·174	·174	·183	·182	·185	·186	·178	·185	·186	·192	·200	·201	·194	·198	·202	·200	·196	·194
Nov	·147	·153	·159	·171	·175	·178	·173	·173	·182	·181	·184	·185	·178	·184	·185	·191	·199	·200	·193	·198	·202	·200	·195	·193
Dec	·141	·147	·153	·165	·169	·172	·168	·168	·176	·175	·179	·179	·172	·178	·179	·186	·193	·195	·187	·192	·196	·194	·189	·188
1995																								
Jan	·141	·147	·153	·165	·169	·172	·168	·168	·176	·175	·179	·179	·172	·178	·179	·186	·193	·195	·187	·192	·196	·194	·189	·188
Feb	·134	·140	·146	·158	·162	·165	·161	·161	·169	·168	·172	·172	·165	·171	·172	·178	·186	·187	·180	·184	·189	·187	·182	·180
Mar	·129	·136	·142	·153	·157	·160	·156	·156	·164	·163	·167	·167	·160	·166	·167	·174	·181	·182	·175	·180	·184	·182	·177	·176
Apr	·118	·124	·130	·142	·146	·148	·144	·144	·152	·152	·155	·156	·148	·154	·156	·162	·169	·170	·163	168	·172	·170	·165	·164
May	·114	·120	·126	·137	·141	·144	·140	·140	·148	·147	·150	·151	·144	·150	·151	·157	·164	·166	·158	·163	·167	·165	·160	·159
June	·112	·118	·124	·136	·140	·142	·138	·138	·146	·146	·149	·150	·142	·148	·150	·156	·163	·164	·157	·162	·166	·164	·159	·158
July	·117	·123	·129	·141	·145	·148	·144	·144	·152	·151	·154	·155	·148	·154	·155	·161	·168	·170	·162	·167	·171	·169	·164	·163
Aug	·111	·117	·123	·135	·139	·141	·137	·137	·145	·145	·148	·149	·141	·147	·149	·155	·162	·163	·156	·161	·165	·163	·158	·157
Sept	·106	·112	·118	·129	·133	·136	·132	·132	·140	·139	·143	·143	·136	·142	·143	·149	·157	·158	·151	·155	·159	·157	·153	·151
Oct	·112	·118	·124	·136	·140	·142	·138	·138	·146	·146	·149	·150	·142	·148	·150	·156	·163	·164	·157	·162	·166	·164	·159	·158
Nov	·112	·118	·124	·136	·140	·142	·138	·138	·146	·146	·149	·150	·142	·148	·150	·156	·163	·164	·157	·162	·166	·164	·159	·158
Dec	·106	·111	·117	·129	·133	·135	·131	·131	·139	·139	·142	·143	·135	·141	·143	·149	·156	·157	·150	·155	·159	·157	·152	·151

Base Month

	2002												2003											
	Jan	Feb	Mar	Apr	May	June	July	Aug	Sept	Oct	Nov	Dec	Jan	Feb	Mar	Apr	May	June	July	Aug	Sept	Oct	Nov	Dec
1991																								
Jan	·331	·335	·340	·349	·353	·353	·351	·355	·364	·366	·369	·371	·370	·377	·382	·392	·394	·392	·392	·395	·402	·402	·403	·409
Feb	·324	·328	·333	·342	·346	·346	·344	·348	·357	·359	·361	·364	·363	·370	·374	·384	·387	·385	·385	·387	·394	·395	·396	·402
Mar	·319	·323	·328	·337	·341	·341	·339	·342	·352	·354	·356	·358	·358	·365	·369	·379	·381	·380	·380	·382	·389	·390	·390	·396
Apr	·302	·306	·311	·320	·324	·324	·322	·325	·334	·337	·339	·341	·340	·347	·352	·361	·364	·362	·362	·364	·371	·372	·373	·379
May	·298	·302	·307	·316	·320	·320	·318	·321	·330	·333	·335	·337	·336	·343	·348	·357	·360	·358	·358	·360	·367	·368	·369	·375
June	·292	·296	·301	·310	·314	·314	·312	·315	·324	·327	·329	·331	·330	·337	·342	·351	·353	·352	·352	·354	·361	·362	·362	·368
July	·295	·299	·304	·313	·317	·317	·315	·318	·327	·330	·332	·334	·333	·340	·345	·354	·357	·355	·355	·357	·364	·365	·365	·371
Aug	·292	·296	·301	·310	·314	·314	·312	·315	·324	·327	·329	·331	·330	·337	·342	·351	·353	·352	·352	·354	·361	·362	·362	·368
Sept	·288	·291	·296	·305	·309	·309	·307	·311	·319	·322	·324	·326	·325	·332	·337	·346	·348	·347	·347	·349	·356	·357	·357	·363
Oct	·283	·286	·292	·301	·304	·304	·302	·306	·315	·317	·319	·321	·321	·327	·332	·341	·343	·342	·342	·344	·351	·352	·352	·358
Nov	·278	·282	·287	·296	·299	·299	·297	·301	·310	·312	·314	·316	·316	·322	·327	·336	·338	·337	·337	·339	·346	·347	·347	·353
Dec	·277	·281	·286	·295	·298	·298	·296	·300	·309	·311	·313	·315	·315	·321	·326	·335	·338	·336	·336	·338	·345	·346	·346	·352
1992																								
Jan	·278	·282	·287	·296	·299	·299	·297	·301	·310	·312	·314	·316	·316	·322	·327	·336	·338	·337	·337	·339	·346	·347	·347	·353
Feb	·271	·275	·280	·289	·293	·293	·291	·294	·303	·305	·307	·310	·309	·315	·320	·329	·332	·330	·330	·332	·339	·340	·340	·346
Mar	·268	·271	·277	·285	·289	·289	·287	·290	·299	·301	·304	·306	·305	·312	·316	·326	·328	·326	·326	·328	·335	·336	·337	·342
Apr	·249	·252	·257	·266	·269	·269	·267	·271	·280	·282	·284	·286	·285	·292	·296	·305	·308	·306	·306	·308	·315	·316	·316	·322
May	·244	·248	·253	·261	·265	·265	·263	·266	·275	·277	·279	·281	·281	·287	·291	·301	·303	·302	·302	·304	·310	·311	·312	·317
June	·244	·248	·253	·261	·265	·265	·263	·266	·275	·277	·279	·281	·281	·287	·291	·301	·303	·302	·302	·304	·310	·311	·312	·317
July	·249	·252	·257	·266	·269	·269	·267	·271	·280	·282	·284	·286	·285	·292	·296	·305	·308	·306	·306	·308	·315	·316	·316	·322
Aug	·248	·251	·256	·265	·269	·269	·266	·270	·279	·281	·283	·285	·284	·291	·295	·305	·307	·305	·305	·307	·314	·315	·315	·321
Sept	·243	·247	·252	·260	·264	·264	·262	·265	·274	·276	·278	·280	·280	·286	·291	·300	·302	·301	·301	·303	·309	·310	·311	·316
Oct	·239	·242	·247	·256	·259	·259	·257	·261	·269	·272	·274	·276	·275	·282	·286	·295	·297	·296	·296	·298	·305	·305	·306	·312
Nov	·241	·244	·249	·258	·261	·261	·259	·263	·271	·273	·276	·278	·277	·283	·288	·297	·299	·298	·298	·300	·306	·307	·308	·314
Dec	·245	·249	·254	·262	·266	·266	·264	·267	·276	·278	280	·282	·282	·288	·292	·302	·304	·302	·302	·305	·311	·312	·313	·318
1993																								
Jan	·257	·260	·265	·274	·278	·278	·276	·279	·288	·290	292	·294	·294	·300	·305	·314	·316	·315	·315	·317	·323	·324	·325	·331
Feb	·249	·252	·257	·266	·269	·269	·267	·271	·280	·282	·284	·286	·285	·292	·296	·305	·308	·306	·306	·308	·315	·316	·316	·32
Mar	·244	·248	·253	·261	·265	·265	·263	·266	·275	·277	279	·281	·281	·287	·291	·301	·303	·302	·302	·304	·310	·311	·312	·317
Apr	·233	·236	·241	·250	·253	·253	·251	·255	·263	·265	267	270	·269	·275	·280	·289	·291	·289	·289	·292	·298	·299	·299	·305
May	·228	·232	·237	·245	·249	·249	·247	·250	·259	·261	263	265	·264	·271	·275	·284	·286	·285	·285	·287	·293	·294	·295	·300
June	·229	·233	·238	·246	·250	·250	·248	·251	·260	·262	·264	·266	·265	·272	·276	·285	·287	·286	·286	·288	·294	·295	·296	·301
July	·232	·235	·240	·249	·252	·252	·250	·254	·262	·264	267	·269	·268	·274	·279	·288	·290	·289	·289	·291	·297	·298	·299	·304
Aug	·226	·230	·235	·243	·247	·247	·245	·248	·257	·259	·261	·263	·263	·269	·273	·282	·285	·283	·283	·285	·292	·292	·293	·299
Sept	·221	·225	·230	·238	·242	·242	·240	·243	·252	·254	·256	·258	·257	·264	·268	·277	·279	·278	·278	·280	·286	·287	·288	·293
Oct	·222	·226	·231	·239	·243	·243	·240	·244	·252	·255	·257	·259	·258	·264	·269	·278	·280	·279	·279	·281	·287	·288	·288	·294
Nov	·224	·227	·232	·241	·244	·244	·242	·246	·254	·256	·258	·261	·260	·266	·270	·280	·282	·280	·280	·282	·289	·290	·290	·296
Dec	·221	·225	·230	·238	·242	·242	·240	·243	·252	·254	·256	·258	·257	·264	·268	·277	·279	·278	·278	·280	·286	·287	·288	·293
1994																								
Jan	·226	·230	·235	·243	·247	·247	·245	·248	·257	·259	·261	·263	·263	·269	·273	·282	·285	·283	·283	·285	·292	·292	·293	·299
Feb	·220	·223	·228	·236	·240	·240	·238	·241	·250	·252	·254	·256	·255	·262	·266	·275	·277	·276	·276	·278	·284	·285	·286	·291
Mar	·216	·220	·225	·233	·236	·236	·234	·238	·246	·248	·251	·253	·252	·258	·262	·272	·274	·272	·272	·274	·281	·281	·282	·288
Apr	·202	·205	·210	·218	·222	·222	·220	·223	·232	·234	·236	·238	·237	·243	·248	·257	·259	·257	·257	·259	·266	·266	·267	·273
May	·198	·201	·206	·214	·218	·218	·216	·219	·227	·229	·232	·234	·233	·239	·243	·252	·254	·253	·253	·255	·261	·262	·263	·268
June	·198	·201	·206	·214	·218	·218	·216	·219	·227	·229	·232	·234	·233	·239	·243	·252	·254	·253	·253	·255	·261	·262	·263	·268
July	·203	·207	·212	·220	·224	·224	·222	·225	·233	·235	·238	·240	·239	·245	·249	·258	·260	·259	·259	·261	·267	·268	·269	·274
Aug	·198	·201	·206	·214	·218	·218	·216	·219	·227	·229	·232	·234	·233	·239	·243	·252	·254	·253	·253	·255	·261	·262	·263	·268
Sept	·195	·199	·203	·212	·215	·215	·213	·217	·225	·227	·229	·231	·230	·237	·241	·250	·252	·250	·250	·252	·259	·259	·260	·266
Oct	·194	·197	·202	·210	·213	·213	·211	·215	·223	·225	·227	·229	·229	·235	·239	·248	·250	·249	·249	·251	·257	·258	·258	·264
Nov	·193	·196	·201	·209	·213	·213	·211	·214	·222	·224	·226	·228	·228	·234	·238	·247	·249	·248	·248	·250	·256	·257	·257	·263
Dec	·187	·190	·195	·203	·207	·207	·205	·208	·216	·218	·221	·223	·222	·228	·232	·241	·243	·242	·242	·244	·250	·251	·251	·257
1995																								
Jan	·187	·190	·195	·203	·207	·207	·205	·208	·216	·218	·221	·223	·222	·228	·232	·241	·243	·242	·242	·244	·250	·251	·251	·257
Feb	·180	·183	·188	·196	·199	·199	·197	·201	·209	·211	·213	·215	·214	·221	·225	·233	·236	·234	·234	·236	·242	·243	·244	·249
Mar	·175	·178	·183	·191	·195	·195	·193	·196	·204	·206	·208	·210	·209	·216	·220	·228	·231	·229	·229	·231	·237	·238	·239	·244
Apr	·163	·166	·171	·179	·183	·183	·181	·184	·192	·194	·196	·198	·197	·203	·207	·216	·218	·217	·217	·219	·225	·226	·226	·232
May	·158	·162	·166	·174	·178	·178	·176	·179	·187	·189	·191	·193	·193	·199	·203	·211	·213	·212	·212	·214	·220	·221	·221	·227
June	·157	·160	·165	·173	·176	·176	·174	·178	·186	·188	·190	·192	·191	·197	·201	·210	·212	·210	·210	·212	·218	·219	·220	·225
July	·162	·166	·170	·178	·182	·182	·180	·183	·191	·193	·195	·197	·197	·203	·207	·215	·217	·216	·216	·218	·224	·225	·225	·231
Aug	·156	·159	·164	·172	·175	·175	·173	·177	·185	·187	·189	·191	·190	·196	·200	·209	·211	·209	·209	·211	·217	·218	·219	·224
Sept	·151	·154	·159	·167	·170	·170	·168	·171	·179	·181	·183	·185	·185	·191	·195	·203	·205	·204	·204	·206	·212	·212	·213	·218
Oct	·157	·160	·165	·173	·176	·176	·174	·178	·186	·188	·190	·192	·191	·197	·201	·210	·212	·210	·210	·212	·218	·219	·220	·225
Nov	·157	·160	·165	·173	·176	·176	·174	·178	·186	·188	·190	·192	·191	·197	·201	·210	·212	·210	·210	·212	·218	·219	·220	·225
Dec	·150	·153	·158	·166	·169	·169	·167	·171	·179	·180	·182	·184	·184	·190	·194	·202	·204	·203	·203	·205	·211	·212	·212	·218

51

Month of disposal

		2004												2005	
	1991	Jan	Feb	Mar	Apr	May	June	July	Aug	Sept	Oct	Nov	Dec	Jan	Feb
B	Jan	·406	·412	·418	·426	·432	·435	.435	.439	.445	.449	.452	.459	.451	
a	Feb	·399	·404	·410	·419	·425	·427	.427	.432	.437	.441	.444	.451	.443	
s	Mar	·393	·399	·405	·413	·419	·422	.422	.426	.432	.435	.438	.445	.438	
e	Apr	·376	·381	·387	·395	·401	·403	.403	.408	.413	.417	.420	.427	.419	
	May	·372	·377	·383	·391	·397	·399	.399	.404	.409	.413	.416	.422	.415	
M	June	·365	·371	·377	·385	·391	·393	.393	.397	.403	.406	.409	.416	.409	
o	July	·368	·374	·380	·388	·394	·396	.396	.401	.406	.410	.413	.419	.412	
n	Aug	·365	·371	·377	·385	·391	·393	.393	.397	.403	.406	.409	.416	.409	
t	Sept	·360	·366	·371	·380	·386	·388	.388	.392	.397	.401	.404	.411	.403	
h	Oct	·355	·360	·366	·375	·380	·383	.383	.387	.392	.396	.399	.406	.398	
	Nov	·350	·355	·361	·369	·375	·378	.378	.382	.387	.391	.394	.400	.393	
	Dec	·349	·354	·360	·368	·374	·377	.377	.381	.386	.390	.393	.399	.392	
	1992														
	Jan	·350	·355	·361	·369	·375	·378	.378	.382	.387	.391	.394	.400	.393	
	Feb	·343	·348	·354	·362	·368	·371	.371	.375	.380	.384	.387	.393	.386	
	Mar	·339	·345	·350	·358	·364	·366	.366	.371	.376	.380	.383	.389	.382	
	Apr	·319	·324	·330	·338	·344	·346	.346	.350	.355	.359	.362	.368	.361	
	May	·314	·319	·325	·333	·339	·341	.341	.345	.350	.354	.357	.363	.356	
	June	·314	·319	·325	·333	·339	·341	.341	.345	.350	.354	.357	.363	.356	
	July	·319	·324	·330	·338	·344	·346	.346	.350	.355	.359	.362	.368	.361	
	Aug	·318	·323	·329	·337	·343	·345	.345	.349	.354	.358	.361	.367	.360	
	Sept	·313	·319	·324	·332	·338	·340	.340	.344	.349	.353	.356	.362	.355	
	Oct	·309	·314	·320	·327	·333	·335	.335	.340	.345	.348	.351	.357	.350	
	Nov	·311	·316	·321	·329	·335	·337	.337	.341	.346	.350	.353	.359	.352	
	Dec	·315	·320	·326	·334	340	·342	.342	.346	.351	.355	.358	.364	.357	
	1993														
	Jan	·328	·333	·339	·347	·352	·355	.355	.359	.364	.368	.371	.377	.370	
	Feb	·319	·324	·330	·338	·344	·346	.346	.350	.355	.359	.362	.368	.361	
	Mar	·314	·319	·325	·333	·339	·341	.341	.345	.350	.354	.357	.363	.356	
	Apr	·302	·307	·313	·321	·326	·329	.329	.333	.338	.341	.344	.351	.344	
	May	·298	·303	·308	·316	·322	·324	.324	.328	.333	.337	.339	.346	.339	
	June	·299	·304	·309	·317	·323	·325	.325	.329	.334	.338	.340	.347	.340	
	July	·301	·306	·312	·320	·326	·328	.328	.332	.337	.340	.343	.350	.343	
	Aug	·296	·301	·306	·314	·320	·322	.322	.326	.331	.335	.338	.344	.337	
	Sept	·290	·295	·301	·309	·314	·316	.316	.321	.326	.329	.332	.338	.331	
	Oct	·291	·296	·302	·310	·315	·317	.317	.322	.327	.330	.333	.339	.332	
	Nov	·293	·298	·304	·311	·317	·319	.319	.323	.328	.332	.335	.341	.334	
	Dec	·290	·295	·301	·309	·314	·316	.316	.321	.326	.329	.332	.338	.331	
	1994														
	Jan	·296	·301	·306	·314	·320	·322	.322	.326	.331	.335	.338	.344	.337	
	Feb	·289	·293	·299	·307	·312	·315	.315	.319	.324	.327	.330	.336	.329	
	Mar	·285	·290	·295	·303	·309	·311	.311	.315	.320	.324	.326	.333	.326	
	Apr	·270	·275	·280	·288	·293	·295	.295	.300	.304	.308	.311	.317	.310	
	May	·265	·270	·276	·283	·289	·291	.291	.295	.300	.303	.306	.312	.305	
	June	·265	·270	·276	·283	·289	·291	.291	.295	.300	.303	.306	.312	.305	
	July	·272	·276	·282	·290	·295	·297	.297	.301	.306	.310	.313	.319	.312	
	Aug	·265	·270	·276	·283	·289	·291	.291	.295	.300	.303	.306	.312	.305	
	Sept	·263	·268	·273	·281	·286	·288	.288	.292	.297	.301	.303	.310	.303	
	Oct	·261	·266	·271	·279	·284	·287	.287	.291	.295	.299	.302	.308	.301	
	Nov	·260	·265	·270	·278	·284	·286	.286	.290	.295	.298	.301	.307	.300	
	Dec	·254	·259	·264	·272	·277	·279	.279	.284	.288	.292	.295	.301	.294	
	1995														
	Jan	·254	·259	·264	·272	·277	·279	.279	.284	.288	.292	.295	.301	.294	
	Feb	·246	·251	·257	·264	·270	·272	.272	.276	.280	.284	.287	.293	.286	
	Mar	·241	·246	·252	·259	·264	·266	.266	.271	.275	.279	.281	.287	.281	
	Apr	·229	·234	·239	·246	·252	·254	.254	.258	.262	.266	.268	.274	.268	
	May	·224	·229	·234	·241	·247	·249	.249	.253	.257	.261	.263	.269	.263	
	June	·222	·227	·232	·240	·245	·247	.247	.251	.256	.259	.262	.268	.261	
	July	·228	·233	·238	·245	·251	·253	.253	.257	.262	.265	.268	.274	.267	
	Aug	·221	·226	·231	·239	·244	·246	.246	.250	.255	.258	.261	.267	.260	
	Sept	·216	·220	·226	·233	·238	·240	.240	.244	.249	.252	.255	.261	.254	
	Oct	·222	·227	·232	·240	·245	·247	.247	.251	.256	.259	.262	.268	.261	
	Nov	·222	·227	·232	·240	·245	·247	.247	.251	.256	.259	.262	.268	.261	
	Dec	·215	·220	·225	·232	·238	·240	.240	.244	.248	.251	.254	.260	.253	

	2000												2001											
1996	Jan	Feb	Mar	Apr	May	June	July	Aug	Sept	Oct	Nov	Dec	Jan	Feb	Mar	Apr	May	June	July	Aug	Sept	Oct	Nov	Dec
Jan	·109	·115	·121	·132	·136	·139	·135	·135	·143	·142	·146	·146	·139	·145	·146	·152	·160	·161	·154	·158	·162	·160	·156	·154
Feb	·104	·110	·116	·127	·131	·134	·130	·130	·138	·137	·140	·141	·134	·140	·141	·147	·154	·156	·148	·153	·157	·155	·150	·149
Mar	·100	·106	·112	·123	·127	·129	·125	·125	·133	·133	·136	·137	·129	·135	·137	·143	·150	·151	·144	·149	·152	·150	·146	·145
Apr	·092	·098	·104	·115	·119	·121	·117	·117	·125	·125	·128	·128	·121	·127	·128	·134	·142	·143	·136	·140	·144	·142	·138	·136
May	·090	·095	·101	·112	·116	·118	·115	·115	·123	·122	·126	·126	·118	·125	·126	·132	·139	·141	·133	·138	·142	·140	·135	·134
June	·089	·095	·101	·112	·116	·118	·114	·114	·122	·122	·125	·125	·118	·124	·125	·131	·139	·140	·133	·137	·141	·139	·135	·133
July	·093	·099	·105	·116	·120	·123	·119	·119	·127	·126	·129	·130	·123	·129	·130	·136	·143	·144	·137	·142	·146	·144	·139	·138
Aug	·088	·094	·100	·111	·115	·118	·114	·114	·121	·121	·124	·125	·118	·123	·125	·131	·138	·139	·132	·137	·140	·138	·134	·133
Sept	·083	·089	·095	·106	·110	·112	·109	·109	·116	·116	·119	·120	·112	·118	·120	·125	·133	·134	·127	·131	·135	·133	·129	·127
Oct	·083	·089	·095	·106	·110	·112	·109	·109	·116	·116	·119	·120	·112	·118	·120	·125	·133	·134	·127	·131	·135	·133	·129	·127
Nov	·083	·088	·094	·105	·109	·112	·108	·108	·116	·115	·118	·119	·112	·118	·119	·125	·132	·133	·126	·131	·135	·133	·128	·127
Dec	·079	·085	·091	·102	·106	·108	·104	·104	·112	·111	·115	·115	·108	·114	·115	·121	·128	·130	·122	·127	·131	·129	·124	·123
1997																								
Jan	·079	·085	·091	·102	·106	·108	·104	·104	·112	·111	·115	·115	·108	·114	·115	·121	·128	·130	·122	·127	·131	·129	·124	·123
Feb	·075	·081	·086	·097	·101	·104	·100	·100	·108	·107	·110	·111	·104	·110	·111	·117	·124	·125	·118	·123	·126	·125	·120	·119
Mar	·072	·078	·084	·095	·098	·101	·097	·097	·105	·104	·107	·108	·101	·107	·108	·114	·121	·122	·115	·120	·124	·122	·117	·116
Apr	·066	·072	·077	·088	·092	·095	·091	·091	·099	·098	·101	·102	·095	·100	·102	·107	·115	·116	·109	·113	·117	·115	·111	·109
May	·062	·068	·073	·084	·088	·091	·087	·087	·094	·094	·097	·098	·091	·096	·098	·103	·110	·112	·105	·109	·113	·111	·106	·105
June	·058	·063	·069	·080	·084	·086	·083	·083	·090	·090	·093	·093	·086	·092	·093	·099	·106	·107	·100	·105	·109	·107	·102	·101
July	·058	·063	·069	·080	·084	·086	·083	·083	·090	·090	·093	·093	·086	·092	·093	·099	·106	·107	·100	·105	·109	·107	·102	·101
Aug	·051	·057	·062	·073	·077	·079	·076	·076	·083	·083	·086	·086	·079	·085	·086	·092	·099	·100	·093	·098	·102	·100	·095	·094
Sept	·046	·051	·057	·068	·072	·074	·070	·070	·078	·077	·080	·081	·074	·080	·081	·087	·094	·095	·088	·092	·096	·094	·090	·089
Oct	·045	·050	·056	·066	·070	·073	·069	·069	·076	·076	·079	·080	·073	·078	·080	·085	·092	·093	·087	·091	·095	·093	·088	·087
Nov	·044	·049	·055	·066	·070	·072	·068	·068	·076	·075	·078	·079	·072	·078	·079	·085	·091	·093	·086	·090	·094	·092	·088	·086
Dec	·041	·047	·053	·063	·067	·069	·066	·066	·073	·073	·076	·076	·069	·075	·076	·082	·089	·090	·083	·088	·091	·089	·085	·084
1998																								
Jan	·045	·050	·056	·066	·070	·073	·069	·069	·076	·076	·079	·080	·073	·078	·080	·085	·092	·093	·087	·091	·095	·093	·088	·087
Feb	·039	·045	·051	·061	·065	·067	·064	·064	·071	·070	·074	·074	·067	·073	·074	·080	·087	·088	·081	·085	·089	·087	·083	·082
Mar	·036	·042	·047	·058	·062	·064	·060	·060	·068	·067	·070	·071	·064	·070	·071	·076	·083	·085	·078	·082	·086	·084	·080	·078
Apr	·025	·030	·036	·046	·050	·052	·049	·049	·056	·055	·058	·059	·052	·058	·059	·065	·071	·073	·066	·070	·074	·072	·068	·066
May	·019	·024	·030	·040	·044	·046	·043	·043	·050	·050	·053	·053	·046	·052	·053	·059	·065	·067	·060	·064	·068	·066	·062	·061
June	·020	·025	·031	·041	·045	·047	·043	·043	·050	·050	·053	·054	·047	·053	·054	·059	·066	·067	·061	·065	·069	·067	·062	·061
July	·022	·028	·033	·044	·047	·050	·046	·046	·053	·053	·056	·056	·050	·055	·056	·062	·069	·070	·063	·067	·071	·069	·065	·064
Aug	·018	·023	·029	·039	·043	·045	·042	·042	·049	·048	·051	·052	·045	·051	·052	·057	·064	·065	·059	·063	·067	·065	·060	·059
Sept	·013	·019	·024	·035	·038	·041	·037	·037	·044	·044	·047	·047	·041	·046	·047	·053	·060	·061	·054	·058	·062	·060	·056	·055
Oct	·013	·018	·024	·034	·038	·040	·036	·036	·044	·043	·046	·047	·040	·046	·047	·052	·059	·060	·053	·058	·061	·060	·055	·054
Nov	·013	·019	·024	·035	·038	·041	·037	·037	·044	·044	·047	·047	·041	·046	·047	·053	·060	·061	·054	·058	·062	·060	·056	·055
Dec	·013	·019	·024	·035	·038	·041	·037	·037	·044	·044	·047	·047	·041	·046	·047	·053	·060	·061	·054	·058	·062	·060	·056	·055
1999																								
Jan	·020	·025	·031	·041	·045	·047	·043	·043	·051	·050	·053	·054	·047	·053	·054	·059	·066	·067	·061	·065	·069	·067	·062	·061
Feb	·018	·023	·029	·039	·043	·045	·042	·042	·049	·048	·051	·052	·045	·051	·052	·057	·064	·065	·059	·063	·067	·065	·060	·059
Mar	·015	·021	·026	·037	·040	·043	·039	·039	·046	·046	·049	·049	·043	·048	·049	·055	·062	·063	·056	·060	·064	·062	·058	·057
Apr	·008	·014	·019	·030	·033	·036	·032	·032	·039	·039	·042	·042	·036	·041	·042	·048	·054	·056	·049	·053	·057	·055	·051	·050
May	·005	·011	·017	·027	·031	·033	·030	·030	·037	·036	·039	·040	·033	·039	·040	·045	·052	·053	·046	·051	·054	·053	·048	·047
June	·005	·011	·017	·027	·031	·033	·030	·030	·037	·036	·039	·040	·033	·039	·040	·045	·052	·053	·046	·051	·054	·053	·048	·047
July	·009	·015	·020	·030	·034	·036	·033	·033	·040	·039	·042	·043	·036	·042	·043	·048	·055	·056	·050	·054	·058	·056	·051	·050
Aug	·007	·012	·018	·028	·031	·034	·030	·030	·037	·037	·040	·040	·034	·039	·040	·046	·053	·054	·047	·051	·055	·053	·049	·048
Sept	·002	·008	·013	·023	·027	·029	·026	·026	·033	·032	·035	·036	·029	·035	·036	·042	·048	·049	·043	·047	·051	·049	·045	·043
Oct	·001	·006	·011	·022	·025	·028	·024	·024	·031	·031	·034	·034	·028	·033	·034	·040	·046	·047	·041	·045	·049	·047	·043	·041
Nov	·000	·005	·010	·020	·024	·026	·023	·023	·030	·029	·032	·033	·026	·032	·033	·038	·045	·046	·040	·044	·047	·046	·041	·040
Dec	·000	·001	·007	·017	·020	·023	·019	·019	·026	·026	·029	·029	·023	·028	·029	·035	·041	·042	·036	·040	·044	·042	·038	·036
2000																								
Jan	–	·005	·011	·021	·025	·027	·023	·023	·031	·030	·033	·034	·027	·032	·034	·039	·046	·047	·040	·044	·048	·046	·042	·041
Feb	–	–	·005	·016	·019	·021	·018	·018	·025	·024	·027	·028	·021	·027	·028	·033	·040	·041	·035	·039	·042	·041	·036	·035
Mar	–	–	–	·010	·014	·016	·012	·012	·020	·019	·022	·023	·016	·021	·023	·028	·034	·036	·029	·033	·037	·035	·031	·030
Apr	–	–	–	–	·004	·006	·002	·002	·009	·009	·012	·012	·006	·011	·012	·018	·024	·025	·019	·023	·026	·025	·021	·019
May	–	–	–	–	–	·002	·000	·000	·006	·005	·008	·009	·002	·008	·009	·014	·021	·022	·015	·019	·023	·021	·017	·016
June	–	–	–	–	–	–	·000	·000	·004	·003	·006	·006	·000	·005	·006	·012	·018	·019	·013	·017	·020	·019	·015	·013
July	–	–	–	–	–	–	–	·000	·007	·006	·009	·010	·004	·009	·010	·015	·022	·023	·016	·021	·024	·022	·018	·017
Aug	–	–	–	–	–	–	–	–	·007	·006	·009	·010	·004	·009	·010	·015	·022	·023	·016	·021	·024	·022	·018	·017
Sept	–	–	–	–	–	–	–	–	–	·000	·002	·003	·000	·002	·003	·008	·015	·016	·009	·013	·017	·015	·011	·010
Oct	–	–	–	–	–	–	–	–	–	–	·003	·003	·000	·002	·003	·009	·015	·016	·010	·014	·017	·016	·012	·010
Nov	–	–	–	–	–	–	–	–	–	–	–	·001	·000	·000	·001	·006	·012	·013	·007	·011	·015	·013	·009	·008
Dec	–	–	–	–	–	–	–	–	–	–	–	–	·000	·000	·000	·005	·012	·013	·006	·010	·014	·012	·008	·007

Base Month

Indexation allowance — continued

Month of disposal

Base Month

	2002												2003											
1996	Jan	Feb	Mar	Apr	May	June	July	Aug	Sept	Oct	Nov	Dec	Jan	Feb	Mar	Apr	May	June	July	Aug	Sept	Oct	Nov	Dec
Jan	·154	·157	·162	·170	·173	·173	·171	·174	·182	·184	·186	·188	·188	·194	·198	·206	·208	·207	·207	·209	·215	·216	·216	·222
Feb	·148	·152	·156	·164	·168	·168	·166	·169	·177	·179	·181	·183	·182	·188	·192	·201	·203	·201	·201	·203	·209	·210	·211	·216
Mar	·144	·147	·152	·160	·163	·163	·161	·164	·172	·174	·176	·178	·178	·183	·187	·196	·198	·197	·197	·199	·205	·205	·206	·211
Apr	·136	·139	·144	·151	·155	·155	·153	·156	·164	·166	·168	·170	·169	·175	·179	·187	·189	·188	·188	·190	·196	·197	·197	·202
May	·133	·137	·141	·149	·152	·152	·150	·154	·162	·164	·165	·167	·167	·173	·177	·185	·187	·186	·186	·188	·194	·194	·195	·200
June	·133	·136	·141	·148	·152	·152	·150	·153	·161	·163	·165	·167	·166	·172	·176	·184	·186	·185	·185	·187	·193	·193	·194	·199
July	·137	·140	·145	·153	·156	·156	·154	·157	·165	·167	·169	·171	·171	·177	·180	·189	·191	·190	·190	·192	·198	·198	·199	·204
Aug	·132	·135	·140	·148	·151	·151	·149	·152	·160	·162	·164	·166	·165	·171	·175	·184	·185	·184	·184	·186	·192	·193	·193	·199
Sept	·127	·130	·135	·142	·146	·146	·144	·147	·155	·157	·159	·161	·160	·166	·170	·178	·180	·179	·179	·181	·187	·187	·188	·193
Oct	·127	·130	·135	·142	·146	·146	·144	·147	·155	·157	·159	·161	·160	·166	·170	·178	·180	·179	·179	·181	·187	·187	·188	·193
Nov	·126	·129	·134	·142	·145	·145	·143	·146	·154	·156	·158	·160	·159	·165	·169	·177	·179	·178	·178	·180	·186	·186	·187	·192
Dec	·122	·126	·130	·138	·141	·141	·139	·142	·150	·152	·154	·156	·155	·161	·165	·174	·176	·174	·174	·176	·182	·183	·183	·188
1997																								
Jan	·122	·126	·130	·138	·141	·141	·139	·142	·150	·152	·154	·156	·155	·161	·165	·174	·176	·174	·174	·176	·182	·183	·183	·188
Feb	·118	·121	·126	·134	·137	·137	·135	·138	·146	·148	·150	·152	·151	·157	·161	·169	·171	·170	·170	·172	·177	·178	·179	·184
Mar	·115	·118	·123	·131	·134	·134	·132	·135	·143	·145	·147	·149	·148	·154	·158	·166	·168	·167	·167	·169	·174	·175	·176	·181
Apr	·109	·112	·116	·124	·127	·127	·125	·129	·136	·138	·140	·142	·141	·147	·151	·159	·161	·160	·160	·162	·168	·168	·169	·174
May	·105	·108	·112	·120	·123	·123	·121	·124	·132	·134	·136	·138	·137	·143	·147	·155	·157	·156	·156	·157	·163	·164	·164	·170
June	·100	·103	·108	·116	·119	·119	·117	·120	·128	·130	·131	·133	·133	·138	·142	·150	·152	·151	·151	·153	·159	·159	·160	·165
July	·100	·103	·108	·116	·119	·119	·117	·120	·128	·130	·131	·133	·133	·138	·142	·150	·152	·151	·151	·153	·159	·159	·160	·165
Aug	·093	·097	·101	·109	·112	·112	·110	·113	·121	·122	·124	·126	·126	·131	·135	·143	·145	·144	·144	·146	·151	·152	·153	·158
Sept	·088	·091	·095	·103	·106	·106	·104	·107	·115	·117	·119	·121	·120	·126	·129	·137	·139	·138	·138	·140	·146	·146	·147	·152
Oct	·087	·090	·094	·102	·105	·105	·103	·106	·113	·115	·117	·119	·118	·124	·128	·136	·138	·137	·137	·139	·144	·145	·145	·150
Nov	·086	·089	·093	·101	·104	·104	·102	·105	·113	·115	·117	·118	·118	·123	·127	·135	·137	·136	·136	·138	·143	·144	·145	·150
Dec	·083	·086	·091	·098	·101	·101	·099	·103	·110	·112	·114	·116	·115	·121	·124	·133	·134	·133	·133	·135	·141	·141	·142	·147
1998																								
Jan	·087	·090	·094	·102	·105	·105	·103	·106	·113	·115	·117	·119	·118	·124	·128	·136	·138	·137	·137	·139	·144	·145	·145	·150
Feb	·081	·084	·089	·096	·099	·099	·097	·100	·108	·110	·112	·114	·113	·119	·122	·130	·132	·131	·131	·133	·138	·139	·140	·145
Mar	·078	·081	·085	·093	·096	·096	·094	·097	·104	·106	·108	·110	·109	·115	·119	·127	·129	·127	·127	·129	·135	·136	·136	·141
Apr	·066	·069	·073	·081	·084	·084	·082	·085	·092	·094	·096	·098	·097	·103	·106	·114	·116	·115	·115	·117	·122	·123	·124	·129
May	·060	·063	·067	·075	·078	·078	·076	·079	·086	·088	·090	·092	·091	·097	·100	·108	·110	·109	·109	·111	·116	·117	·117	·122
June	·061	·064	·068	·075	·078	·078	·076	·080	·087	·089	·091	·092	·092	·097	·101	·109	·111	·110	·110	·111	·117	·118	·118	·123
July	·063	·066	·071	·078	·081	·081	·079	·082	·090	·091	·093	·095	·094	·100	·104	·112	·113	·112	·112	·114	·120	·120	·121	·126
Aug	·059	·062	·066	·073	·076	·076	·075	·078	·085	·087	·089	·090	·090	·095	·099	·107	·109	·108	·108	·109	·115	·115	·116	·121
Sept	·054	·057	·061	·069	·072	·072	·070	·073	·080	·082	·084	·086	·085	·091	·094	·102	·104	·103	·103	·105	·110	·111	·111	·116
Oct	·053	·057	·061	·068	·071	·071	·069	·072	·080	·081	·083	·085	·084	·090	·094	·102	·103	·102	·102	·104	·109	·110	·111	·116
Nov	·054	·057	·061	·069	·072	·072	·070	·073	·080	·082	·084	·086	·085	·091	·094	·102	·104	·103	·103	·105	·110	·111	·111	·116
Dec	·054	·057	·061	·069	·072	·072	·070	·073	·080	·082	·084	·086	·085	·091	·094	·102	·104	·103	·103	·105	·110	·111	·111	·116
1999																								
Jan	·061	·064	·068	·075	·078	·078	·076	·080	·087	·089	·091	·092	·092	·097	·101	·109	·111	·110	·110	·111	·117	·118	·118	·123
Feb	·059	·062	·066	·073	·076	·076	·075	·078	·085	·087	·089	·090	·090	·095	·099	·107	·109	·108	·108	·109	·115	·115	·116	·121
Mar	·056	·059	·063	·071	·074	·074	·072	·075	·082	·084	·086	·088	·087	·093	·096	·104	·106	·105	·105	·107	·112	·113	·113	·118
Apr	·049	·052	·056	·064	·067	·067	·065	·068	·075	·077	·079	·081	·080	·085	·089	·097	·099	·097	·097	·099	·105	·105	·106	·111
May	·046	·050	·054	·061	·064	·064	·062	·065	·072	·074	·076	·078	·077	·083	·086	·094	·096	·095	·095	·097	·102	·103	·103	·108
June	·046	·050	·054	·061	·064	·064	·062	·065	·072	·074	·076	·078	·077	·083	·086	·094	·096	·095	·095	·097	·102	·103	·103	·108
July	·050	·053	·057	·064	·067	·067	·065	·068	·076	·078	·079	·081	·081	·086	·090	·098	·099	·098	·098	·100	·105	·106	·107	·111
Aug	·047	·050	·054	·062	·065	·065	·063	·066	·073	·075	·077	·079	·078	·083	·087	·095	·097	·095	·095	·097	·103	·103	·104	·109
Sept	·043	·046	·050	·057	·060	·060	·058	·061	·069	·070	·072	·074	·073	·079	·082	·090	·092	·091	·091	·093	·098	·099	·099	·104
Oct	·041	·044	·048	·055	·058	·058	·056	·059	·067	·068	·070	·072	·071	·077	·080	·088	·090	·089	·089	·091	·096	·097	·097	·102
Nov	·040	·043	·047	·054	·057	·057	·055	·058	·065	·067	·069	·071	·070	·076	·079	·087	·089	·088	·088	·089	·095	·095	·096	·101
Dec	·036	·039	·043	·050	·053	·053	·051	·054	·062	·063	·065	·067	·066	·072	·075	·083	·085	·084	·084	·085	·091	·091	·092	·097
2000																								
Jan	·040	·043	·047	·055	·058	·058	·056	·059	·066	·068	·070	·071	·071	·076	·080	·088	·089	·088	·088	·090	·095	·096	·097	·101
Feb	·035	·038	·042	·049	·052	·052	·050	·053	·060	·062	·064	·066	·065	·070	·074	·082	·084	·082	·082	·084	·090	·090	·091	·096
Mar	·029	·032	·036	·043	·046	·046	·045	·048	·055	·056	·058	·060	·059	·065	·068	·076	·078	·077	·077	·078	·084	·084	·085	·090
Apr	·019	·022	·026	·033	·036	·036	·034	·037	·044	·046	·048	·049	·049	·054	·058	·065	·067	·066	·066	·068	·073	·073	·074	·079
May	·015	·018	·022	·029	·032	·032	·030	·033	·040	·042	·044	·046	·045	·050	·054	·062	·063	·062	·062	·064	·069	·070	·070	·075
June	·013	·016	·020	·027	·030	·030	·028	·031	·038	·040	·041	·043	·043	·048	·051	·059	·061	·060	·060	·061	·067	·067	·068	·072
July	·016	·019	·023	·030	·033	·033	·032	·035	·042	·043	·045	·047	·046	·052	·055	·063	·065	·063	·063	·065	·070	·071	·072	·076
Aug	·016	·019	·023	·030	·033	·033	·032	·035	·042	·043	·045	·047	·046	·052	·055	·063	·065	·063	·063	·065	·070	·071	·072	·076
Sept	·009	·012	·016	·023	·026	·026	·024	·027	·034	·036	·038	·040	·039	·044	·048	·055	·057	·056	·056	·058	·063	·063	·064	·069
Oct	·010	·013	·017	·024	·027	·027	·025	·028	·035	·037	·038	·040	·040	·045	·048	·056	·058	·057	·057	·058	·064	·064	·065	·069
Nov	·007	·010	·014	·021	·024	·024	·022	·025	·032	·034	·035	·037	·037	·042	·045	·053	·055	·053	·053	·055	·060	·061	·062	·066
Dec	·006	·009	·013	·020	·023	·023	·021	·024	·031	·033	·035	·037	·036	·041	·045	·052	·054	·053	·053	·055	·060	·060	·061	·066

Indexation allowance — continued

Month of disposal

	2004												2005	
1996	Jan	Feb	Mar	Apr	May	June	July	Aug	Sept	Oct	Nov	Dec	Jan	Feb
Jan	.219	.224	.229	.236	.242	.244	.244	.248	.252	.253	.258	.264	.258	
Feb	.213	.218	.223	.231	.236	.238	.238	.242	.247	.250	.252	.258	.252	
Mar	.209	.213	.218	.226	.231	.233	.233	.237	.242	.245	.248	.253	.247	
Apr	.200	.204	.210	.217	.222	.224	.224	.228	.233	.236	.239	.244	.238	
May	.198	.202	.207	.215	.220	.222	.222	.226	.230	.233	.236	.242	.235	
June	.197	.201	.207	.214	.219	.221	.221	.225	.229	.233	.235	.241	.235	
July	.201	.206	.211	.219	.224	.226	.226	.230	.234	.238	.240	.246	.240	
Aug	.196	.201	.206	.213	.218	.220	.220	.224	.229	.232	.234	.240	.234	
Sept	.191	.195	.200	.207	.213	.215	.215	.218	.223	.226	.229	.235	.228	
Oct	.191	.195	.200	.207	.213	.215	.215	.218	.223	.226	.229	.235	.228	
Nov	.190	.194	.199	.207	.212	.214	.214	.218	.222	.225	.228	.234	.227	
Dec	.186	.190	.196	.203	.208	.210	.210	.214	.218	.222	.224	.230	.223	
1997														
Jan	.186	.190	.196	.203	.208	.210	.210	.214	.218	.222	.224	.230	.223	
Feb	.181	.186	.191	.198	.203	.205	.205	.209	.214	.217	.219	.225	.219	
Mar	.178	.183	.188	.195	.200	.202	.202	.206	.210	.214	.216	.222	.216	
Apr	.171	.176	.181	.188	.193	.195	.195	.199	.203	.207	.209	.215	.209	
May	.167	.171	.177	.184	.189	.191	.191	.194	.199	.202	.205	.210	.204	
June	.163	.167	.172	.179	.184	.186	.186	.190	.194	.197	.200	.206	.199	
July	.163	.167	.172	.179	.184	.186	.186	.190	.194	.197	.200	.206	.199	
Aug	.155	.160	.165	.172	.177	.179	.179	.182	.187	.190	.192	.198	.192	
Sept	.149	.154	.159	.166	.171	.173	.173	.176	.181	.184	.186	.192	.186	
Oct	.148	.152	.157	.164	.169	.171	.171	.175	.179	.182	.185	.191	.184	
Nov	.147	.152	.157	.164	.169	.170	.170	.174	.179	.182	.184	.190	.184	
Dec	.144	.149	.154	.161	.166	.168	.168	.171	.176	.179	.181	.187	.181	
1998														
Jan	.148	.152	.157	.164	.169	.171	.171	.175	.179	.182	.185	.191	.184	
Feb	.142	.147	.152	.158	.163	.165	.165	.169	.173	.177	.179	.185	.178	
Mar	.139	.143	.148	.155	.160	.162	.162	.165	.170	.173	.175	.181	.175	
Apr	.126	.130	.135	.142	.147	.149	.149	.153	.157	.160	.162	.168	.162	
May	.120	.124	.129	.136	.141	.143	.143	.146	.150	.154	.156	.161	.155	
June	.121	.125	.130	.136	.141	.143	.143	.147	.151	.154	.157	.162	.156	
July	.123	.128	.133	.139	.144	.146	.146	.150	.154	.157	.160	.165	.159	
Aug	.119	.123	.128	.134	.139	.141	.141	.145	.149	.152	.155	.160	.154	
Sept	.114	.118	.123	.130	.134	.136	.136	.140	.144	.147	.150	.155	.149	
Oct	.113	.117	.122	.129	.134	.136	.136	.139	.143	.147	.149	.154	.148	
Nov	.114	.118	.123	.130	.134	.136	.136	.140	.144	.147	.150	.155	.149	
Dec	.114	.118	.123	.130	.134	.136	.136	.140	.144	.147	.150	.155	.149	
1999														
Jan	.121	.125	.130	.136	.141	.143	.143	.147	.151	.154	.157	.162	.156	
Feb	.119	.123	.128	.134	.139	.141	.141	.145	.149	.152	.155	.160	.154	
Mar	.116	.120	.125	.132	.137	.138	.138	.142	.146	.149	.152	.157	.151	
Apr	.108	.113	.117	.124	.129	.131	.131	.134	.139	.142	.144	.150	.143	
May	.106	.110	.115	.121	.126	.128	.128	.132	.136	.139	.141	.147	.141	
June	.106	.110	.115	.121	.126	.128	.128	.132	.136	.139	.141	.147	.141	
July	.109	.113	.118	.125	.130	.131	.131	.135	.139	.142	.145	.150	.144	
Aug	.106	.111	.115	.122	.127	.129	.129	.132	.137	.140	.142	.147	.141	
Sept	.102	.106	.111	.117	.122	.124	.124	.128	.132	.135	.137	.143	.137	
Oct	.100	.104	.109	.115	.120	.122	.122	.126	.130	.133	.135	.141	.135	
Nov	.098	.103	.107	.114	.119	.121	.121	.124	.128	.131	.134	.139	.133	
Dec	.094	.099	.103	.110	.115	.117	.117	.120	.124	.127	.130	.135	.129	
2000														
Jan	.099	.103	.108	.115	.119	.121	.121	.125	.129	.132	.134	.140	.134	
Feb	.093	.097	.102	.109	.113	.115	.115	.119	.123	.126	.128	.134	.128	
Mar	.087	.091	.096	.103	.107	.109	.109	.113	.117	.120	.122	.128	.122	
Apr	.076	.081	.085	.092	.096	.098	.098	.102	.106	.109	.111	.116	.111	
May	.073	.077	.081	.088	.093	.094	.094	.098	.102	.105	.107	.112	.107	
June	.070	.074	.079	.085	.090	.092	.092	.095	.099	.102	.105	.110	.104	
July	.074	.078	.083	.089	.094	.096	.096	.099	.103	.106	.109	.114	.108	
Aug	.074	.078	.083	.089	.094	.096	.096	.099	.103	.106	.109	.114	.108	
Sept	.066	.070	.075	.082	.086	.088	.088	.091	.096	.098	.101	.106	.100	
Oct	.067	.071	.076	.082	.087	.089	.089	.092	.096	.099	.101	.107	.101	
Nov	.064	.068	.073	.079	.084	.085	.085	.089	.093	.096	.098	.103	.098	
Dec	.063	.067	.072	.078	.083	.085	.085	.088	.092	.095	.098	.103	.097	

Base Month

Indexation allowance — continued

Month of disposal

(Rows: month of acquisition — "Base Month". Columns: month of disposal, grouped by year.)

Month of disposal — 2001

Acquisition	Jan	Feb	Mar	Apr	May	June	July	Aug	Sept	Oct	Nov	Dec
2001 Jan	—	·005	·006	·012	·018	·019	·013	·017	·020	·019	·015	·013
Feb		—	·001	·006	·013	·014	·008	·012	·015	·013	·009	·008
Mar			—	·005	·012	·013	·006	·010	·014	·012	·008	·007
Apr				—	·006	·007	·001	·005	·009	·007	·003	·002
May					—	·001	·000	·004	·008	·006	·002	·001
Jun						—	·000	·003	·007	·005	·002	·000
Jul							—	·000	·004	·002	·000	·000
Aug								—	·004	·002	·000	·000
Sep									—	·003	·000	·000
Oct										—	·000	·000
Nov											—	·000
Dec												—

Month of disposal — 2002

Acquisition	Jan	Feb	Mar	Apr	May	June	July	Aug	Sept	Oct	Nov	Dec
2001 Jan	·013	·016	·020	·027	·030	·030	·028	·031	·038	·040	·041	·043
Feb	·008	·010	·015	·022	·024	·024	·023	·026	·033	·034	·036	·038
Mar	·007	·009	·013	·020	·023	·021	·021	·024	·031	·033	·035	·037
Apr	·002	·004	·008	·015	·018	·016	·016	·019	·026	·028	·029	·031
May	·000	·000	·002	·009	·011	·011	·010	·013	·020	·021	·023	·025
Jun	·000	·000	·001	·007	·011	·010	·009	·011	·018	·020	·021	·024
Jul	·000	·000	·001	·009	·010	·011	·009	·012	·019	·021	·022	·024
Aug		·000	·000	·005	·010	·011	·007	·011	·018	·019	·022	·024
Sep			·000	·003	·007	·009	·005	·009	·016	·017	·019	·021
Oct				·002	·006	·007	·002	·006	·013	·015	·017	·019
Nov					·002	·004	·000	·004	·011	·012	·015	·017
Dec						·000	·000	·002	·009	·011	·013	·015
2002 Jan	·013	·016	·020	·027	·030	·030	·028	·031	·038	·040	·041	·043
Feb		·003	·007	·014	·017	·017	·015	·018	·025	·027	·028	·030
Mar			·004	·011	·014	·014	·012	·015	·022	·024	·025	·027
Apr				·007	·010	·010	·008	·011	·018	·019	·021	·023
May					·003	·003	·001	·004	·011	·013	·014	·016
June						·000	·000	·003	·010	·011	·013	·015
July							·000	·002	·009	·011	·013	·014
Aug								·000	·007	·008	·010	·013
Sept									·000	·002	·003	·006
Oct										·000	·000	·003
Nov											·000	·002
Dec												·000

Month of disposal — 2003

Acquisition	Jan	Feb	Mar	Apr	May	June	July	Aug	Sept	Oct	Nov	Dec
2001 Jan	·043	·048	·051	·059	·061	·060	·060	·061	·067	·067	·068	·072
Feb	·037	·042	·046	·053	·055	·054	·054	·056	·061	·062	·062	·067
Mar	·036	·041	·045	·052	·054	·053	·053	·055	·060	·060	·061	·066
Apr	·031	·036	·039	·047	·049	·047	·047	·049	·054	·055	·055	·060
May	·024	·029	·033	·040	·042	·041	·041	·042	·048	·048	·049	·053
Jun	·023	·028	·032	·039	·041	·040	·040	·041	·046	·047	·047	·052
Jul	·029	·035	·038	·046	·047	·046	·046	·048	·053	·054	·054	·059
Aug	·025	·030	·034	·041	·043	·042	·042	·044	·049	·049	·050	·055
Sep	·022	·027	·030	·038	·040	·038	·038	·040	·045	·046	·046	·051
Oct	·022	·029	·032	·040	·041	·040	·040	·042	·047	·046	·048	·053
Nov	·028	·033	·037	·044	·046	·044	·044	·046	·051	·052	·052	·057
Dec	·029	·034	·037	·045	·047	·046	·046	·047	·052	·053	·054	·058
2002 Jan	·029	·035	·038	·046	·047	·046	·046	·048	·053	·054	·054	·059
Feb	·026	·032	·035	·043	·044	·043	·043	·045	·050	·051	·051	·056
Mar	·022	·028	·031	·039	·039	·039	·039	·041	·046	·046	·047	·052
Apr	·015	·020	·024	·031	·033	·032	·032	·034	·039	·039	·040	·044
May	·012	·018	·021	·028	·030	·029	·029	·031	·036	·036	·037	·041
June	·012	·018	·021	·028	·029	·029	·029	·031	·036	·036	·037	·041
July	·014	·019	·023	·030	·032	·031	·031	·032	·038	·037	·039	·043
Aug	·011	·016	·020	·027	·029	·028	·028	·029	·035	·035	·036	·040
Sept	·011	·016	·019	·027	·028	·027	·027	·029	·035	·035	·036	·040
Oct	·005	·011	·014	·021	·023	·022	·022	·023	·028	·029	·029	·033
Nov	·003	·008	·011	·019	·021	·019	·019	·021	·026	·026	·027	·031
Dec	·001	·006	·010	·017	·019	·017	·017	·018	·024	·025	·025	·030
2003 Jan		·005	·008	·016	·017	·016	·016	·018	·023	·024	·024	·029
Feb			·003	·011	·012	·011	·011	·013	·018	·018	·019	·023
Mar				·007	·009	·008	·008	·009	·014	·015	·016	·020
Apr					·002	·001	·000	·001	·007	·008	·008	·013
May						·000	·000	·001	·006	·006	·007	·011
June							·000	·002	·007	·007	·008	·012
July								·002	·007	·007	·008	·012
Aug									·005	·006	·007	·012
Sept										·001	·006	·010
Oct											·001	·006
Nov												·005
Dec												—

Month of disposal

	2004												2005	
2001	Jan	Feb	Mar	Apr	May	June	July	Aug	Sept	Oct	Nov	Dec	Jan	Feb
Jan	·070	·074	·079	·085	·090	·092	.092	.095	.099	.102	.105	.110	.104	
Feb	·065	·069	·073	·080	·084	·086	.086	.090	.094	.097	.099	.104	.098	
Mar	·063	·067	·072	·078	·083	·085	.085	.088	.092	.095	.098	.103	.097	
Apr	·058	·062	·066	·073	·077	·079	.079	.083	.087	.090	.092	.097	.091	
May	·051	·055	·060	·066	·071	·072	.072	.076	.080	.083	.085	.090	.084	
June	·050	·054	·058	·065	·069	·071	.071	.075	.079	.081	.084	.089	.083	
July	·057	·061	·065	·072	·076	·078	.078	.081	.085	.088	.091	.096	.090	
Aug	·052	·056	·061	·067	·072	·074	.074	.077	.081	.084	.086	.091	.086	
Sept	·049	·053	·057	·064	·068	·070	.070	.073	.077	.080	.082	.088	.082	
Oct	·050	·055	·059	·065	·070	·072	.072	.075	.079	.082	.084	.090	.084	
Nov	·055	·059	·063	·070	·074	·076	.076	.079	.084	.086	.089	.094	.088	
Dec	·056	·060	·065	·071	·076	·077	.077	.081	.085	.088	.090	.095	.089	
2002														
Jan	·057	·061	·065	·072	·076	·078	.078	.081	.085	.088	.091	.096	.090	
Feb	·054	·058	·062	·068	·073	·075	.075	.078	.082	.085	.087	.093	.087	
Mar	·049	·053	·058	·064	·069	·070	.070	.074	.078	.081	.083	.088	.083	
Apr	·042	·046	·051	·057	·061	·063	.063	.067	.071	.073	.076	.081	.075	
May	·039	·043	·048	·054	·058	·060	.060	.064	.068	.070	.073	.078	.072	
June	·039	·043	·048	·054	·058	·060	.060	.064	.068	.070	.073	.078	.072	
July	·041	·045	·049	·056	·060	·062	.062	.065	.069	.072	.074	.080	.074	
Aug	·038	·042	·046	·053	·057	·059	.059	.062	.066	.069	.071	.077	.071	
Sept	·031	·035	·039	·046	·050	·052	.052	.055	.059	.062	.064	.069	.064	
Oct	·029	·033	·038	·044	·048	·050	.050	.053	.057	.060	.062	.067	.062	
Nov	·027	·031	·036	·042	·047	·048	.048	.052	.056	.058	.061	.066	.060	
Dec	·026	·030	·034	·040	·045	·046	.046	.050	.054	.057	.059	.064	.058	
2003														
Jan	·026	·030	·035	·041	·045	·047	.047	.050	.054	.057	.059	.064	.059	
Feb	·021	·025	·030	·036	·040	·042	.042	.045	.049	.052	.054	.059	.054	
Mar	·018	·022	·026	·032	·037	·038	.038	.042	.046	.048	.051	.056	.050	
Apr	·010	·014	·019	·025	·029	·031	.031	.034	.038	.041	.043	.048	.042	
May	·009	·013	·017	·023	·028	·029	.029	.033	.036	.039	.041	.046	.041	
June	·010	·014	·018	·024	·029	·030	.030	.034	.038	.040	.042	.047	.042	
July	·010	·014	·018	·024	·029	·030	.030	.034	.038	.040	.042	.047	.042	
Aug	·008	·012	·017	·023	·027	·029	.029	.032	.036	.039	.041	.046	.040	
Sept	·003	·007	·012	·018	·022	·024	.024	.027	.031	.033	.036	.041	.035	
Oct	·003	·007	·011	·017	·021	·023	.023	.026	.030	.033	.035	.040	.035	
Nov	·002	·006	·010	·016	·021	·022	.022	.026	.030	.032	.034	.039	.034	
Dec	·000	·002	·006	·012	·016	·018	.018	.021	.025	.028	.030	.035	.029	
2004														
Jan	–	·004	·008	·014	·019	·020	.020	.023	.027	.030	.032	.037	.032	
Feb	–	–	·004	·010	·015	·016	.016	.020	.023	.026	.028	.033	.028	
Mar	–	–	·000	·006	·010	·012	.012	.015	.019	.022	.024	.029	.023	
Apr	–	–	–	·000	·004	·006	.006	.009	.013	.016	.018	.023	.017	
May	–	–	–	–	·000	·002	.002	.005	.009	.011	.013	.018	.013	
June	–	–	–	–	–	·000	.000	.003	.007	.010	.012	.017	.011	
July	–	–	–	–	–	–	.000	.003	.007	.010	.012	.017	.011	
Aug	–	–	–	–	–	–	–	.000	.004	.006	.009	.013	.008	
Sept	–	–	–	–	–	–	–	–	.000	.003	.005	.010	.004	
Oct	–	–	–	–	–	–	–	–	–	.000	.002	.007	.002	
Nov	–	–	–	–	–	–	–	–	–	–	.000	.005	.000	
Dec	–	–	–	–	–	–	–	–	–	–	–	.000	.000	
2005														
Jan	–	–	–	–	–	–	–	–	–	–	–	–	.000	
Feb	–	–	–	–	–	–	–	–	–	–	–	–	–	

Base Month

Retail prices index

	Jan	Feb	Mar	Apr	May	June	July	Aug	Sept	Oct	Nov	Dec
1950	8·73	8·73	8·73	8·81	8·81	8·81	8·81	8·73	8·81	8·89	8·97	8·97
1951	9·03	9·11	9·19	9·35	9·59	9·67	9·72	9·80	9·88	9·96	9·96	10·04
1952	10·20	10·28	10·28	10·44	10·44	10·65	10·65	10·04	9·96	10·11	10·11	10·11
1953	10·11	10·19	10·67	10·34	10·27	10·34	10·34	10·27	10·27	10·27	10·27	10·27
1954	10·27	10·27	10·34	10·42	10·34	10·42	10·62	10·57	10·49	10·57	10·62	10·62
1955	10·70	10·70	10·70	10·77	10·77	11·00	11·00	10·93	11·00	11·15	11·28	11·28
1956	11·25	11·25	11·38	11·56	11·53	11·51	11·48	11·51	11·48	11·56	11·58	11·63
1957	11·74	11·74	11·71	11·76	11·76	11·89	11·99	11·96	11·94	12·04	12·12	12·17
1958	12·17	12·09	12·19	12·32	12·29	12·40	12·19	12·19	12·19	12·29	12·34	12·40
1959	12·42	12·40	12·40	12·32	12·27	12·29	12·27	12·29	12·22	12·29	12·37	12·40
1960	12·37	12·37	12·34	12·40	12·40	12·47	12·50	12·42	12·42	12·52	12·60	12·62
1961	12·62	12·62	12·67	12·75	12·78	12·90	12·90	13·00	13·00	13·00	13·16	13·18
1962	13·21	13·23	13·28	13·46	13·51	13·59	13·54	13·43	13·41	13·41	13·46	13·51
1963	13·56	13·69	13·71	13·74	13·74	13·74	13·66	13·61	13·66	13·71	13·74	13·76
1964	13·84	13·84	13·89	14·02	14·14	14·20	14·20	14·25	14·25	14·27	14·37	14·42
1965	14·47	14·47	14·52	14·80	14·85	14·90	14·90	14·93	14·93	14·96	15·01	15·08
1966	15·11	15·11	15·13	15·34	15·44	15·49	15·41	15·51	15·49	15·51	15·61	15·64
1967	15·67	15·67	15·67	15·79	15·79	15·84	15·74	15·72	15·69	15·86	15·92	16·02
1968	16·07	16·15	16·20	16·50	16·50	16·58	16·58	16·60	16·63	16·70	16·76	16·96
1969	17·06	17·16	17·21	17·41	17·39	17·47	17·47	17·41	17·47	17·59	17·64	17·77
1970	17·90	18·00	18·10	18·38	18·43	18·48	18·63	18·61	18·71	18·91	19·04	19·16
1971	19·42	19·54	19·70	20·13	20·25	20·38	20·51	20·53	20·56	20·66	20·79	20·89
1972	21·01	21·12	21·19	21·39	21·50	21·62	21·70	21·88	22·00	22·31	22·38	22·48
1973	22·64	22·79	22·92	23·35	23·52	23·65	23·75	23·83	24·03	24·51	24·69	24·87
1974	25·35	25·78	26·01	26·89	27·28	27·55	27·81	27·83	28·14	28·69	29·20	29·63
1975	30·39	30·90	31·51	32·72	34·09	34·75	35·11	35·31	35·61	36·12	36·55	37·01
1976	37·49	37·97	38·17	38·91	39·34	39·54	39·62	40·18	40·71	41·44	42·03	42·59
1977	43·70	44·24	44·56	45·70	46·06	46·54	46·59	46·82	47·07	47·28	47·50	47·76
1978	48·04	48·31	48·62	49·33	49·61	49·99	50·22	50·54	50·75	50·98	51·33	51·76
1979	52·52	52·95	53·38	54·30	54·73	55·67	58·07	58·53	59·11	59·72	60·25	60·68
1980	62·18	63·07	63·93	66·11	66·72	67·35	67·91	68·06	68·49	68·92	69·48	69·86
1981	70·29	70·93	71·99	74·07	74·55	74·98	75·31	75·87	76·30	76·98	77·78	78·28
1982	78·73	78·76	79·44	81·04	81·62	81·85	81·88	81·90	81·85	82·26	82·66	82·51
1983	82·61	82·97	83·12	84·28	84·64	84·84	85·30	85·68	86·06	86·36	86·67	86·89
1984	86·84	87·20	87·48	88·64	88·97	89·20	89·10	89·94	90·11	90·67	90·95	90·87
1985	91·20	91·94	92·80	94·78	95·21	95·41	95·23	95·49	95·44	95·59	95·92	96·05
1986	96·25	96·60	96·73	97·67	97·85	97·79	97·52	97·82	98·30	98·45	99·29	99·62
1987	100·00	100·40	100·60	101·80	101·90	101·90	101·80	102·10	102·40	102·90	103·40	103·30
1988	103·30	103·70	104·10	105·80	106·20	106·60	106·70	107·90	108·40	109·50	110·00	110·30
1989	111·00	111·80	112·30	114·30	115·00	115·40	115·50	115·80	116·60	117·50	118·50	118·80
1990	119·50	120·20	121·40	125·10	126·20	126·70	126·80	128·10	129·30	130·30	130·00	129·90
1991	130·20	130·90	131·40	133·10	133·50	134·10	133·80	134·10	134·60	135·10	135·60	135·70
1992	135·60	136·30	136·70	138·80	139·30	139·30	138·80	138·90	139·40	139·90	139·70	139·20
1993	137·90	138·80	139·30	140·60	141·10	141·00	140·70	141·30	141·90	141·80	141·60	141·90
1994	141·30	142·10	142·50	144·20	144·70	144·70	144·00	144·70	145·00	145·20	145·30	146·00
1995	146·00	146·90	147·50	149·00	149·60	149·80	149·10	149·90	150·60	149·80	149·80	150·70
1996	150·20	150·90	151·50	152·60	152·90	153·00	152·40	153·10	153·80	153·80	153·90	154·40
1997	154·40	155·00	155·40	156·30	156·90	157·50	157·50	158·50	159·30	159·50	159·60	160·00
1998	159·50	160·30	160·80	162·60	163·50	163·40	163·00	163·70	164·40	164·50	164·40	164·40
1999	163·40	163·70	164·10	165·20	165·60	165·60	165·10	165·50	166·20	166·50	166·70	167·30
2000	166·60	167·50	168·40	170·10	170·70	171·10	170·50	170·50	171·70	171·60	172·10	172·20
2001	171·10	172·00	172·20	173·10	174·20	174·40	173·30	174·00	174·60	174·30	173·60	173·40
2002	173·30	173·80	174·50	175·70	176·20	176·20	175·90	176·40	177·60	177·90	178·20	178·50
2003	178·40	179·30	179·90	181·20	181·50	181·30	181·30	181·60	182·50	182·60	182·70	183·50
2004	183·10	183·80	184·60	185·70	186·50	186·80	186·80	187·40	188·10	188·60	189·00	189·90
2005	188·90											

Corporation tax

Rates of corporation tax and advance corporation tax

Financial year	1997	1998	1999	2000	2001	2002	2003	2004	2005
Corporation tax (full rate)	31%	31%	30%	30%	30%	30%	30%	30%	30%
Non-corporate distribution rate[2]	—	—	—	—	—	—	—	19%	19%
Advance corporation tax: from 6 April	¼	¼	—[1]	—	—	—	—	—	—
Tax credit: from 6 April[3]	20%	20%	10%	10%	10%	10%	10%	10%	10%

[1] Advance corporation tax is abolished from 6 April 1999.
[2] Applies where the underlying corporation tax rate is less than 19% (TA 1988 s 13AB, Sch A2).
[3] Individual shareholders not subject to tax at the higher rate will have no further tax to pay. The abolition of the repayment of the tax credit to charities is phased in over five years at 21% for 1999–2000, 17% for 2000–01, 13% for 2001–02, 8% for 2002–03 and 4% for 2003–04.

Starting and small companies' rates (TA 1988 ss 13, 13AA)

Financial year:	1999	2000	2001	2002	2003	2004	2005
Starting rate	—	10%	10%	0%	0%	0%	0%
first relevant amount*	—	£10,000	£10,000	£10,000	£10,000	£10,000	£10,000
second relevant amount*	—	£50,000	£50,000	£50,000	£50,000	£50,000	£50,000
marginal relief fraction	—	$\frac{1}{40}$	$\frac{1}{40}$	$\frac{19}{400}$	$\frac{19}{400}$	$\frac{19}{400}$	$\frac{19}{400}$
effective marginal rate†	—	22.5%	22.5%	23.75%	23.75%	23.75%	23.75%
Small companies' rate	20%	20%	20%	19%	19%	19%	19%
lower relevant amount*	£300,000	£300,000	£300,000	£300,000	£300,000	£300,000	£300,000
upper relevant amount*	£1,500,000	£1,500,000	£1,500,000	£1,500,000	£1,500,000	£1,500,000	£1,500,000
marginal relief fraction	$\frac{1}{40}$	$\frac{1}{40}$	$\frac{1}{40}$	$\frac{11}{400}$	$\frac{11}{400}$	$\frac{11}{400}$	$\frac{11}{400}$
effective marginal rate†	32.5%	32.5%	32.5%	32.75%	32.75%	32.75%	32.75%

* Reduced proportionally for accounting periods of less than 12 months. Associated companies: divide limits by total number of associated companies (including the company in question).
1) The starting and the small companies' rate apply to *basic profits* ("I") where *profits* ("P") do not exceed the first (in the case of the starting rate) and lower (small companies' rate) relevant amounts.
2) Where *profits* ("P") exceed the first or lower relevant amounts but not the second or upper relevant amounts, corporation tax on *basic profits* ("I") is reduced by—

(second or upper relevant amount $- P) \times \dfrac{I}{P} \times$ fraction

For the purposes of 1) and 2) above:
P = profits as finally computed for corporation tax purposes *plus* franked investment income *excluding* franked investment income from UK companies in the same group or from UK companies owned by a consortium of which the recipient is a member (TA 1988 s 13(7) amended by FA 1998 Sch 3 para 7 for distributions made after 5 April 1999).
I = profits on which corporation tax is actually borne (income plus chargeable gains).
† Where there is no franked investment income, an alternative to the above formula is to apply the starting or small companies' rate up to the first or lower relevant amount and the marginal rate to the balance of the profits.

Corporate venturing scheme (FA 2000 s 63, Schs 15, 16; FA 2001 s 64, Sch 16; FA 2004 s 95, Sch 20)

Relief on amounts invested in new ordinary unquoted shares in small higher-risk trading companies	1.4.00–6.3.01	7.3.01 onwards
Rate of corporation tax relief	20%	20%
Minimum investee company's ordinary share capital to be held by individuals	20%	20%
Investing company's maximum stake in investee company	30%	30%
Minimum investment period	3 years	3 years
Minimum of investment to be employed in qualifying business within 12 months	100%	80%

Research and development (FA 2000 ss 68, 69, Schs 19, 20; FA 2002 s 53, Sch 12; FA 2003 s 168, Sch 31)

Minimum threshold on spending[1]	£10,000
Large companies (from 1 April 2002) Rate of corporation tax relief	125%
Small and medium-sized companies (from 1 April 2000) Rate of corporation tax relief	150%
Maximum turnover limit	£25 million

[1] The threshold is reduced from £25,000 to £10,000 for accounting periods beginning after 8 April 2003 for large companies and for accounting periods beginning after 26 September 2003 for SMEs.
Companies not yet in profit or which have not yet started to trade can claim the relief up front.
See also the 100% capital allowance for research and development, p 62.
Research into vaccines and medicines for the prevention and treatment of specified diseases: extra 50% relief from 22 April 2003 (FA 2002 s 54, Schs 13, 14; FA 2003 s 168, Sch 31).

Community Amateur Sports Clubs see page 70.

Community Investment Tax Relief see page 75.

Urban Regeneration Companies see page 73.

Capital allowances

Rates

Agricultural and forestry land

	Expenditure incurred after	% Rate
Initial allowance	31 March 1986	Nil
	31 October 1992[1]	20
	31 October 1993	Nil
Writing-down allowance	31 March 1986	4

Note:
[1] Initial allowances were temporarily reintroduced for 1 year in respect of capital expenditure on agricultural buildings or works. The allowances applied to buildings or works constructed under a contract entered into between 1 November 1992 and 31 October 1993, and brought into use for the purposes of the farming trade by 31 December 1994. See CAA 1990 s 124A.

Dredging

	Expenditure incurred after	% Rate
Initial allowance	31 March 1986	Nil
Writing-down allowance	5 November 1962	4

Industrial buildings and structures

	Expenditure[1] incurred after	% Rate
Initial allowance		
Generally:	31 March 1986	Nil
	31 October 1992[2]	20
	31 October 1993	Nil
Exceptions:		
Enterprise zones	within 10 years of site being included in zone[3]	100
Writing-down allowance		
Generally:	5 April 1946	2
	5 November 1962[4]	4
Exception:		
Enterprise zones	within 10 years of site being included in zone[5]	25

Notes:
[1] The amount qualifying for allowance is the price paid for the relevant interest *minus* (i) the value of the land element and (ii) any value attributable to elements over and above those which would feature in a normal commercial lease negotiated in the open market: FA 1995 s 100 confirming previous practice.
[2] Initial allowances were temporarily reintroduced for 1 year in respect of capital expenditure on industrial buildings and qualifying hotels. The allowances applied to buildings constructed under, or bought unused under, a contract entered into after 31 October 1992 and before 1 November 1993, and brought into use in qualifying trade by 31 December 1994. Balance of relief by 4% pa writing-down allowance. All or part of the initial allowance could be disclaimed. See CAA 1990 ss 2A, 10C.
[3] CAA 2001 s 306. Includes expenditure on qualifying hotels. See p 56 for a list of enterprise zones.
[4] Includes expenditure on qualifying hotels (other than in an enterprise zone).
Also includes expenditure on the construction of toll roads incurred for accounting periods or basis periods ending after 5 April 1991.
[5] CAA 2001 s 310. Includes expenditure on qualifying hotels. See p 62 for a list of enterprise zones.

Films

From 10 March 1992, pre-production expenditure on films produced with sufficient EU content is relieved as it occurs. 100% write-off is available for expenditure incurred after 1 July 1997 and before 2 July 2005 on a qualifying British film completed after 1 July 1997. See F(No 2)A 1992 ss 41, 42; F(No 2)A 1997 s 48; FA 2001 s 72; Statement of Practice SP1/98. The rules are amended for certain films completed after 16 April 2002 and to certain acquisition expenditure incurred after 29 June 2002 (FA 2002 ss 99–101).

Flat conversions

	Expenditure incurred after	% Rate
Initial allowance	10 May 2001[1]	100

Note:
[1] Expenditure incurred on renovating or converting vacant or storage space above commercial properties to provide low value flats for rent (CAA 2001 ss 393A–393W; FA 2001 s 67, Sch 19).

Know-how
Writing-down allowance

Expenditure incurred after 31 March 1986: annual 25% writing-down allowance (reducing balance basis).

Plant and machinery

Expenditure incurred	after	before	% Rate
First-year allowance (FYA)			
Universal	31 October 1993[1]		Nil
Small and medium-sized businesses	1 July 1998[2]		40
	1 July 1997[2]	2 July 1998	50
in Northern Ireland *only*	11 May 1998[3]	12 May 2002	100
Small businesses			
for income tax purposes	5 April 2004[4]	6 April 2005	50
for corporation tax purposes	31 March 2004[4]	1 April 2005	50
ICT	31 March 2000[5]	1 April 2004	100
Long-life assets			
Generally	25 November 1996		Nil
Small and medium-sized businesses	1 July 1997[2]	2 July 1998	12
Energy-saving plant or machinery	31 March 2001[6]		100
New low-emission cars and refuelling equipment	16 April 2002[7]	1 April 2008	100
Environmentally beneficial plant or machinery	31 March 2003[8]		100
Writing-down allowance (WDA)[9]			
Generally	26 October 1970		25
Leasing to non-residents	9 March 1982		10
Long-life assets[10]	25 November 1996		6

Notes:

[1] FYAs available universally had been generally abolished for expenditure after 31 March 1986 but were reintroduced temporarily at the rate of 40% for expenditure in the 12 months to 31 October 1993. Thereafter, FYAs have been specifically targeted as below.

[2] *Small and medium-sized businesses:* 40% FYAs for qualifying expenditure incurred after 1 July 1998. It does not apply to certain expenditure including that on plant and machinery for leasing, motor cars, ships, railway assets or long-life assets. After the first year, allowances revert to the normal WDA of 25% (or 6% for long-life assets). The higher rate of 50% applied only for expenditure incurred during the year ended 1 July 1998 when a 12% FYA applied to long-life assets. (See footnotes 4 and 10 below.) Small and medium-sized businesses are, broadly, those satisfying any two of the following conditions: (a) turnover £11,200,000 or less (b) assets £5,600,000 or less (c) not more than 250 employees (CAA 1990 ss 22(3C)(6B), 22A, 44, 46–49). For accounting periods ending after 29 January 2004, the thresholds are increased to: (a) turnover £22,800,000 or less (b) assets £11,400,000 or less.

[3] The conditions for relief were similar to those outlined in footnote 2 above, but goods vehicles used in freight haulage businesses did not qualify (CAA 2001 ss 40–43, 46).

[4] *Small businesses:* 50% FYAs for qualifying expenditure incurred after 5 April 2004 for income tax purposes or after 31 March 2004 for corporation tax purposes and before 6 April 2005 or 1 April 2005 respectively. The conditions for relief are similar to those outlined in footnote 2 above. After April 2005, the FYA reverts to 40% as for small and medium-sized enterprises. Small businesses are, broadly, those satisfying any two of the following conditions: (a) turnover £2,800,000 (b) assets £1,400,000 or less (c) not more than 50 employees. For accounting periods ending after 29 January 2004, the thresholds are increased to: (a) turnover £5,600,000 or less (b) assets £2,800,000 or less. (FA 2004 s 142).

[5] *ICT (information and communications technology):* 100% FYAs for *small businesses* (see footnote 4 above) buying computers or investing in e-commerce and new information technology. (CAA 2001 ss 45, 46).

[6] *Energy-saving plant or machinery:* 100% FYAs available for investment by *any* business in designated energy-saving plant and machinery in accordance with the Government's Energy Technology Product List (CAA 2001 ss 45A–45C; FA 2001 s 65, Sch 17; SI 2001/2541). For expenditure incurred after 16 April 2002 the List is extended, and the 100% allowance is available where the asset is for leasing, letting or hire (CAA 2001 s 46). The product lists are available at www.eca.gov.uk.

[7] For expenditure incurred after 16 April 2002 and before 1 April 2008, the allowance is given on (a) new cars which are either electrically propelled or emit not more than 120g/km of carbon dioxide, registered after 16 April 2002 and (b) new plant and machinery to refuel vehicles with natural gas or hydrogen fuels. The allowance is also available where the asset is to be leased, let or hired (CAA 2001 ss 45D, 45E, 46).

[8] *Environmentally beneficial plant or machinery:* 100% FYAs are available for expenditure after 31 March 2003 by *any* business on new and unused designated technologies and products which satisfy the relevant environmental criteria in accordance with the Government's technologies or products lists (FA 2003 s 167, Sch 30). The product lists are available at www.eca.gov.uk.

[9] On reducing balance basis. Generally, CAA 2001 s 56; leasing to non-residents, CAA 2001 s 109.

[10] Applies to plant or machinery with an expected working life, when new, of 25 years or more. Applies where expenditure on long-life assets in a year is £100 000 or more (in the case of companies the de minimis limit is £100,000 divided by one plus the number of associated companies). Transitional provisions apply to maintain a 25% allowance for expenditure incurred before 1 January 2001 under a contract entered into before 26 November 1996 and to expenditure on second-hand plant or machinery if old rules applied to vendor. It does not apply to plant or machinery in a building used wholly or mainly as, or for purposes ancillary to, a dwelling-house, retail shop, showroom, hotel or office, cars, or sea-going ships and railway assets acquired before 1 January 2011 (CAA 2001 ss 90–104, Sch 3 para 20).

Cars: See p 62 and Expensive cars p 69.

Mineral extraction (CA 2001 s 418)

	Expenditure incurred after	% Rate
Initial allowance	31 March 1986	Nil
Writing-down allowance		

Expenditure incurred after 31 March 1986: annual writing-down allowance on reducing balance basis—10% for certain pre-trading expenditure and expenditure on the acquisition of a mineral asset, otherwise 25%.

Motor cars available for private use

	Expenditure incurred after	% Rate
Writing-down allowance (WDA)	11 March 1992	25%[1]

[1] Restricted to £3,000 for cars costing more than £12,000 and bought outright, on hire purchase or by way of a lease with an option to purchase (CAA 2001 ss 74, 75).

[2] The requirement that expenditure on cars costing £12,000 or less goes into a separate pool was removed from the start of the chargeable period which includes 1 April 2000 (corporation tax) or 6 April 2000 (income tax) or the start of the chargeable period which includes 1 (or 6) April 2001 at the option of the taxpayer (CAA 1990 s 41; FA 2000 s 74).

[1] See also note 7, p 61 and Expensive cars, p 69.

Patent rights (CA 2001 s 472)

Writing-down allowance

Expenditure incurred before 1 April 1986 spread equally over 17 years or, if less
    (a)   the period for which the rights are acquired, or
    (b)   17 years less the number of complete years from the commencement of the patent to the acquisition.

Expenditure incurred after 31 March 1986: annual 25% writing-down allowance (reducing balance basis).

Research and development (formerly scientific research)*

	Expenditure incurred after	% Rate
Allowance in year 1	5 November 1962	100

Note: Land and houses are excluded from 1 April 1985.
*See also corporation tax relief, p 59.

Disadvantaged areas

Renovation of business premises

	Expenditure incurred after	% Rate
First-year allowance	Approval of state aid	100

The expenditure must be incurred on renovating or converting vacant business properties in the designated disadvantaged areas in the UK that have been vacant for at least a year to bring the property back into business use. The enhanced rate will apply to any expenditure currently qualifying for plant and machinery, industrial buildings or agricultural buildings allowances and also to expenditure on commercial buildings (such as shops and offices). (FA 2005 s 92, Sch 6).

Enterprise zones

The following areas have been designated as enterprise zones. The designation applies for 10 years from the commencement date. Previous enterprise zones, the designation of which has lapsed, are not shown.

Area	*Commencement date*
Dearne Valley	3 November 1995
East Midlands (North East Derbyshire)	3 November 1995
East Midlands (Bassetlaw)	16 November 1995
East Midlands (Ashfield)	21 November 1995
East Durham	29 November 1995
Tyne Riverside (North Tyneside)	19 February 1996
Tyne Riverside (North Tyneside and South Tyneside)	21 October 1996

Time limits for capital allowances claims see p 26.

Income tax

Starting, basic and higher rates and rate applicable to trusts

Band of taxable income £	Band £	Rate %	Tax £	Cumulative tax £
2005–06				
0–2,090	2,090	10	209.00	209.00
2,091–32,400	30,310	22	6,668.20	6,877.20
over 32,400	—	40	—	—
2004–05				
0–2,020	2,020	10	202.00	202.00
2,021–31,400	29,380	22	6,463.60	6,665.60
over 31,400	—	40	—	—
2003–04				
0–1,960	1,960	10	196.00	196.00
1,961–30,500	28,540	22	6,278.80	6,474.80
over 30,500	—	40	—	—
2002–03				
0–1,920	1,920	10	192.00	192.00
1,921–29,900	27,980	22	6,155.60	6,347.60
over 29,900	—	40	—	—
2001–02				
0–1,880	1,880	10	188.00	188.00
1,881–29,400	27,520	22	6,054.40	6,242.40
over 29,400	—	40	—	—
2000–01				
0–1,520	1,520	10	152.00	152.00
1,521–28,400	26,880	22	5,913.60	6,065.60
over 28,400	—	40	—	—
1999–2000				
0–1,500	1,500	10	150	150
1,501–28,000	26,500	23	6,095	6,245
over 28,000	—	40	—	—

Taxation of savings: From 6 April 1999, savings income is chargeable at the rates of 10% (if within the starting rate band), 20% and/or 40% (TA 1988 s 1A; FA 2000 s 32).

Savings income includes interest from banks and building societies, interest distributions from authorised unit trusts, interest on gilts and other securities including corporate bonds, purchased life annuities and discounts.

Where income does not exceed the basic rate limit, there will be no further tax to pay on savings income from which the 20% tax rate has been deducted, and any tax over-deducted is repayable. Higher rate taxpayers are liable to pay tax at 40% or that part of their savings income falling above the higher rate limit.

Savings income is generally treated as the second top slice of income behind dividends.

Non-taxpayers may apply to have interest paid without deduction of tax where their total income is expected to be covered by personal allowances. Taxpayers who are entitled to a refund of tax deducted from interest can claim the refund using form R40. The Revenue have launched a *Taxback* website page to simplify repayments: www.inlandrevenue.gov.uk/taxback.

Taxation of dividends: UK and foreign dividends (except those foreign dividends taxed under the remittance basis) form the top slice of taxable income. Where income does not exceed the basic rate limit the rate is 10% (applied to the dividend grossed-up by a tax credit of ⅑th) so that the liability is met by the tax credit. Higher rate taxpayers are liable to pay tax at 32.5% on that part of their dividend income falling above the higher rate limit.
See TA 1988 s 1A.

Construction industry sub-contractors rate of deduction at source: 2000–01 onwards: 18%, 1999–2000 and before: basic rate of tax.

Taxation of trusts

	Rate applicable to trusts	Dividend trust rate
From 2004–05 onwards	40%	32.5%
1999–2000 to 2003–04	34%	25%

From 2005–06 onwards: The first £500 of income arising to a trust chargeable at the rate applicable to trusts or the dividend trust rate, is instead chargeable at the basic, lower or dividend ordinary rate depending on the type of income (TA 1988 s 686D; FA 2005 s 14).

Vulnerable beneficiaries: From 2004–05 onwards, trustees can be taxed (on election) on trust income as if it were income of the vulnerable beneficiary taking into account the beneficiary's personal allowances, starting and basic rate bands (FA 2005 ss 23–45).

Table of income tax reliefs

	2005–06	2004–05
Personal allowance (age under 65)	£4,895	£4,745
Age allowance: Allowance reduced by £1 for every £2 over	£19,500	£18,900
Personal allowance age 65–74 .... Not beneficial if individual's total income exceeds	£7,090 £23,890	£6,830 £23,070
Personal allowance age 75 and over .... Not beneficial if individual's total income exceeds	£7,220 £24,150	£6,950 £23,310
Married couple's allowance[1] From 6 April 2000 available only where either spouse is aged 65 or over at 5 April 2000 .... Monthly reduction in year of marriage....................................	— —	— —
Age allowance: Allowance reduced by £1 for every £2 over .... Minimum allowance where income exceeds limit...........................	£19,500 £2,280	£18,900 £2,210

Elder spouse aged under 75 and
  either spouse born before 6 April 1935 ....
Not beneficial if husband:
  under 65 and his total income exceeds.................................
  65–74 and his total income exceeds.................................
	£5,905
	
	£26,750
	£31,140
		£5,725
		
		£25,930
		£30,100

Either spouse aged 75 and over...
Not beneficial if husband:
  under 65 and his total income exceeds.................................
  65–74 and his total income exceeds.................................
  75 or over and his total income exceeds.............................
	£5,975
	
	£26,890
	£31,280
	£31,540
		£5,795
		
		£26,070
		£30,240
		£30,480

Children's tax credit[2] Baby rate[3]	— —	— —
Widow's bereavement allowance[1] (available only where the death occurred before 6 April 2000 and the wife had not remarried before that date)	—	—
Additional relief for children[1]	—	—
Blind person	£1,610	£1,560
Mortgage interest relief Limit on amount available for relief... Relief restricted to..	— —	— —
Life assurance relief For contracts made before 14 March 1984 *only*, given by deduction	12.5%	12.5%
NI Class 2 Small earnings exception	£4,345	£4,215

NI Class 4 Band
 	
        Amount payable to upper limit
        Charge on earnings above upper limit
	£4,895–£32,760
	£27,865 @ 8%
	£2,229.20
	1%
		£4,745–£31,720
		£26,975 @ 8%
		£2,158
		1%

Starting rate (before 1999–2000, lower rate) of tax Band	10% £2,090	10% £2,020
Basic rate of tax Band	22% £30,310	22% £29,380

[1]Relief is restricted to 10% of figure quoted.
[2]The relief is withdrawn at the rate of £2 for every £3 of income chargeable to income tax at the higher rate and is restricted to 10% of the resulting figure. From 2003–04 the allowance has been replaced by the Child Tax Credit which is paid direct to the main carer.
[3]From 6 April 2002 the amount per claimant is higher for the year of birth. From 2003–04, the allowance has been replaced by the Child Tax Credit which is paid direct to the main carer.

2003–04	2002–03	2001–02	2000–01	1999–2000
£4,615	£4,615	£4,535	£4,385	£4,335
£18,300	£17,900	£17,600	£17,000	£16,800
£6,610	£6,100	£5,990	£5,790	£5,720
£22,290	£20,870	£20,510	£19,810	£19,570
£6,720	£6,370	£6,260	£6,050	£5,980
£22,510	£21,410	£21,050	£20,330	£20,090
—	—	—	—	£1,970
—	—	—	—	£164.16
£18,300	£17,900	£17,600	£17,000	£16,800
£2,150	£2,110	£2,070	£2,000	£1,970
£5,565	£5,465	£5,365	£5,185	£5,125
£25,130	£24,610	£24,190	£23,370	£23,110
£29,120	£27,580	£27,100	£26,180	£25,880
£5,635	£5,535	£5,435	£5,255	£5,195
£25,270	£24,750	£24,330	£23,510	£23,250
£29,260	£27,720	£27,240	£26,320	£26,020
£29,480	£28,260	£27,780	£26,840	£26,540
—	£5,290	£5,200	—	—
—	£10,490	—	—	—
—	—	—	£2,000	£1,970
—	—	—	—	£1,970
£1,510	£1,480	£1,450	£1,400	£1,380
—	—	—	—	£30,000
—	—	—	—	10%
12.5%	12.5%	12.5%	12.5%	12.5%
£4,095	£4,025	£3,955	£3,825	£3,770
£4,615–£30,940	£4,615–£30,420	£4,535–£29,900	£4,385–£27,820	£7,530–£26,000
£26,325 @ 8%	£25,805 @ 7%	£25,365 @ 7%	£23,435 @ 7%	£18,470 @ 6%
£2,106	£1,806·35	£1,775·55	£1,640·45	£1,108·20
1%	—	—	—	—
10%	10%	10%	10%	10%
£1,960	£1,920	£1,880	£1,520	£1,500
22%	22%	22%	22%	23%
£28,540	£27,980	£27,520	£26,880	£26,500

Car benefits

From 6 April 2002: The income tax charge is based on a percentage of the car's price graduated according to the level of the car's carbon dioxide emissions measured in grams per kilometre (g/km) and rounded down to the nearest 5 g/km: ITEPA 2003 ss 114–148, 169; FA 2003 s 138.

CO₂ emissions in grams per kilometre				% of list price	
2002/03	2003/04	2004/05	2005/06–2007/08	Petrol	Diesel*
165	155	145	140	15%	18%
170	160	150	145	16%	19%
175	165	155	150	17%	20%
180	170	160	155	18%	21%
185	175	165	160	19%	22%
190	180	170	165	20%	23%
195	185	175	170	21%	24%
200	190	180	175	22%	25%
205	195	185	180	23%	26%
210	200	190	185	24%	27%
215	205	195	190	25%	28%
220	210	200	195	26%	29%
225	215	205	200	27%	30%
230	220	210	205	28%	31%
235	225	215	210	29%	32%
240	230	220	215	30%	33%
245	235	225	220	31%	34%
250	240	230	225	32%	35%
255	245	235	230	33%	35%
260	250	240	235	34%	35%
265	255	245	240	35%	35%

Cars registered after 28 February 2001
For cars registered on or after 1 March 2001, the definitive CO₂ emissions figure is recorded on the vehicle registration document. For cars first registered between 1 January 1998 and 28 February 2001, the Vehicle Certification Agency supply relevant information on their website at www.vcacarfueldata.org.uk and in their free, twice-yearly edition of the 'New Car Fuel Consumption & Emission Figures' booklet.

Cars registered after 31 December 1997 with no CO₂ emission figures

Cylinder capacity of car	Appropriate percentage*
1,400cc or less	15%
Over 1,400cc up to 2,000cc	25%
Over 2,000cc	35%
Electrically propelled vehicle	9%

Cars registered before 1 January 1998 with no CO₂ emission figures

Cylinder capacity of car	Appropriate percentage
1,400cc or less	15%
Over 1,400cc up to 2,000cc	22%
Over 2,000cc	32%
No cylinder capacity	Appropriate percentage
Electrically propelled vehicle	15%
Other vehicles	32%

* **Diesel cars:** A 3% supplement applies to diesel cars first registered after 31 December 1997 up to a maximum of 35%. The supplement does not apply to diesel cars meeting the Euro IV emissions standards until 5 April 2006 after which time it will apply to such cars registered on or after 1 January 2006.

Notes
List price of car:
(1) Includes any optional accessories supplied with the car when first made available to the employee and any further accessories costing £100 or more (ITEPA 2003 ss 122–131).
(2) Reduced by capital contributions made by the employee (up to a maximum of £5,000) (ITEPA 2003 s 132).
(3) Capped at £80,000 (ITEPA 2003 s 121).
(4) Classic cars (aged 15 years or more and with a market value of £15,000 or more at the end of the year of assessment): substitute market value at end of year of assessment if this is higher than the adjusted list price. £80,000 cap and reduction for capital contributions apply (ITEPA 2003 s 147).
(5) There are discounts for cars which run on alternative fuels.

Automatic car made available to a disabled driver: CO₂ figure reduced to that for an equivalent manual car (ITEPA 2003 s 138).

Car unavailable for part of year: Value of the benefit is reduced proportionately (ITEPA 2003 s 143).

National Insurance: Also used to calculate the national insurance contributions payable by employers on the benefit of cars they provide for the private use of their employees, see p 94.

Basic cash equivalent 1999–2000 to 2001–02

List price of car plus extra qualifying accessories[1] *less* capital contributions[2] by employee[3,4].

Multiplied by –
35% where business mileage is under 2,500[5] miles.
25% where business mileage is at least 2,500[5] but less than 18,000[5] miles.
15% where business mileage is 18,000[5] miles or more[6].

Adjustments

1 Reduce cash equivalent by –
¼ where car is 4 years old or more at end of year of assessment.

2 Reduce adjusted cash equivalent in **1** proportionately where car is not available throughout year of assessment.

3 Reduce adjusted cash equivalent in **2** by amount of payments by employee for private use.

Notes

[1] Excluding an accessory provided after car was made available if its list price was less than £100. Accessories designed for use only by disabled people are also excluded. Where a car is manufactured so as to be capable of running on road fuel gas, its price is proportionately reduced by so much of that price as is reasonably attributable to it being manufactured in that way. Where a new car is converted to run on road fuel gas, the equipment is not regarded as an accessory.

[2] Up to £5,000.

[3] List price as adjusted capped at £80,000.

[4] Classic cars (aged 15 years or more and with a market value of £15,000 or more at end of year of assessment): substitute market value at end of year of assessment if this is higher than adjusted list price. £80,000 cap and reduction for capital contributions apply.

[5] Mileage figures are reduced proportionately where car is not available for whole year.

[6] For second and subsequent cars there is no reduction if business mileage is under 18,000 miles; **from 1999–2000** reduce basic cash equivalent to 25% if business mileage is 18,000 miles or more.

Vans: private use

(ITEPA 2003 ss 114–118, 154–166, 168, 169A, 170)

	Under 4 years old[1]	4 years old or more[1]
1993–94 to 2006–07: Vehicle weight up to 3,500 kgs	£500	£350

[1] At the end of the relevant year of assessment. Includes fuel.

From 6 April 2005 no charge will apply to employees who have to take their van home and private use is restricted other than for ordinary commuting (insignificant use is disregarded).

From 6 April 2007 the scale charge will increase to £3,000 irrespective of the age of the van. An additional fuel charge of £500 will also apply for unrestricted private use (FA 2004 s 80, Sch 14).

On-call emergency vehicles

From 6 April 2004 onwards: No tax or NIC charge arises where emergency service workers have private use of their emergency vehicle when on call (ITEPA 2003 s 248A).

Bus services

From 6 April 2002 onwards: No taxable benefit in respect of the provision of works buses with a seating capacity of 9 or more, provided to employees (or their children) to travel to and from work (ITEPA 2003 s 242). (Before 5 April 2002 the minimum seating capacity was 12.) From 6 April 2002 there is no tax or NIC charge where employees are carried free or at reduced rates on employer-subsidised local bus services (ITEPA 2003 s 243).

Cycles and cyclist's safety equipment

No taxable benefit in respect of the provision to employees of bicycles or cycling safety equipment for travel to and from work (ITEPA 2003 s 244) nor, from 6 April 2005, for subsequent transfer to the employee at market value (ITEPA 2003 s 206).

Parking facilities

No taxable benefit for work place provision of car parking spaces, or parking for bicycles or motorcycles, or from 6 April 2005, vans (ITEPA 2003 s 237).

Car fuel benefits

(ITEPA 2003 ss 149–153; TA 1988 s 158)

CO₂ emissions grams per kilometre			Petrol	Diesel
2003/04	**2004/05**	**2005/06**	£	£
155	145	140	2,160	2,592
160	150	145	2,304	2,736
165	155	150	2,448	2,880
170	160	155	2,592	3,024
175	165	160	2,736	3,168
180	170	165	2,880	3,312
185	175	170	3,024	3,456
190	180	175	3,168	3,600
195	185	180	3,312	3,744
200	190	185	3,456	3,888
205	195	190	3,600	4,032
210	200	195	3,744	4,176
215	205	200	3,888	4,320
220	210	205	4,032	4,464
225	215	210	4,176	4,608
230	220	215	4,320	4,752
235	225	220	4,464	4,896
240	230	225	4,608	5,040
245	235	230	4,752	5,040
250	240	235	4,896	5,040
255	245	240	5,040	5,040

From 2003–04, the same percentage figures on page 66 used to calculate the car benefit charge for the company car, which are directly linked to the car's CO₂ emissions, are used to calculate the benefit charge for fuel provided for private motoring. The relevant percentage figure is multiplied by £14,400 from 2003–04 onwards.

The benefit is reduced to nil if the employee is required to, and does, make good all fuel provided for private use. There is no taxable benefit where the employer only provides fuel for business travel. From 2003–04, the charge is proportionately reduced where the employee stops receiving free fuel part way through the tax year, but where free fuel is subsequently provided in the same tax year, the full year's charge is payable.

The benefit is proportionately reduced where a car is not available or is incapable of being used for part of a year (being at least 30 days).

2002–03		
Cylinder capacity: (non-diesel cars)	1,400cc or less	£2,240
	Over 1,400cc up to 2,000cc	£2,850
	Over 2,000cc	£4,200
Cylinder capacity: (diesel cars)	2,000cc or less	£2,850
	Over 2,000cc	£4,200
No internal combustion engine		£4,200
2001–02		
Cylinder capacity: (non-diesel cars)	1,400cc or less	£1,930
	Over 1,400cc up to 2,000cc	£2,460
	Over 2,000cc	£3,620
Cylinder capacity: (diesel cars)	2,000cc or less	£2,460
	Over 2,000cc	£3,620
No internal combustion engine		£3,620
2000–01		
Cylinder capacity: (non-diesel cars)	1,400cc or less	£1,700
	Over 1,400cc up to 2,000cc	£2,170
	Over 2,000cc	£3,200
Cylinder capacity: (diesel cars)	2,000cc or less	£2,170
	Over 2,000cc	£3,200
No internal combustion engine		£3,200

Advisory fuel rates for company cars

Engine size	Cost per mile		
2004–05 onwards	*Petrol*	*Diesel*	*LPG*
1,400cc or less	10p	9p	7p
1,401–2,000cc	12p	9p	8p
Over 2,000cc	14p	12p	10p
2002–03 and 2003–04[1]	*Petrol*	*Diesel*	*LPG*
1,400cc or less	10p	9p	6p
1,401–2,000cc	12p	9p	7p
Over 2,000cc	14p	12p	9p

Notes
[1] The advisory fuel rates can be used to negotiate dispensations for mileage payments from 28 January 2002 where employers:
  (a) reimburse employees for business travel in their company cars; or
  (b) require employees to repay the cost of fuel used for private travel.
  (In the case of (b) the figures may be used for private travel from 6 April 2001.)
[2] Payments at these rates give rise to no income tax or Class 1 NIC liability. The table figures will be accepted for VAT purposes.
[3] Other rates may be used if the employer can demonstrate that they are justified.
[4] The rates will be reviewed if fuel prices vary by more than 10% from the prices used when the rates were set. The rates will continue to apply from 6 April 2003 until further notice.

Authorised mileage rates: cars and vans

2002–03 onwards				Rate per mile[1]	
Annual business mileage up to 10,000 miles				40p	
Each additional mile over 10,000 miles				25p	
Each passenger making same business trip				5p	

Business mileage	Engine size Up to 1,000cc	1,001–1,500cc	1,501–2,000cc	Over 2,000cc	One rate[3]
2001–02[2]					
Up to 4,000 miles	40p	40p	45p	63p	—
Excess over 4,000 miles	25p	25p	25p	36p	—
1997–98 to 2000–01:[2,4]					
Up to 4,000 miles	28p	35p	45p	63p	40p
Excess over 4,000 miles	17p	20p	25p	36p	22·5p

[1] ITEPA 2003 ss 229–236. Except in the case of the rate applying in respect of passengers, if the employer pays less than the statutory rate, the employee can claim tax relief on the difference.
[2] Employees using their own car may claim these rates as a tax-free allowance or as a deduction whether or not their employer operates the scheme (1995) SWTI 1879.
[3] Where the same rate of mileage allowance is paid irrespective of the engine size, a fixed rate based on the average of the two middle bands is used.
[4] Subject to transitional relief.

Authorised mileage rates: pedal cycles and motorcycles

	Pedal cycles Rate per mile	Motorcycle Rate per mile
2002–03 onwards	20p	24p
2000–01 and 2001–02	12p	24p
1999–2000	12p	—

When the employee is not paid by the employer for using the pedal cycle or motorcycle the employee is able to claim the appropriate rate per mile (or on the balance up to the appropriate rate per mile if the employer pays less than this rate) ITEPA 2003 ss 230–232.

Expensive cars: restricted allowances

Restriction on deduction for hire charge
(TA 1988 ss 578A, 578B)
Contracts made after 10 March 1992
If a car with a retail price when new of more than £12,000 is acquired under a rental lease the maximum allowable deduction in computing trading profits is —

$$\frac{£12,000 + P}{2P} \times R$$

P = retail price of car when new
R = annual rental
Capital allowances see p 62.

Charities

Gift aid
(FA 2002 s 58; FA 2000 ss 39, 40; FA 1990 s 25; FA 1998 s 48)

The gift aid scheme gives higher rate relief for an individual donor and corporation tax relief for a corporate donor. The charity claims repayment of basic rate income tax on the grossed up amount of the donation.

From 6 April 2000 for individuals and from 1 April 2000 for companies, gift aid was extended to all donations to charity, including one-off gifts, made by UK-taxpayers. There is no minimum limit for donations. Donors (who may be resident or non-resident) have to make a declaration that they are UK taxpayers if the charity is to claim the repayment of basic rate income tax on the gift. One declaration can cover a series of donations to the same charity. Donors are able to join the scheme by phone or the internet. It is no longer necessary for companies to deduct income tax from their donations and for the recipient charity to claim back the tax.

From 6 April 2002, gift aid was extended to gifts to Community Amateur Sports Clubs (CASCs) (FA 2002 s 58).

Before 6 April 2000 the minimum amount which could be donated by gift aid was £250 (and £100 after 30 July 1998 under the Millennium Gift Aid Scheme, introduced by FA 1998 s 47 for businesses to donate goods to help education projects and projects undertaken for medical purposes in eighty 'low income countries').

Covenants
Because of the extension of the gift aid scheme from 6 April 2000, charitable covenants are in effect treated as regular donations by gift aid. For payments under a charitable covenant falling due before 6 April 2000 to be tax-effective, the covenant had to be for a period capable of exceeding three years (there are no monetary limits). With the introduction of the extended gift aid provisions, however, the separate tax relief for payments under covenants is withdrawn and all relief for such payments falling due on or after 6 April 2000 is given under the gift aid scheme (FA 2000 s 41).

Payroll giving
(ITEPA 2003, ss 713–715; SI 1986 No 2211; FA 2000 s 38; FA 2003 s 146)

Under the payroll giving scheme, employees authorise their employer to deduct charitable donations from their pay and receive tax relief on their donation at their top rate of tax. The government added a supplement to donations from 6 April 2000 to 5 April 2004. Before 6 April 2000, there was a maximum amount which could be donated in this way of £1,200.

Small and medium-sized enterprises with fewer than 500 employees, which set up a payroll giving scheme between April 2004 and December 2006 are entitled to receive a grant of up to £500 to offset the costs of setting up the scheme. In addition, the first £10 donated by each employee every month will be matched for a period of six months. (See www.payrollgivinggrants.org.uk for further details.)

Gifts in kind
From 27 July 1999, relief is available for gifts by traders to educational establishments of goods produced or sold or of plant or machinery used for the purposes of the trade (TA 1988 s 84; CAA 2001 s 63(2)–(4)).

Gifts of real property
From 6 April 2002 (individuals) and 1 April 2002 (companies), income or corporation tax relief is available for gifts of freehold or leasehold property which a charity agrees to accept (FA 2002 s 97).

Gifts of shares and securities
From 6 April 2000, relief is available where a person disposes of listed shares and securities, unit trust units, AIM shares, etc to a charity by way of a gift or sale at an undervalue. The amount deductible from total income is the market value of the shares etc on the date of disposal plus incidental disposal costs less any consideration or value of benefits received by the donor or a connected person. This is in addition to any capital gains tax relief (TA 1988 s 587B; FA 2000 s 43).

Tax return giving: For gifts made after 5 April 2003 under gift aid, donors may elect to have the donation treated as though made in the previous year of assessment (FA 2002 s 98).

From 2003–04, taxpayers can nominate a charity (from a published list of participating charities) to receive all or part of any tax repayments due to them, the nomination to be made on the self-assessment tax return (FA 2004 s 83).

Community amateur sports clubs (CASCs)
From 1 April 2002 registered CASCs are exempt from tax on bank and building society interest and from corporation tax on chargeable gains reinvested in the club. They are also exempt from corporation tax on profits from trading if their trading income is less than £30,000 and on profits derived from property if their property income is less than £20,000. For accounting periods ending before 1 April 2004, these thresholds were £15,000 and £10,000 respectively. (FA 2002, Sch 18; FA 2004 s 56).

Inheritance tax relief see p 88.

Capital gains tax see p 42.

Fixed rate expenses

For most classes of industry fixed rate allowances for the upkeep of tools and special clothing have been agreed between the Revenue and the trade unions concerned. Alternatively, the individual employee may claim as a deduction his or her actual expenses (ITEPA 2003, s 367) The rates are published by the Treasury and are as previously set out in Concession A1.

Industry code	Industry	Occupation	Deduction from 1995–96
10	Agriculture	All workers	70
100	Aluminium	(a) Continual casting operators, process operators, de-dimplers, driers, drill punchers, dross unloaders, firemen, furnace operators and their helpers, leaders, mouldmen, pourers, remelt department labourers, roll flatteners	130
		(b) Cable hands, case makers, labourers, mates, truck drivers and measurers, storekeepers	60
		(c) Apprentices	45
		(d) All other workers	100
330	Banks	Uniformed bank employees	40
90	Brass and Copper	All workers	100
270	Building	(a) Joiners and carpenters	105
		(b) Cement works and roofing felt and asphalt labourers	55
		(c) Labourers and navvies	40
		(d) All other workers	85
250	Building Materials	(a) Stone-masons	85
		(b) Tilemakers and labourers	40
		(c) All other workers	55
190	Clothing	(a) Lacemakers, hosiery bleachers, dyers, scourers and knitters, knitwear bleachers and dyers	45
		(b) All other workers	30
150	Constructional Engineering	(a) Blacksmiths and their strikers, burners, caulkers, chippers, drillers, erectors, fitters, holders up, markers off, platers, riggers, riveters, rivet heaters, scaffolders, sheeters, template workers, turners, welders	115
		(b) Banksmen, labourers, shop-helpers, slewers, straighteners	60
		(c) Apprentices and storekeepers	45
		(d) All other workers	75
170	Electrical and Electricity Supply	(a) Those workers incurring laundry costs only (generally CEGB employees)	25
		(b) All other workers	90
110	Engineering	(a) Pattern makers	120
		(b) Labourers, supervisory and unskilled workers	60
		(c) Apprentices and storekeepers	45
		(d) Motor mechanics in garage repair shops	100
		(e) All other workers	100
Not known	Fire service	Uniformed fire fighters and fire officers	60
220	Food	All workers	40
20	Forestry	All workers	70
240	Glass	All workers	60
Not known	Healthcare	(a) Ambulance staff on active service	110
		(b) Nurses and midwives, chiropodists, dental nurses, occupational, speech and other therapists, phlebotomists, physiotherapists, radiographers	70
		(c) Plaster room orderlies, hospital porters, ward clerks, sterile supply workers, hospital domestics, hospital catering staff	60
		(d) Laboratory staff, pharmacists, pharmacy assistants	45
		(e) Uniformed ancillary staff maintenance workers, grounds staff, drivers, parking attendants and security guards, receptionists and other uniformed staff	45
280	Heating	(a) Pipe fitters and plumbers	100
		(b) Coverers, laggers, domestic glaziers, heating engineers and their mates	90
		(c) All gas workers, all other workers	70
50	Iron Mining	(a) Fillers, miners and underground workers	100
		(b) All other workers	75
70	Iron and Steel	(a) Day labourers, general labourers, stockmen, time keepers, warehouse staff and weighmen	60
		(b) Apprentices	45
		(c) All other workers	120

Industry code	Industry	Occupation	Deduction from 1995–96
210	Leather	(a) Curriers (wet workers), fellmongering workers, tanning operatives (wet)	55
		(b) All other workers	40
140	Particular Engineering	(a) Pattern makers	120
		(b) All chainmakers; cleaners, galvanisers, tinners and wire drawers in the wire drawing industry; tool-makers in the lock making industry	100
		(c) Apprentices and storekeepers	45
		(d) All other workers	60
355	Police Force	Uniformed police officers (ranks up to and including Chief Inspector)	55
160	Precious Metals	All workers	70
230	Printing	(a) Letterpress Section Electrical engineers (rotary presses), electrotypers, ink and roller makers, machine minders (rotary), maintenance engineers (rotary presses) and stereotypers	105
		(b) Bench hands (P & B), compositors (Lp), readers (Lp), T & E Section wire room operators, warehousemen (Ppr box)	30
		(c) All other workers	70
320	Prisons	Uniformed prison officers	55
300	Public Service	(i) Dock and Inland Waterways	
		(a) Dockers, dredger drivers, hopper steerers	55
		(b) All other workers	40
		(ii) Public Transport	
		(a) Garage hands (including cleaners)	55
		(b) Conductors and drivers	40
60	Quarrying	All workers	70
290	Railways	(See the appropriate category for craftsmen, e.g. engineers, vehicle builders etc.) All other workers	70
30	Seamen	(a) Carpenters (Seamen) Passenger liners	165
		(b) Carpenters (Seamen) Cargo vessels, tankers, coasters and ferries	130
		(c) Other seamen Passenger liners	nil
		(d) Other seamen Cargo vessels, tankers, coasters and ferries	nil
120	Shipyards	(a) Blacksmiths and their strikers, boilermakers, burners, carpenters, caulkers, drillers, furnacemen (platers), holders up, fitters, platers, plumbers, riveters, sheet iron workers, shipwrights, tubers, welders	115
		(b) Labourers	60
		(c) Apprentices and storekeepers	45
		(d) All other workers	75
200	Textile Prints	All workers	60
180	Textiles	(a) Carders, carding engineers, overlookers (all), technicians in spinning mills	85
		(b) All other workers	60
130	Vehicles	(a) Builders, railway wagon etc. repairers, and railway wagon lifters	105
		(b) Railway vehicle painters and letterers, railway wagon etc. builders' and repairers' assistants	60
		(c) All other workers	40
260	Wood & Furniture	(a) Carpenters, cabinet makers, joiners, wood carvers and woodcutting machinists	115
		(b) Artificial limb makers (other than in wood), organ builders and packing case makers	90
		(c) Coopers not providing own tools, labourers, polishers and upholsterers	45
		(d) All other workers	75

(1) 'Industry code' is an industry identification term used for Inland Revenue computer purposes.
(2) The expressions 'all workers' and 'all other workers' refer only to manual workers who have to bear the cost of upkeep of tools and special clothing. They do not extend to other employees such as office staff.

Investment reliefs

Enterprise investment scheme

(Shares issued after 31 December 1993: TA 1988 ss 289–312; FA 1997 Sch 8 as revised from 1998–99 by FA 1998 ss 70, 71, 74, Sch 13 and as amended from 1999–2000 by FA 1999 ss 71–73, Schs 7, 8; FA 2000 s 64, Sch 17; FA 2001 s 63, Sch 15; FA 2004 s 93, Sch 18.)

Relief on investment

Maximum investment:	From 2004–05 From 1998–99 to 2003–04	£200,000 £150,000
Minimum investment:	From 1993–94	£500
Maximum carryback to preceding year	From 1998–99	½ amount invested between 6 April and 5 October (maximum £25,000)
Rate of relief	From 1993–94	20% (given as a reduction in income tax liability)

Other reliefs

(a) A gain on a disposal of shares on which EIS relief has been given and not withdrawn is exempt from capital gains tax.

(b) Deferral relief is available for gains on assets where the disposal proceeds are reinvested in eligible shares in a qualifying company. (CGT taper relief is calculated in accordance with the combined periods of ownership of the first and second investments (and any subsequent qualifying periods of reinvestment) where the shares in the first EIS company were issued after 5 April 1998 and disposed of after 5 April 1999: TCGA 1992 Sch 5BA.)

(c) A loss on a disposal of shares on which EIS relief has been given may be relieved against income tax or capital gains tax.

Main conditions for relief

1. The relief is available for subscriptions in cash to new ordinary fully paid-up shares in a qualifying company with no present or future right of redemption and no present or future preferential right to dividends or to the company's assets on a winding-up, throughout a five-year period from the date of issue.

2. The investor must hold the shares for three years from the date of issue (or from the commencement of trade, if later) where shares are issued after 5 April 2000. (The previous limit was five years from date of issue.) The investor must not be connected with the issuing company at any time in the period beginning two years before the issue of the shares and ending immediately before the third anniversary of the issue date (or, if later, the date of commencement of trade) (for shares issued after 5 April 2000). He must not receive value from the company at any time in the period beginning one year before the issue date and ending immediately before the third anniversary of the issue date (or, if later, the date of commencement of trade) (for shares issued after 6 March 2001 and also as regards value received after that date in respect of shares issued on or before that date). From 7 March 2001 such receipts may be ignored where the amount is insignificant or if equivalent replacement value is given.

3. The money subscribed must be used wholly for the purpose of a qualifying business activity within 12 months of the share issue date (or, where the company commences a qualifying trade within 12 months of the share issue date, within 12 months of the commencement). From 7 March 2001 only 80% of the money subscribed has to be used in a qualifying business within that time limit, though the remainder must be used within the subsequent 12 months.

4. The business activity must be carried on wholly or mainly in the UK for three years after the share issue date (or after the commencement of the trade, if later), unless there is a bona fide liquidation or receivership.

5. Throughout the period beginning with the share issue date and ending three years after that date (or, if later, three years after the date on which its qualifying business activity commences), the company must
   (a) exist for a qualifying purpose;
   (b) have fully paid up capital; and
   (c) not be controlled by another company, or control another company (apart from a qualifying subsidiary).

   Under the provisions of FA 1997 Sch 8, a parent company may qualify if non-qualifying activities do not form a substantial part of the group's activities *as a whole*.

   Before 7 March 2001 it was a condition for relief that the company be unquoted throughout the three-year period. From that date it is necessary only that the company be unquoted at the time the shares are issued, provided that there are at that time no arrangements for the company to cease to be unquoted.

6. For shares issued after 1 July 1997, no arrangement must exist before or at the time of issue for the disposal of shares in the company, the disposal of the company's assets, the ending of the company's trade or a guarantee of the shareholders' investment.

Urban Regeneration Companies

Relief is available from 1 April 2003 for expenditure incurred by businesses in making contributions to designated Urban Regeneration Companies (TA 1988 s 79B; FA 2003 s 180).

Corporate venturing scheme see p 59.

Venture capital trusts

(TA 1988 ss 332A, 842AA, Sch 15B, Sch 28B; TCGA 1992 ss 151A, 151B, Sch 5C; FA 1997 Sch 9; FA 1998 ss 70, 72, 73, Sch 12; FA 1999 ss 69, 70; FA 2000 s 65, Sch 18; FA 2002 s 109, Sch 33; FA 2004 s 94, Sch 19.)

Relief on investment

Maximum annual investment:	From 2004–05	£200,000
	1995–96 to 2003–04	£100,000
Rate of relief:	2004–05 to 2005–06	40%
	1995–96 to 2003–04	20%[1]

[1] Given as a reduction in income tax liability. From 1995–96 to 2003–04 the rate of relief is an amount equal to the 'lower rate' of income tax for the year of assessment in respect of which the claim is made (TA 1988 Sch 15B para 1). This is to be increased to 40% for shares issued in 2004–05 and 2005–06.

Other reliefs
(a) Dividends on shares within investment limit exempt from income tax (unless the investor's main purpose is tax avoidance – from 9 March 1999).
(b) Gains on share disposals exempt from capital gains tax (subject to investment limit).
(c) Deferral relief is available on gains on assets where the disposal proceeds are reinvested in VCT shares issued on or before 5 April 2004 and within one year before or after the disposal. This relief is withdrawn for shares issued after that date.

Main conditions for relief
1   The investment must be in new eligible shares: that is, ordinary shares which, in the five-year period from the issue date, carry no present or future preferential right to dividends or to a return of assets on the winding-up of the trust and no present or future right to redemption.
2   The investor must be an individual, aged 18 or over. He or she must hold the shares for three years from the date of issue where the shares are issued after 5 April 2000. (The previous minimum holding period was five years.)
3   The trust must satisfy the following conditions for approval by the Revenue –
     (a) it must not be a close company;
     (b) its income must be derived wholly or mainly (at least 70%) from investments in shares or securities;
     (c) at least 70% by value of its investments must comprise 'qualifying holdings' (newly issued shares in unquoted companies carrying on qualifying trades – the provisions relating to parent companies are relaxed by FA 1997). Special provisions apply where a company in which the VCT has invested goes into bona fide liquidation or receivership, or where the company is sold, merges or undergoes a capital reconstruction;
     (d) at least 30% by value of its qualifying holdings must comprise 'eligible shares' (see above);
     (e) it may not hold more than 15% by value of its total investment portfolio in any one company;
     (f) each class of its shares must be quoted on the Stock Exchange;
     (g) it must distribute at least 85% of the income derived from shares and securities and 100% of income derived from other sources in each accounting period;
     (h) at least 10% of the total investment in any one company must be held in ordinary, non-preferential shares (accounting periods ending after 1 July 1997);
     (i) no part of a qualifying holding may consist of securities relating to a guaranteed loan (accounting periods ending after 1 July 1997).

Business expansion scheme

(Shares issued before 1 January 1994: TA 1988 ss 289–312 as originally enacted)

Relief on investment

Maximum investment:	£40,000[1]
Minimum investment:	£500
Maximum carryback to preceding year:	½ amount invested between 6 April and 5 October (maximum £5,000)
Rate of relief:	Up to 40%[2]

[1] Applied to total enterprise investment and business expansion scheme investments for 1993–94.
[2] Given as a deduction from total income.

Other reliefs

Capital gains relief: gains on the first disposal of shares on which BES relief has not been withdrawn are exempt from capital gains tax.

Community investment tax credit

(FA 2002 s 57, Sch 16)
Investments made after 16 April 2002 by an individual or company in an accredited community development finance institution (CDFI) are eligible for tax relief. The investment may be by a loan to the CDFI or by a subscription for shares in or securities of a CDFI. Tax relief may be claimed for the tax year in which the investment is made and each of the four subsequent years. Relief for each year is the smaller of:

    (a) 5% of the invested amount, or
    (b) the amount which reduces the investor's income tax liability for the year to nil.

Individual savings accounts

(TA 1988 s 333; FA 1998 s 75; SI 1998/1870; SI 1998/1871; SI 1998/1869; SI 1998/1872; SI 2000/809; SI 2001/908; SI 2004/2996)
The overall annual subscription limit will remain at £7,000 and the cash limit will remain at £3,000 until 2009–10 inclusive (Budget 2005, Revenue Note 2).

(From 6 April 1999)

Overall annual subscription limit	1999–2000 to 2009–10	£7,000
Cash limit	1999–2000 to 2009–10	£3,000
Life insurance limit	6 April 1999 to 5 April 2005	£1,000

Reliefs

(a) Investments under the scheme are free from income tax and capital gains tax.
(b) 10% tax credit paid until 5 April 2004 on dividends from UK equities.
(c) Withdrawals may be made without loss of tax relief.

Main conditions for relief

1   Until 5 April 2005, the account can include three components:
    (a) cash (including National Savings),
    (b) life insurance,
    (c) stocks and shares.
    From 6 April 2005, the insurance component is merged with the cash and stocks and shares components.
2   Savers are subject to the subscription limits set out above. If the subscription limit is reached in a year, no further subscriptions can be made in that year irrespective of any amounts withdrawn.
3   Accounts must be administered by a single manager or by separate managers for each component.

Tax-exempt special savings accounts

(Accounts opened **before 6 April 1999**: TA 1988 ss 326A–326C; FA 1998 s 78)

Reliefs

Interest and bonuses payable on the account over a five-year period from the date on which it was opened are exempt from income tax. The capital of a TESSA maturing on or before 5 April 1999 can be transferred to a follow-up TESSA or to an ISA after that date (without affecting the amount that can be subscribed to an ISA).

Main conditions for relief

1   No capital may be withdrawn from the account during the initial five-year period.
2   TESSAs could be opened until 5 April 1999. Payments into them may be made for the full five-year period. After five years the account ceases to be tax exempt, but the capital (ie a maximum of £9,000) may be reinvested in full within six months in an ISA. The capital in a TESSA that matured between 6 January 1999 and 5 April 1999 could be transferred into an ISA after 5 April 1999 rather than invested into another TESSA before that date.

Personal equity plans

(Subscriptions made **before 6 April 1999**: TA 1988 s 333; FA 1998 s 76; SI 1989/469; SI 1998/1869)

Reliefs

(a) Dividends on shares held in a plan are exempt from income tax.
(b) Interest on plan investments is exempt from income tax if reinvested; interest on cash deposits is paid gross.
(c) Gains on the disposal of assets held in a plan are exempt from capital gains tax.
(d) PEPs held at 5 April 1999 can be held outside the new ISA, but with the same tax advantages as the ISA: (1998) SWTI 388; FA 1998 ss 75, 76.
(e) 10% tax credits paid until 5 April 2004 on dividends from UK equities.

Loan benefits and official rate of interest

A director, or an employee earning £8,500 or more a year, who receives a loan by reason of his or her employment may be charged to tax on the cash equivalent of the benefit for the year (ITEPA 2003 ss 173–191).

There is no charge to tax if either:
  (a) all the beneficial loans provided by reason of the employment; or
  (b) all the beneficial loans, excluding loans qualifying for tax relief, do not exceed £5,000.

The cash equivalent is calculated using the difference between the interest paid (if any) and the official rate of interest.

In January 2000 it was announced that the official rate of interest will be set, in advance, for the whole of the following tax year (although this policy will not be followed if typical mortgage rates fall sharply during the year). Under this policy, the official rate of interest remained at 6.25% for 1999–00, 2000–01 and 2001–02: (2000) SWTI 95, (2001) SWTI 192. The rate was reduced to 5% from 6 January 2002 following reductions in mortgage rates. It remained at this rate for 2002–03 and 2003–04 and it is intended to keep it at this rate for 2004–05: (2004) SWTI 90.

The official rate of interest is set out below.

Date	Rate
From 6 January 2002	5%
6 March 1999–5 January 2002	6.25%
6 August 1997–5 March 1999	7.25%
6 November 1996–5 August 1997	6.75%

	2000–01	2001–02	2002–03	2003–04	2004–05	2005–06
Average official rate of interest	6·25%	5·94%	5%	5%	5%	5%

Note
Loans made on commercial terms by employers who lend predominantly to the general public are generally exempt.

Foreign currency loans

Currency	Date	Rate
Swiss franc	From 6 July 1994	5·5%
Japanese yen	From 6 June 1994	3·9%

Loans of equipment

Computer equipment: No taxable benefit in respect of loan to employees (provided loans are not restricted to directors or senior staff) of computer equipment for private home use, the value of the equipment and related expenses not to exceed £2,500 (ITEPA 2003 s 320). Nor does a taxable benefit arise on the subsequent transfer of the equipment to the employee at its market value (ITEPA 2003 s 206).

Bicycles and cycle safety equipment: No taxable benefit arises on the loan to employees of bicycles and cycling safety equipment for travel to and from work (ITEPA 2003 s 244) nor, from 6 April 2005, on the subsequent transfer to the employee at market value (ITEPA 2003 s 206).

Equipment for disabled employees: No taxable benefit from 9 July 2002 in respect of equipment and facilities provided by employers (such as hearing aids and wheelchairs) to allow disabled employees to perform their duties of employment (the Revenue has indicated it will not pursue past liabilities) (SI 2002/1596).

Maintenance payments

From 6 April 2000: Relief for maintenance payments was withdrawn from 6 April 2000, *except* where either party to the marriage was born before 6 April 1935. In this case *only*, relief continues to be given under the rules for arrangements made after 15 March 1988 even if the obligation existed on or before that date. Under these rules the payer can claim tax relief in respect of the lesser of (a) the amount of the payments in the year concerned and (b) the minimum amount of the married couple's allowance for the year concerned (£2,110 for 2002–03). From 1999–2000 the relief has been given at the rate of 10% on the relevant amount.

The payment must be made to the divorced or separated spouse. It is made gross and is not taxable in the hands of the recipient. (TA 1988 ss 347A, 347B.)

Mobile telephones

No taxable benefit arises on the provision (other than a transfer) of a mobile phone even where used for private calls (ITEPA 2003 s 319).

National Savings Bank interest

First £70 of interest on deposits (other than investment deposits) is exempt (TA 1988 s 325).

PAYE and national insurance thresholds

	1999–00	2000–01	2001–02	2002–03	2003–04	2004–05	2005–06
PAYE[1]: Weekly	£83·00	£84·00	£87·00	£89·00	£89·00	£91·00	£94·00
Monthly	£361·00	£365·00	£378·00	£385·00	£385·00	£395·00	£408·00
National Insurance[2]: Weekly	£66·00	£76·00	£87·00	£89·00	£89·00	£91·00	£94·00
Monthly	£286·00	£329·00	£378·00	£385·00	£385·00	£395·00	£408·00

[1] From 1999–2000 these are also the earnings thresholds for employers for national insurance contributions.
[2] For employees only from 1999–2000.

PAYE codes

Code suffix	Meaning
L	Basic personal allowance
P	Personal allowance age 65–74
Y	Personal allowance aged 75+
V	Personal allowance (65–74) plus married couple's allowance (born before 6.4.35) aged under 75 and estimated taxable at the basic rate
T	Code to be changed where specific notification received from tax office or used where taxpayer wants status to remain private

Code prefix	Meaning
K	Total allowances less than total deductions: amount to be added to pay (tax deducted cannot exceed 50% of monetary pay)
D0	Tax to be deducted at higher rate on Week 1/Month 1 basis
BR	Tax to be deducted at basic rate; no allowances given
NT	No tax to be deducted
0T	No allowances available; tax to be deducted at appropriate rate

Relocation expenses and benefits

Qualifying removal benefits and expenses

The statutory relief covers the following expenses and benefits (ITEPA 2003 ss 271–289), subject to an £8,000 limit—

(a) *disposal expenses and benefits* (legal and advertising expenses in connection with the disposal of accommodation, penalty for redeeming a mortgage, auctioneers' and estate agents' fees, disconnection of public utilities, rent, maintenance and insurance costs while the property is unoccupied);

(b) *acquisition expenses and benefits* (legal expenses in connection with the acquisition of an interest in a new main residence, loan fees, mortgage indemnity insurance costs, survey and land registry fees, stamp duty, connection of public utilities). (NB: similar expenses and benefits are covered in respect of abortive acquisitions, if the property would have been the employee's new residence but the acquisition does not proceed either for reasons outside the employee's control or because he or she reasonably declines to proceed);

(c) *transportation of domestic belongings* (including insurance costs);

(d) *travelling and subsistence expenses and benefits* (for temporary visits to new residence before relocation; travel from old residence to new place of work or from new residence to old place of work where date of move and relocation of work do not coincide; subsistence and travel costs of child under 19 relocating before or after parents for educational reasons; benefit of a car or van for use in connection with the relocation where it is not otherwise available for private use);

(e) *bridging loan expenses and cheap bridging loans* (relief is given on any charge to interest at the official rate on a beneficial loan to the extent that the aggregate value of other qualifying benefits and expenses falls short of the maximum exempt amount);

(f) *duplicate expenses and benefits in respect of new residence* (replacement domestic items).

Rent-a-room scheme

Gross annual receipts from letting furnished accommodation in the only or main home are exempt from tax up to a maximum of £4,250. If the receipts exceed £4,250, the taxpayer can pay tax on the gross receipts after deduction of expenses or on the amount by which the receipts exceed that amount, without relief for the actual expenses. An individual's maximum is halved to £2,125 if during the basis period for the year some other person received income from letting accommodation in that property. (F(No 2)A 1992 Sch 10).

Pension provision from 6 April 2006
(FA 2004 ss 149–284, Schs 28–36)

From 6 April 2006, a new pension scheme tax regime fully replaces pre-existing rules for occupational pension schemes, personal (and stakeholder) pension schemes and retirement annuity schemes.

Tax relief on contributions
Individual contributions: Contributions to registered schemes are not limited by reference to a fraction of earnings and there is no earnings cap. There is no provision for the carry-back or carry-forward of contributions to tax years other than the year of payment.

An individual may make unlimited contributions and tax relief is available on contributions up to the higher of:
- the full amount of relevant earnings; or
- £3,600 provided the scheme operates tax relief at source.

Employer contributions: Employer contributions to registered schemes are deductible for tax purposes, with statutory provision for spreading abnormally large contributions over a period of up to four years. The contributions are not treated as taxable income of the employee.

Taxable benefits
'Tax-free' lump sum: The maximum 'tax-free' lump sum that can be paid to a member under a registered scheme is broadly the lower of
- 25% of the value of the pension rights; and
- 25% of the member's lifetime allowance.

Lifetime allowance: Each individual has a lifetime allowance for contributions as set out in the table below. The excess over the lifetime allowance of the benefits crystallising (usually when a pension begins to be paid) is taxable at the following rates:
- at 55% if taken as a lump sum
- at 25% in other cases

Any tax due may be deducted from the individual's benefits.

Lifetime allowance	£
2006–07	1,500,000

Annual allowance: Each individual has an annual contributions allowance as set out in the table below. If the annual increase in an individual's rights under all registered schemes exceeds the annual allowance, the excess is chargeable at 40%, the individual being liable for the tax.

Annual allowance	£
2006–07	215,000

Transitional. There are transitional provisions for the protection of lump sum and other pension rights accrued before 6 April 2006.

Age restrictions
Minimum pension age: The minimum pension age is 50 (rising to 55 on 6 April 2010). A pension cannot be paid before the minimum age except on grounds of ill health. Those with existing contractual rights to draw a pension earlier will have those rights protected and there is special protection for members of pre-6 April 2006 approved schemes with early retirement ages (see page 80). A reduced lifetime allowance will apply in the case of early retirement before age 50 except in the case of certain professions such as the police and the armed forces (to be prescribed by regulations).

Maximum benefit age: Benefits must be taken by the age of 75 at the latest. A member of a money purchase scheme may take a pension from the age of 75 by way of income withdrawal (known as an 'alternatively secured pension') instead of taking a scheme pension or purchasing a lifetime annuity. The maximum alternatively secured pension is 70% of a comparable annuity.

Personal pension schemes, stakeholder pensions and retirement annuities

1 July 1988: Retirement annuity contracts were replaced by personal pension schemes, although retirement annuity premiums may continue to be paid, and tax relief obtained (TA 1988 ss 618–629). There are provisions for the carrying back (TA 1988 s 619) and the carrying forward (TA 1988 s 625) of relief, and these are not affected by FA 2000.

6 April 2001: The personal pension scheme rules were adapted to accommodate the stakeholder pensions provisions (TA 1988 ss 630–655, FA 2000 s 61, Sch 13). From that date, personal pension and stakeholder pension contributions are subject to the same rules.

6 April 2006: For provision from 6 April 2006, see page 78.

Tax relief on contributions to 5 April 2006

Retirement annuities: Premiums continue to be deducted from or set off against relevant earnings (TA 1988 s 619). The amount of relief available is based on a percentage of net relevant earnings (see maximum amount, below).

Personal pension schemes: Before 6 April 2001, premiums were deducted from or set off against relevant earnings (TA 1988 s 639, as enacted). The amount of relief available was based on a percentage of net relevant earnings (see maximum amount, below).

Personal pension schemes/stakeholder pensions:

Contributions not exceeding the earnings threshold:

(1) Contributions of up to £3,600 gross ('the earnings threshold') may be paid into a stakeholder pension by anyone who is not a member of an occupational pension scheme, regardless of the amount (if any) of their earnings (TA 1988 s 632A).

(2) An individual who is a member of an occupational pension scheme but who is not a controlling director and whose total annual remuneration is no more than £30,000 is allowed to pay into both an occupational scheme and a stakeholder pension and will receive tax relief on an annual contribution of up to £3,600 (gross) into the stakeholder pension (TA 1988 s 632B).

Contributions exceeding the earnings threshold:

(1) Contributions in excess of the earnings threshold may be made. Tax relief is given on contributions up to a maximum based on a percentage of net relevant earnings (see maximum percentage below).

(2) For the purpose of supporting contributions in excess of the earnings threshold, a tax year for which evidence of relevant earnings can be provided may be nominated as the basis year and contributions based on the amount of those earnings may be paid in each of the next 5 years (TA 1988 s 646B). The provisions enable an individual to make pension contributions for up to 5 years after the relevant earnings ceased, by reference to the net relevant earnings of a basis year which may be any one of the 6 tax years preceding the first year for which there are no relevant earnings (TA 1988 s 646D).

Carry-back of relief:

Carry-back of relief is provided for in TA 1988 s 641A. There is no carry forward of relief (FA 2000 Sch 13 para 19).

Basic and higher rate relief:

From 6 April 2001, contributions are payable net of basic rate tax relief. Tax relief at the higher rate is given by extending the basic rate band by the amount of the contribution paid in the year of assessment (TA 1988 s 639, as amended by FA 2000 Sch 13 para 15).

From 2001–02, relief for contributions is given up to a maximum which is the greater of:
  (a) the 'earnings threshold'; and
  (b) the 'maximum percentage' of net relevant earnings for the year

(TA 1988 s 640, as amended by FA 2000 Sch 13 para 16). For the purposes of calculating the maximum percentage, net relevant earnings are subject to an earnings cap (TA 1988 s 640A).

Earnings threshold: from 6 April 2001 onwards £3,600 (TA 1988 s 630(1), as amended)

Maximum amount

Personal pension schemes/ stakeholder pensions (TA 1988 s 640)		
	Age in years at beginning of year of assessment	*Maximum percentage*
	35 and below	17½
	36 to 45	20
	46 to 50	25
	51 to 55	30
	56 to 60	35
	61 or more	40
Earnings cap	£	
2005–06	105,600	
2004–05	102,000	
2003–04	99,000	
2002–03	97,200	
2001–02	95,400	
2000–01	91,800	

Retirement annuities (TA 1988 s 626)

Age in years at beginning of year of assessment	Maximum percentage
50 and below	17½
51 to 55	20
56 to 60	22½
61 or more	27½

Life insurance element (TA 1988 s 640(3), as amended)

The maximum amount of contributions in respect of life insurance on which tax relief can be given is limited to a percentage of net relevant earnings (retirement annuities; personal pension contracts taken out before 6 April 2001) or of total amount of relevant pension contributions (personal pensions/stakeholder pension contracts taken out after 5 April 2001).

	Maximum percentage of net relevant earnings
Retirement annuities (contracts for dependants or life insurance)	5%
Personal pension schemes (contract of life insurance made before 6 April 2001)	5%
	Maximum percentage of total relevant pension contributions
Personal pension schemes/stakeholder pensions Contract of life insurance made after 5 April 2001	10%

Approval of contracts – early retirement ages

Trades and professions for which an early retirement age has been agreed by the Revenue under TA 1988 s 620(4)(c) for the purpose of the approval of retirement annuity contracts are set out below. Under the personal and stakeholder pensions legislation, individuals may not take benefits from their pension arrangements before the age of 50. The trades and professions listed below for which the Revenue has approved an earlier retirement age of 30, 35, 40 or 45 have been approved under TA 1988 s 634(3)(b) for the purposes of personal pension schemes and stakeholder pensions.

Retirement age	Profession or occupation		
30	downhill skiers		
35	athletes	ice hockey players	table tennis players
	badminton players	models	tennis players (including real tennis players)
	boxers	national hunt jockeys	wrestlers
	cyclists	rugby league players	
	dancers	rugby union players	
	footballers	squash players	
40	cricketers	golfers	speedway drivers
	divers (saturation, deep sea and free swimming)	motorcycle riders (motorcross or road racing)	trapeze artists
		motor racing drivers	WPBSA snooker players
45	flat racing jockeys	members of the reserve forces	
50	circus animal trainers	off-shore riggers (mechanical fitters, pipe fitters, riggers, platers, welders and roustabouts)	rugby league referees
	croupiers		territorial army members
	interdealer brokers		TV newsreaders
	martial arts instructors	Royal Navy reservists	
	moneybroker dealers		
55	air pilots	inshore fishermen	psychiatrists (who are also maximum part-time specialists employed within the NHS solely in the treatment of the mentally disordered)
	brass instrumentalists	midwives (female)	
	distant water trawlermen	moneybroker dealer managers and directors responsible for dealers	
	firemen (part-time)	nurses (female)	singers
	health visitors (female)	physiotherapists (female)	

Share schemes

Inland Revenue share schemes web page: www.inlandrevenue.gov.uk/shareschemes

Share incentive plans

(TCGA 1992 ss 236A, 238A, Schs 7C, 7D Pt 1; ITEPA 2003 ss 488–515, Sch 2; FA 2003 s 139, Sch 21)
Applications for approval of Share Incentive Plans could be made from 28 July 2000.

Free share plan

2000–01 onwards	annual maximum	£3,000

Partnership share plan

2000–01 to 2002–03	monthly maximum	£125 or 10% of monthly salary if lower
2003–04 onwards	annual maximum	£1,500 or 10% of annual salary if lower

Matching shares

2000–01 onwards	Maximum number of shares given by employer to employee for each partnership share bought	2

Main conditions

1 All employees must be eligible to participate on similar terms and not discouraged from doing so. Free shares may be awarded by reference to remuneration, length of service or hours worked, or allocated by reference to performance, and benefits must not be conferred wholly or mainly on directors or employees receiving higher levels of remuneration.
2 Free and matching shares must be kept in the plan normally for three years and not more than five (partnership shares can be taken out of the plan at any time).
3 Shares must be taken out of the plan when an employee ceases to be employed by the company (if this happens within three years of getting the share, the free and matching shares may be lost).

Reliefs

Where the conditions of the scheme are complied with –
   (a) Free share plans: employers can give shares to employees free of income tax and national insurance contributions. (Some or all of these shares may be awarded for reaching performance targets.)
   (b) Partnership share plans: employees may allocate part of their pre-tax salary to buy shares in their employing company without income tax or national insurance contributions being payable.
   (c) Generally, all shares held in a plan for five years, will be free of income tax and national insurance contributions.
   (d) No capital gains tax is payable on the withdrawal of shares from the plan and they are deemed to be acquired at their market value at that time.
   (e) There is no stamp duty charge when the employee buys shares from trustees of the plan (FA 2000 Sch 8 para 116A; FA 2001 s 95; ITEPA 2003 Sch 6 para 257).
   (f) If shares are taken out of a plan within between three and five years, income tax and national insurance contributions will be payable on the lower of their initial value and their value on leaving the plan.
   (g) Dividends paid on the shares are tax free (up to a £1,500 annual limit) provided they are used to acquire additional shares in the company.
   (h) The costs of the plan will be deductible from profits for tax purposes.

Enterprise management incentives

(TCGA 1992 s 238A, Sch 7D Pt 4; ITEPA 2003 ss 527–541, Sch 5)

With effect from 28 July 2000, certain independent trading companies with gross assets not exceeding £15 million may grant share options then worth up to £100,000 to an eligible employee. The total value of shares in respect of which unexercised qualifying options exist must not exceed £3 million. (For options granted before 11 May 2001 the number of employees who could hold options at any one time was limited to 15, giving an overall limit of £1·5 million.)

Reliefs

Where the conditions of the scheme are complied with –
   (a) There is no charge to tax or NICs when the option is granted provided the option to acquire the shares is not at less than their market values at that date, and there is no charge on exercise providing the option is exercised within ten years.
   (b) Capital gains tax will be payable when the shares are sold, but business assets taper relief (see p 38) will be available and will begin to run from the date on which the options are granted.

Approved save as you earn (SAYE) share option schemes

(TCGA 1992 s 238A, Sch 7D Pt 2; ITEPA 2003 ss 516–520, Sch 3; FA 2003 s 139, Sch 21)

The scheme is linked to an approved savings scheme, on which interest and bonuses are exempt from tax, to provide funds for the acquisition of shares when the option is exercised at the end of a 3 or 5-year contract. A 5-year contract may offer the option of repayment on the 7th anniversary.

All employees must be eligible to participate on similar terms (subject to a minimum service requirement of up to 5 years and material interest exclusions). Scheme shares must be fully paid up, not redeemable and not subject to special restrictions.

Monthly contributions to SAYE scheme

Minimum	£5–£10[1]
Maximum	£250

[1] The company may choose a minimum savings contribution between £5 and £10.

Reliefs

Where the conditions of the scheme are complied with, no income tax charge arises on the employee in respect of –

(a) the grant of an option to acquire shares at a discount of up to 20% of the share price at time of the grant;

(b) the exercise of the option[1]; or

(c) any increase in the value of the shares.

Capital gains tax is chargeable on disposal of the shares: the CGT base cost is the consideration given by the employee for both the shares and the option.

[1] Share options must not be exercised before the bonus date subject to cessation of employment due to injury, disability, redundancy, retirement or death.

Interest payments on termination

Contracts joined from	24.1.04	1.9.03 to 23.1.04	27.4.03 to 31.8.03	1.9.02 to 26.4.03	1.10.01 to 31.8.02	1.10.98 to 30.9.01
3-year contract bonus rate – number of monthly payments	1·7	0·9	1	1·8	2	2·75
effective interest rate	3·02%	1·61%	1·74%	3·18%	3·67%	4·83%
simple interest rate on termination after 1 but less than 3 years	1%	1%	2%	2%	2%	3%
5-year contract bonus rate – number of monthly payments	5·4	3·4	3·7	5·7	6·2	7·5
effective interest rate	3·4%	2·17%	2·34%	3·57%	3·99%	4·65%
simple interest rate on termination after 1 but less than 5 years	1%	1%	2%	2%	2%	3%
7-year contract bonus rate – number of monthly payments	10·4	7·1	7·6	11	11·9	13·5
effective interest rate	3·55%	2·48%	2·64%	3·69%	4·07%	4·52%
compound interest rate on termination after 5 but less than 7 years	1%	1%	2%	2%	2%	3%

A new mechanism for adjusting the bonus rates for the 3, 5 and 7-year SAYE contracts was introduced from 1 October 2001 and the rates will in future be adjusted automatically on an annual basis from 1 September by linking them to the 3, 5 and 7-year market swap rates. The mechanism will allow bonus rates to be adjusted during the 12-month period if there is a dramatic rise or fall in the market reference swap rates. Existing employees who entered SAYE contracts before the implementation of the new mechanism will continue to receive the bonus and interest rates in force when they joined the scheme.

Company share option plans

(TCGA 1992 s 238A, Sch 7D Pt 3; ITEPA 2003 ss 521–526, Sch 4; FA 2003 s 139, Sch 21)

Limit on value of shares under option held by employee at any one time

From 29 April 1996	£30,000

Scheme shares must be fully paid up, not redeemable and not subject to special restrictions. Only full-time directors or qualifying employees may participate in the scheme.

Reliefs

Where the conditions of the scheme are complied with, no tax charge arises on the employee in respect of –

(a) the grant of an option to acquire shares[1];
(b) the exercise of the option[2]; or
(c) any increase in the value of the shares.

Capital gains tax is chargeable on disposal of the shares: the CGT base cost is the consideration given by the employee for both the shares and the option.

[1] At the time the option is granted the price at which shares can be acquired must not be less than the market value of shares of the same class at that time.
[2] The option must be exercised between 3 and 10 years after the grant (or may be exercised less than 3 years after the grant where the individual ceases to be an employee due to injury, disablement, redundancy or retirement). For options granted before 9 April 2003, the options must be exercised between 3 and 10 years after the grant (without exception) and not less than 3 years after a previous exempt exercise of another option under the same or another approved company share option scheme.

Approved profit sharing schemes

(TA 1988 ss 186, 187, Sch 9, 10)

NOTE: The income tax relief in respect of awards of shares under approved profit sharing schemes was withdrawn for awards of shares made after 31 December 2002: FA 2000 s 49.

Annual limit on shares appropriated

From 1991–92:	Greater of £3,000 or 10% of salary, up to £8,000

Schedule E charge on early disposal or receipt of capital from shares

Time of disposal or capital receipt	Percentage charge[1]
Before 3rd anniversary of appropriation	100%[2]

[1] Calculated on the appropriate percentage of the initial market value of the shares when appropriated (or the sales proceeds if less).
[2] The charge is reduced to 50% where the employee reaches the retirement age specified in the scheme rules or leaves the employment due to injury, disability or redundancy before the shares are sold or capital is received.

Reliefs

Where the conditions of the scheme are satisfied, no tax charge arises on the employee in respect of –

(a) the value of the shares at the time of appropriation;
(b) any increase in the value of the shares; or
(c) any gain on the disposal of the shares (although capital gains tax is chargeable on any gain over the market value on appropriation).

Executive share option schemes

(TA 1988 ss 185, 187, Sch 9)

NOTE: The income tax relief in respect of the grant and exercise of options under executive schemes was withdrawn with effect for options granted after 17 July 1995, subject to transitional provisions (see Revenue Press Release dated 28 November 1995). In general, options granted under an approved scheme after 16 July 1995 qualify for tax relief only if they meet the conditions for approved company share option plans (see above).

Limit on market value of unexercised options

Greater of £100,000 or 4 times emoluments subject to PAYE (excluding benefits).

Reliefs

Where the conditions of the scheme are satisfied, no tax charge arises on the employee in respect of –

(a) the grant or exercise of the option; or
(b) any increase in value of the shares.

Capital gains tax is chargeable on disposal of the shares: the CGT base cost is the consideration given by the employee for both the shares and the option.

Tax credits

Child tax credit and working tax credit

Child tax credit	2005–06 Annual amount	2004–05 Annual amount
	£	£
Family element[1]	545	545
Addition for child under age of 1[1]	545	545
Child element (for each child or young person)	1,690	1,625
Addition for disabled child or young person	2,285	2,215
Enhancement for severe disabled child or young person	920	890

Working tax credit	2005–06 Annual amount	2004–05 Annual amount
	£	£
Basic element	1,620	1,570
Lone parent and couple element	1,595	1,545
30-hour element	660	640
Disability element	2,165	2,100
Severe disability element	920	890
50+ element—16 to 29 hours worked	1,110	1,075
50+ element—30 or more hours worked[2]	1,660	1,610
Childcare element (up to 70% of eligible costs)	**Weekly**	**Weekly**
—maximum eligible cost for 1 child	175.00	135.00
—maximum eligible cost for 2 or more children	300.00	200.00

Income thresholds	2005–06 Annual amount	2004–05 Annual amount
	£	£
First income threshold	£5,220	£5,060
First withdrawal rate	37%	37%
Second income threshold	£50,000	£50,000
Second withdrawal rate	6.67%	6.67%
First threshold for those entitled to Child Tax Credit only	£13,910	£13,480
Income disregarded	£2,500	£2,500

Notes
[1] Only one family element available per family. The baby element is payable in addition in the first year of the child's life.
[2] Where an individual qualifies for the 50 plus (30+ hours) payment, they cannot also qualify for the 50 plus (16–29 hours) payment.

Payments. Tax credits are non-taxable and are awarded on an annual basis. Child tax credit (CTC) and the childcare element of working tax credit (WTC) is paid by the Revenue direct to the main carer at weekly or four-weekly intervals. WTC, apart from any childcare cost element, is paid through the employer or direct to a self-employed person by bank credit.

Basis of claim. Tax credits are initially based on the income of the claimant or joint claimants for the preceding tax year and then adjusted based on actual income in the tax year in which the credit is claimed (subject to the £2,500 tolerance rule).

Who can claim. CTC is payable to UK resident single parents and couples responsible for a child or young person and whose income is within a set limit.

WTC is payable to UK residents who are at least 16 years old and who work (or in the case of a couple, one of whom who works) at least 16 hours a week and whose income is within a set limit. Additionally, the claimant (or one of them if a couple) must either:

- be at least 25 years old and work at least 30 hours a week; or
- have a dependent child or children; or
- be over 50 and qualify for the 50+ element; or
- have a mental or physical disability which puts them at a disadvantage in getting a job and have previously been in receipt of some form of disability benefit.

Time limits. Claims must be made after the commencement of the tax year but within three months after commencement if maximum entitlement is to be awarded, as claims can only be backdated for a maximum of three months (providing the claimant is entitled to the tax credit in that earlier period).

End-of-year returns and notifiable changes. A return must be made, by notice from the Revenue and normally by 6 July following the tax year to which the claim relates, confirming the claimant's circumstances and income for that year. Certain in-year changes of circumstances must be notified to the Revenue, normally within three months of the change, if tax credit entitlement will fall to be reduced as a result.

Underpayments and overpayments. After the year-end, once entitlement to tax credits for the tax year has been determined, any underpayment will be paid by the Revenue in a lump sum to the designated claimant. Overpayments are recovered by deduction from tax credit entitlement in the following year, or through the PAYE system, or by assessment as if they were unpaid tax.

Penalties and interest apply for fraud or neglect or the provision of incorrect information.

Taxable earnings – income from employment

(ITEPA 2003 ss 14–43)

	Services performed			
Persons domiciled in UK	Wholly in UK	Partly in UK	Partly abroad	Wholly abroad
Non-resident	All	That part	None	None
Resident but not ordinarily resident	All	That part	Remittances	Remittances
Resident and ordinarily resident	All	All[1]	All[1]	All[1]
Persons domiciled outside UK	UK employer Foreign employer	As for person domiciled in UK. *Non-resident* All UK earnings. *Resident (not ordinarily resident)* – All UK earnings. (Remittances for duties performed outside UK.) *Resident (and ordinarily resident)* All earnings. (Remittances if all duties performed outside UK.)		

[1] Before 17 March 1998, exempt if qualifying period of over 364 days mostly abroad. The relief for seafarers continues after that date (FA 1998 s 63; ITEPA 2003 ss 378–385). Special relief for employees forced to return early from Kuwait or Iraq who had intended to work abroad for over 364 days.
It was further announced in the Budget Speech made on 9 April 2003 that the Government is reviewing the residence and domicile rules as they affect the tax liabilities of individuals; a background paper having been published on the same day (Budget 2003 PN 01).

Termination payments

Exempt lump sum payments

(a) Payments in connection with the cessation of employment on the death, injury or disability of the employee.
(b) Payments under unapproved retirement benefits schemes where the employee has been taxed on the actual or notional contributions to provide the benefit.
(c) Payments under approved retirement benefits schemes which can properly be regarded as a benefit earned by past service.
(d) Certain payments of terminal grants to members of the armed forces.
(e) Certain benefits under superannuation schemes for civil servants in Commonwealth overseas territories.
(f) Payments in respect of foreign service where the period of foreign service comprises –
    (i)   75% of the whole period of service; or
    (ii) the whole of the last 10 years of service; or
    (iii) where the period of service exceeded 20 years, one-half of that period, including any 10 of the last 20 years.
Otherwise, a proportion of the payment is exempt, as follows –

$$\frac{\text{length of foreign service}}{\text{length of total service}} \times \text{amount otherwise chargeable}$$

(g) The first £30,000 of genuine ex gratia payments (where there is no 'arrangement' by the employer to make the payment): ITEPA 2003 ss 401–413.
(h) Statutory redundancy payments (included in computing £30,000 limit in (f) above).

Inheritance tax

Delivery of accounts: due dates

Type of transfer	Due date
Chargeable lifetime transfers	Later of – (a) 12 months after the end of the month in which the transfer took place; and (b) 3 months after the date on which the person delivering the account became liable
PETs which become chargeable	12 months after the end of the month in which the transferor died
Gifts with reservation chargeable on death	12 months after the end of the month in which the death occurred
Transfers on death	Later of – (a) 12 months after the end of the month in which the death occurred; and (b) 3 months after the date on which the personal representatives first act or the person liable first has reason to believe that he is liable to deliver an account
National heritage property	6 months after the end of the month in which the chargeable event occurred

Delivery of accounts: excepted transfers, estates and settlements
(SI 2002 No 1733, SI 2004 No 2543)

Date of transfer or death	6 April 1996–5 April 1998	6 April 1998–5 April 2000	6 April 2000–5 April 2002	6 April 2002–5 April 2003	After 5 April 2003
Excepted transfers:	*Value below:*	*Value below:*	*Value below:*	*Value below:*	*Value below:*
Total chargeable transfers since 6 April	£10,000	£10,000	£10,000	£10,000	£10,000
Total chargeable transfers during last 10 years	£40,000	£40,000	£40,000	£40,000	£40,000
Excepted estates:					
Total gross value	£180,000[1]	£200,000[1]	£210,000[1]	£220,000[1]	£240,000[1]
Total gross value of property outside UK	£30,000	£50,000	£50,000	£75,000	£75,000
Aggregate value of 'specified transfers'[2]	£50,000	£75,000	£75,000	£100,000	£100,000
Settled property passing on death	—	—	—	£100,000	£100,000

Excepted estates: For deaths occurring after 5 April 2004, no account need be delivered where the deceased died domiciled in the UK provided either conditions (a) or (b) below are met, and both conditions (c) and (d) below are met.

(a) the aggregate of the gross value of the estate, and of any 'specified transfers' or 'specified exempt transfers'[3] does not exceed the appropriate IHT threshold;

(b) the aggregate of the gross value of the estate, and of any 'specified transfers' or 'specified exempt transfers'[3] does not exceed £1,000,000; and after deducting from that aggregate figure any exempt spouse and charity transfers and total estate liabilities, it does not exceed the appropriate IHT threshold;

(c) the gross value of settled property or foreign assets do not exceed the above limits; and

(d) there were no chargeable lifetime transfers in the 7 years before death other than specified transfers not exceeding the above limits.

For deaths after 5 April 2002 and before 6 April 2004, no account need be delivered where the deceased died domiciled in the UK provided that:

(i) the aggregate of the gross value of the estate, and of any 'specified transfers' does not exceed the above limits; and

(ii) the gross value of settled property or foreign assets do not exceed the above limits; and

(iii) there were no chargeable lifetime transfers in the 7 years before death other than specified transfers not exceeding the above limits.

Where the deceased was never domiciled in the UK, no account need be delivered for deaths after 5 April 2002 provided the value of the estate in the UK is wholly attributable to cash and quoted shares and securities not exceeding £100,000.

Notes:
[1] This limit applies to the aggregate gross value of the estate and of 'specified transfers'.
[2] 'Specified transfers' are transfers of cash, quoted shares and securities and, after 6 April 2002, interests in or over land and, after 5 April 2004, personal chattels or corporeal moveable property.
[3] 'Specified exempt transfers' are transfers in the 7 years before death between spouses, gifts to charity, political parties or housing associations, transfers to maintenance funds for historical buildings, etc. or to employee trusts.

Excepted settlements: No account need be delivered of property comprised in excepted settlements where a chargeable event occurs after 5 April 2002. 'Excepted settlements' is one comprising solely of cash not exceeding £1,000 and in which there is no interest in possession. The trustees must be UK resident throughout the life of the trust and there must be no related settlements.

Rates of tax

From 15 March 1988 onwards

Tax rates on cumulative gross transfers	% rate on gross
Gross transfers on death	
Up to cumulative chargeable transfer limit	0
Over cumulative chargeable transfer limit	40
Gross lifetime transfers	
Up to cumulative chargeable transfer limit	0
Over cumulative chargeable transfer limit	20

Grossing-up rate on net transfers	Rate on net fraction
Net transfers on death not bearing own tax	
Up to cumulative chargeable transfer limit	nil
For each £1 over chargeable transfer limit	⅔
Net lifetime transfers	
Up to cumulative chargeable transfer limit	nil
For each £1 over chargeable transfer limit	¼

Cumulative chargeable transfer limits

Period	Limit
	£
2005–06	275,000
2004–05	263,000
2003–04	255,000
2002–03	250,000
2001–02	242,000
2000–01	234,000
1999–2000	231,000
1998–99	223,000
1997–98	215,000
1996–97	200,000
1995–96	154,000
10.3.92–5.4.95	150,000
6.4.91–9.3.92	140,000
1990–91	128,000
1989–90	118,000

Note
The nil-rate band for 2006–07 has been set at £285,000 and for 2007–08 at £300,000 (FA 2005 s 98).

Reliefs

The following is a summary of the main reliefs and exemptions for 2005–06 under the Inheritance Tax Act 1984. The legislation should be referred to for conditions and exceptions.

Agricultural property
Transfer with vacant possession (or right to obtain it within 12 months); transfer on or after 1 September 1995, of land let (or treated as let) on or after that date. — 100% of agricultural value
Any other case — 50% of agricultural value
(Under IHTA 1984 s 124C, as inserted by FA 1997 s 94, land managed according to terms of certain Habitat Schemes is treated as farm land, and qualifies for relief after 26 Nov. 1996.)

Charges arising and transfers occurring after 9 March 1992 and before 1 September 1995:
Transfer with vacant possession (or right to obtain within 12 months) — 100% of agricultural value
Most other cases — 50% of agricultural value

Note: The 100% relief is extended in limited circumstances by Concession F17.

Annual exemption
From 6 April 1981 — £3,000

Business property
Unincorporated business
Unquoted shares (including shares in AIM or USM companies) (held for 2 years or more)[1]
Unquoted securities which alone, or together with other such securities and unquoted shares, give the transferor control of the company (held for 2 years or more)[1]
Settled property used in life tenant's business — 100%

Controlling holding in fully quoted companies
Land, buildings, machinery or plant used in business of company or partnership — 50%

[1] Tax charges arising and transfers occurring after 5 April 1996. 10 March 1992–5 April 1996 minority holding of shares or securities of up to 25% in unquoted or USM company qualified for 50% relief; larger holdings qualified for 100% relief.

Charities, gifts to
From 15 March 1983 — Exempt

Community Amateur Sports Clubs (CASCs), gifts to
From 6 April 2002 — Exempt

Marriage gifts
Made by: parent — £5,000
remoter ancestor — £2,500
party to marriage — £2,500
other person — £1,000

Political parties, gifts to
From 15 March 1988 — Exempt

Quick succession relief
Estate increased by chargeable transfer followed by death within 5 years
Death within first year — 100%
Each additional year: decreased by — 20%

Small gifts to same person
From 6 April 1981 — £250

Spouses with separate domicile (one not being in the UK)
Total exemption — £55,000

Tapering relief
The value of the estate on death is taxed as the top slice of cumulative transfers in the 7 years before death. Transfers on or within 7 years of death are taxed on their value at the date of the gift on the death rate scale, but using the scale in force at the date of death, subject to the following taper—

Years between gift and death	Percentage of full charge at death rates
0–3	100
3–4	80
4–5	60
5–6	40
6–7	20

Penalties see p 20.

National insurance & State benefits

Taxable and non-taxable state benefits

State benefits of an income nature are in principle taxable in the same way as other sources of income, but the majority of such benefits are not in fact taxed.

Benefits taxed as earned income

Bereavement allowance[1]
Carer's allowance[2]
Incapacity benefit – short-term higher rate
Incapacity benefit – long-term[3]
Industrial death benefit pensions
Invalidity allowance paid with state pension
Jobseeker's allowance[4]

Retirement pension[2]
Statutory adoption pay
Statutory maternity pay
Statutory paternity pay
Statutory sick pay
Widowed parents' allowance and widows' pension

Notes:
[1] Replaced widow's pension from 9 April 2001. Paid up to 52 weeks.
[2] Invalid care allowance before 6 April 2003. Child dependency additions are not taxable (see (2) below).
[3] Not taxable if transferred from invalidity benefit.
[4] In practice limited to the smaller of the jobseeker's allowance 'personal allowance' (for a couple or single person as appropriate) and the weekly amount to which the claimant is entitled: IR41 Income tax and jobseekers.

Benefits which are not taxed

(1) *Short-term benefits*
    Maternity allowance

(2) *Benefits in respect of children*
    Child benefit
    Child dependency additions paid with
        retirement pension, bereavement allowance,
        incapacity benefit, carer's allowance, severe
        disablement allowance, higher-rate
        industrial death benefit
    Child tax credit
    Child's special allowance
    Guardian's allowance
    One-parent benefit

(3) *Industrial injury benefits*
    Constant attendance allowance
    Industrial death benefit
    Industrial injuries disablement pension
    Pneumoconiosis and miscellaneous disease
        benefits
    Reduced earnings allowance

(4) *War disablement benefits*
    Constant attendance allowance
    Disablement pension
    Severe disablement allowance

(5) *Other benefits*
    Attendance allowance
    Bereavement payment
    Christmas bonus
    Cold weather payments
    Council tax benefit
    Disability living allowance
    Earnings top-up
    Housing benefit
    Incapacity benefit (short-term, lower rate)
    Income support (not if involved in a trade dispute)
    Jobfinder's grant
    Pension Credit
    Redundancy payment
    Social fund payments
    Television licence payment
    Vaccine damage (lump sum)
    War pensions
    Widow's payment (replaced by bereavement
        payment from 9 April 2001)
    Winter fuel payment
    Working tax credit

Taxable benefits – rates from 11 April 2005

	Qualifying average weekly earnings	Rate	Maximum no weeks paid
Statutory adoption pay[1]	£82	lower of 90% of average weekly earnings and £106·00	26
Statutory maternity pay[1]	baby due 6.4.05–22.7.05 £79 23.7.05–5.4.06 £82	first six weeks: 90% of average weekly earnings after first six weeks: lower of 90% of average weekly earnings or £106·00	26
Statutory paternity pay[1]	baby due 6.4.05–22.7.05 £79 23.7.05–5.4.06 £82	lower of 90% of average weekly earnings and £106·00	2
Statutory sick pay	£82	£68.20 daily rate is the weekly rate divided by number of qualifying days in week (commencing on the Sunday) in which day to be paid occurs	–

[1] For babies expected, or where children are matched or start to live with adoptive parents, after 5 April 2005

Taxable benefits

	Weekly 11.4.05 onwards £	Total 2005–06 (52 weeks) £	Weekly 12.4.04 onwards £	Total 2004–05 (52 weeks) £
Retirement pensions				
Single person	82.05	4,266.60	79.60	4,139.20
Married couple:				
both contributors—each	82.05	4,266.60	79.60	4,139.20
wife non-contributor—addition	49.15	2,555.80	47.65	2,477.80
wife non-contributor—joint	131.20	6,822.40	127.25	6,617.00
Age addition (over 80)—each	0.25	13.00	0.25	13.00
Bereavement benefits[1]				
Bereavement allowance				
—standard	82.05	4,266.60	79.60	4,139.20
Widowed parent's allowance	82.05	4,266.60	79.60	4,139.20
Non-contributory retirement pension				
Single person (category C or D)	49.15	2,555.80	47.65	2,477.80
Married couple (category C)	78.55	4,084.60	76.15	3,959.80
Married couple (category D—over 80)	98.30	5,111.60	95.30	4,955.60
Age addition	0.25	13.00	0.25	13.00
Incapacity benefit				
Long-term	76.45	3,975.40	74.15	3,855.80
Increased for age: Higher rate	16.05	834.60	15.55	808.60
Lower rate	8.05	418.60	7.80	405.60
Short-term[2] (under pension age) higher rate	68.20	—	66.15	—
(over pension age) higher rate	76.45	—	74.15	—
Invalidity allowance when paid with retirement pension				
Higher rate	16.05	834.60	15.55	808.60
Middle rate	10.30	535.60	10.00	520.00
Lower rate	5.15	267.80	5.00	260.00
Industrial death benefit[3]				
Widow's pension:				
Higher permanent rate	82.05	4,266.60	79.60	4,139.20
Lower permanent rate	24.62	1,280.24	23.88	1,241.76
Widower's pension	82.05	4,266.60	79.60	4,139.20
Carer's allowance[4]				
Each qualifying individual	45.70	2,376.40	44.35	2,306.20
Earnings limit	82.00	—	79.00	—
Adult dependency increase	27.30	1,419.60	26.50	1,378.00
Jobseeker's allowance				
Single: under 18	33.85	—	33.50	—
18 to 24	44.50	—	44.05	—
25 or over	56.20	—	55.65	—

[1] Paid to widows and widowers for up to 52 weeks.
[2] Lower rate (tax-free) paid up to week 28 (see below). Higher rate (taxable) paid weeks 29 to 52. New claims cannot be made by persons over pensionable age.
[3] Deaths before 11.4.88.
[4] Invalid care allowance before April 2003.

Child dependency additions (from 11.4.05): £9·40 a week where higher rate child benefit payable £11·35 a week for each other child (tax free).

The Revenue generally apply the basis of 52 weeks at the new rate. In certain cases, however, it may be to the advantage of the recipient to calculate the amount actually received within the year of assessment where this includes one week at the old rate.

Non-taxable benefits – rates from 11 April 2005

Attendance allowance:	Higher rate	£60·60 a week
	Lower rate	£40·55 a week
Child benefit:	£17·00 for eldest eligible child (couple)	
	£17·55 for eldest eligible child (lone parent, existing claimants only)	
	£11·40 (each) for other eligible children	
Guardian's allowance:	£12·20 for each qualifying child	
Disability living allowance:		
Care component:	Higher rate	£60·60 a week
	Middle rate	£40·55 a week
	Lower rate	£16·05 a week
Mobility component:	Higher rate	£42·30 a week
	Lower rate	£16·05 a week
Incapacity benefit:		
Short term (under pension age)	Lower rate	£57·65 a week
Short term (over pension age)	Lower rate	£73·35 a week
Maternity allowance:	Lower earnings limit	£82·00 a week (average)
	Standard rate	£106·00 a week
	Earnings threshold	£30·00 a week (average)
	Lower rate	90% average weekly earnings (at least £106·00)
Bereavement payment:	£2,000 lump sum (Paid to widows and widowers.)	

National insurance contributions

From 6 April 2005

Class 1
Lower earnings limit £82 a week; £356 a month; £4,264 a year
Earnings threshold (employees and employers) £94 a week; £408 a month; £4,895 a year
Upper earnings limit £630 a week; £2,730 a month; £32,760 a year

	Not contracted out	Contracted out	
Employees' contributions[1]			
Weekly earnings: £94·01–£630	11%	9·4%[2]	
Over £630	1%	1%	
Employers' contributions[2]		*Salary-related schemes*	*Money purchase schemes*
Weekly earnings: £94·01–£630	12·8%	9·3%	11·8%
Over £630	12·8%	12.8%	12·8%

[1] Employees' rates are nil for children under 16, men over 65 and women over 60. Rates for married women and widows with valid certificates of election are reduced to 4.85% for earnings between £94.01 and £630 pw but the 1% rate still applies to amounts above £630. Normal employers' contributions are payable. NICs are not payable on the first £94 of earnings per week.

[2] Employers receive a rebate of 3.5% for salary-related schemes and 1% for money purchase schemes on earnings from £82 to £94 pw. A rebate of 1.6% on earnings from £82 to £94 pw is given to employees (or employers to the extent that insufficient contributions have been paid for offset). NICs are not payable on the first £94 of earnings pw.

Class 1A and Class 1B:	12·8%
Class 2 (Self-employed):	Flat rate £2·10 a week Volunteer development workers £4·10 a week Share fishermen £2·75 a week Small earnings exception £4,345 a year
Class 3 (Voluntary contributions):	£7·35 a week
Class 4 (Self-employed):	profits £4,895–£32,760 a year: 8%; over £32,760 a year: 1% Exempt if pensionable age reached by beginning of tax year

Maximum Contributions
Class 1 or Class 1/Class 2 £3,124.88 plus 1% of earnings over the upper earnings limit
Class 4 limiting amount £2,340.50 plus 1% of profits over £32,760 a year

---

6 April 2004–5 April 2005

Class 1
Lower earnings limit £79 a week; £343 a month; £4,108 a year
Earnings threshold (employees and employers) £91 a week; £395 a month; £4,745 a year
Upper earnings limit £610 a week; £2,644 a month; £31,720 a year

	Not contracted out	Contracted out	
Employees' contributions[1]			
Weekly earnings: £91·01–£610	11%	9·4%[2]	
Over £610	1%	1%	
Employers' contributions[2]		*Salary-related schemes*	*Money purchase schemes*
Weekly earnings: £91·01–£610	12·8%	9·3%	11·8%
Over £610	12·8%	12·8%	12·8%

[1] Employees' rates are nil for children under 16, men over 65 and women over 60. Rates for married women and widows with valid certificates of election are reduced to 4·85% for earnings between £91·01 and £610 pw but the 1% rate still applies to amounts above £610. Normal employers' contributions are payable. NICs are not payable on the first £91 of earnings pw.

[2] Employers receive a rebate of 3·5% for salary-related schemes and 1% for money purchase schemes on earnings from £79 to £91 pw. A rebate of 1·6% on earnings from £79 to £91 pw is given to employees (or employers to the extent that insufficient contributions have been paid for offset). NICs are not payable on the first £91 of earnings pw.

Class 1A and Class 1B:	12·8%
Class 2 (self-employed):	Flat rate £2.05 a week Volunteer development workers £3·95 a week Share fishermen £2·70 a week Small earnings exception £4,215 a year
Class 3 (voluntary contributions):	£7·15 a week
Class 4 (self-employed):	profits £4,745–£31,720 a year: 8%; over £31,720 a year: 1% Exempt if pensionable age reached by beginning of tax year

Maximum Contributions
Class 1 or Class 1/Class 2 £3,025·77   plus 1% of earnings over the upper earnings limit
Class 4 limiting amount £2,266·65   plus 1% of profits above £31,720 a year

6 April 2003–5 April 2004

Class 1

Lower earnings limit	£77 a week; £334 a month; £4,004 a year	
Earnings threshold (employees and employers)	£89 a week; £385 a month; £4,615 a year	
Upper earnings limit	£595 a week; £2,579 a month; £30,940 a year	

	Not contracted out	Contracted out
Employees' contributions[1]		
Weekly earnings: £89·01–£595	11%	9·4%[2]
Over £595	1%	1%

	Not contracted out	Salary-related schemes	Money purchase schemes
Employers' contributions[2]			
Weekly earnings: £89·01–£595	12·8%	9·3%	11·8%
Over £595	12·8%	12·8%	12·8%

[1] Employees' rates are nil for children under 16, men over 65 and women over 60. Rates for married women and widows with valid certificates of election are reduced to 4·85% for earnings between £89·01 and £595 pw but the 1% rate still applies to amounts above £595. Normal employers' contributions are payable. NICs are not payable on the first £89 of earnings pw.

[2] Employers receive a rebate of 3·5% for salary-related schemes and 1% for money purchase schemes on earnings from £77 to £89 pw. A rebate of 1·6% on earnings from £77 to £89 pw is given to employees (or employers to the extent that insufficient contributions have been paid for offset). NICs are not payable on the first £89 of earnings pw.

Class 1A and Class 1B:	12·8%

Class 2 (self-employed):	Flat rate £2 a week Volunteer development workers £3·85 a week Share fishermen £2·65 a week Small earnings exception £4,095 a year

Class 3 (voluntary contributions):	£6·95 a week

Class 4 (self-employed):	profits £4,615–£30,940 a year: 8%; over £30,940 a year: 1% Exempt if pensionable age reached by beginning of tax year

Maximum Contributions		
Class 1 or Class 1/Class 2	£2,949·98	plus 1% of earnings over the upper earnings limit
Class 4 limiting amount	£2,212	plus 1% of profits above £30,940 a year

6 April 2002–5 April 2003

Class 1

Lower earnings limit	£75 a week; £325 a month; £3,900 a year	
Earnings threshold (employees and employers)	£89 a week; £385 a month; £4,615 a year	
Upper earnings limit	£585 a week; £2,535 a month; £30,420 a year	

	Not contracted out	Contracted out
Employees' contributions[1]		
Weekly earnings: £89·01–£585	10%	8·4%[2]
Over £585	no additional liability	no additional liability

	Not contracted out	Salary-related schemes	Money purchase schemes
Employers' contributions[2]			
Weekly earnings: £89·01–£585	11·8%	8·3%	10·8%
Over £585	11·8%	11·8%	11·8%

[1] Employees' rates are nil for children under 16, men over 65 and women over 60. Rates for married women and widows with valid certificates of election are reduced to 3·85% for earnings between £89·01 and £585 pw. Normal employers' contributions are payable. NICs are not payable on the first £89 of earnings pw.

[2] Employers receive a rebate of 3·5% for salary-related schemes and 1% for money purchase schemes on earnings from £75 to £89 pw. A rebate of 1·6% on earnings from £75 to £89 pw is given to employees (or employers to the extent that insufficient contributions have been paid for offset). NICs are not payable on the first £89 of earnings pw.

Class 1A and Class 1B:	11·8%

Class 2 (self-employed):	Flat rate £2 a week Volunteer development workers £3·75 a week Share fishermen £2·65 a week Small earnings exception £4,025 a year

Class 3 (voluntary contributions):	£6·85 a week

Class 4 (self-employed):	7% of profits between £4,615 and £30,420 a year Exempt if pensionable age reached by beginning of tax year

Maximum Contributions	
Class 1 or Class 1/Class 2	£2,628·80
Class 4 limiting amount	£1,912·35

6 April 2001–5 April 2002

Class 1

Lower earnings limit	£72 a week; £312 a month; £3,744 a year
Employees' earnings (primary) threshold	£87 a week; £378 a month; £4,535 a year
Employers earnings (secondary) threshold	£87 a week; £378 a month; £4,535 a year
Upper earnings limit	£575 a week; £2,492 a month; £29,900 a year

	Not contracted out	Contracted out	
Employees' contributions[1]			
Weekly earnings: £87·01–£575	10%	8·4%[2]	
Over £575	no additional liability	no additional liability	

	Not contracted out	*Salary-related schemes*	*Money purchase schemes*
Employers' contributions[2]			
Weekly earnings: £87·01–£575	11·9%	8·9%	11·3%
Over £575	11·9%	11·9%	11·9%

[1] Employees' rates are nil for children under 16, men over 65 and women over 60. Rates for married women and widows with valid certificates of election are reduced to 3·85% for earnings between £87·01 and £575 pw. Normal employers' contributions are payable. NICs are not payable on the first £87 of earnings pw.

[2] Employers receive a rebate of 3% for salary-related schemes and 0·6% for money purchase schemes on earnings from £72 to £87 pw. A rebate of 1·6% on earnings from £72 to £87 pw is given to employees (or employers to the extent that insufficient contributions have been paid for offset). NICs are not payable on the first £87 of earnings pw.

Class 1A and Class 1B:	11·9%
Class 2 (self-employed):	Flat rate £2 a week Volunteer development workers £3·60 a week Share fishermen £2·65 a week Small earnings exception £3,955 a year
Class 3 (voluntary contributions):	£6·75 a week
Class 4 (self-employed):	7% of profits between £4,535 and £29,900 a year Exempt if pensionable age reached by beginning of tax year

Maximum Contributions

Class 1 or Class 1/Class 2	£2,586·40
Class 4 limiting amount	£1,881·55

6 April 2000–5 April 2001

Class 1

Lower earnings limit	£67 a week; £291 a month; £3,484 a year
Employees' earnings (primary) threshold	£76 a week; £329 a month; £3,952 a year
Employers earnings (secondary) threshold	£84 a week; £365 a month; £4,385 a year
Upper earnings limit	£535 a week; £2,319 a month; £27,820 a year

	Not contracted out	Contracted out	
Employees' contributions[1]			
Weekly earnings: £76·01–£535	10%	8·4%[2]	
Over £535	no additional liability	no additional liability	

	Not contracted out	*Salary-related schemes*	*Money purchase schemes*
Employers' contributions[2]			
Weekly earnings: £84·01–£535	12·2%	9·2%	11·6%
Over £535	12·2%	12·2%	12·2%

[1] Employees' rates are nil for children under 16, men over 65 and women over 60. Rates for married women and widows with valid certificates of election are reduced to 3·85% for earnings between £76·01 and £535 pw. Normal employers' contributions are payable. NICs are not payable on the first £76 of earnings pw.

[2] Employers receive a rebate of 3% for salary-related schemes and 0·6% for money purchase schemes on earnings from £67 to £84 pw. A rebate of 1·6% on earnings from £67 to £76 pw is given to employees (or employers to the extent that insufficient contributions have been paid for offset). Employers' NICs are not payable on the first £84 of earnings pw. Employees' NICs are not payable on the first £76 of earnings pw.

Class 1A and Class 1B:	12·2%
Class 2 (self-employed):	Flat rate £2 a week Volunteer development workers £3·35 a week Share fishermen £2·65 a week Small earnings exception £3,825 a year
Class 3 (voluntary contributions):	£6·55 a week
Class 4 (self-employed):	7% of profits between £4,385 and £27,820 a year Exempt if pensionable age reached by beginning of tax year

Maximum Contributions

Class 1 or Class 1/Class 2	£2,432·70
Class 4 limiting amount	£1,746·45

Employers' contributions: benefits in kind

From *6 April 2000*, **Class 1A** national insurance contributions are payable by employers (at 12·8% for 2005–06) on most taxable benefits in kind, excluding benefits:

(1) which are covered by a dispensation; or
(2) included in a PAYE settlement agreement; or
(3) provided to employees not earning more than £8,500 pa (including benefits in kind and expenses payments); or
(4) otherwise not required to be included on a PIID; or
(5) on which Class 1 national insurance contributions were due.

Expenses payments and certain benefits are not liable to Class 1A national insurance contributions.

Before 6 April 2000, national insurance contributions were payable by employers only where the benefits in kind were of cars and free fuel provided for the private use of employees (where the latter were liable to the income tax charge on cars). The benefit of cars and free fuel continues to be chargeable (see above).

From *6 April 1999*, **Class 1B** contributions are payable by employers (at 12·8% for 2005–06) by reference to the value of any items included in a PAYE settlement agreement (PSA) which would otherwise be earnings for Class 1 or Class 1A, including the amount of tax paid. Income tax and Class 1B contributions on a PSA are payable by 19 October after the end of the tax year to which the PSA relates.

Benefits subject to Class 1 and Class 1A national insurance contributions		
Benefit	**NICs Class**	**PAYE or P11D**
Assets/gifts given to employees	1A	P11D
Assets loaned to employees	1A	P11D
Car or van fuel supplied for private motoring	1A	P11D
Cars or vans available for private use	1A	P11D
Childcare vouchers – over £50 where qualifying conditions met or any amount where conditions not met	1	P11D
Christmas gifts – cash	1	PAYE
– benefits	1A	P11D
Clothing and uniforms		
– cash payment for clothing that can be worn at any time	1	PAYE
– cash payment for clothing that can only be worn at work or non-durable items such as tights or stockings	–	PAYE
– clothing provided by employer that can be worn at any time	1A	P11D
Credit cards and tokens – personal expenses not reimbursed	1	PAYE
Credit card reward payments – made to employees for detecting and withdrawing lost or stolen cards (no NICs due if made by a third party)	1	PAYE
Entertaining – non-business staff expenses/allowances	1A	P11D
– staff expenses where employee contracts	1	P11D
Living accommodation (beneficial)	1A	P11D
Loans – at low interest or interest-free	1A	P11D
– written off	1	P11D
Medical insurance or treatment provided in the UK by employer	1A	P11D
Notional payments	1	PAYE
Payments in kind convertible to cash	1	PAYE
Payments of employees personal liabilities	1	PAYE
Personal incidental expense payments	1	P11D
Prize money	1	PAYE
Relocation payments – qualifying over £8,000	1A	P11D
– non-qualifying benefits	1A	P11D
– non-qualifying expenses	1	P11D
Round sum allowances (not identified as business expense)	1	PAYE
Services supplied	1A	P11D
Telephone rental and private calls – employee subscribes	1	P11D
– employer subscribes	1A	P11D

National insurance contributions leaflets

Leaflets regarding National Insurance contributions are issued by the Revenue. They are available from the Revenue website: http://www.inlandrevenue.gov.uk and can be obtained from local Revenue offices (including those which were Contributions Agency offices before 1 April 1999) except where indicated:

* Available only from the Revenue website (see above).

† Available from the Employer's Orderline Tel: 0845 7646646 or from the Revenue website (see above).

‡ Inland Revenue National Insurance Contributions Office, Services to Pension Industry, Benton Park View, Newcastle Upon Tyne NE98 1ZZ (Tel: 08459 150 150).

Further leaflets are available, including rates and tables within the PAYE and NIC Employer's Annual Pack, which can be ordered online or from the orderline on 08457 646 646.

National Insurance

Leaflet	Date	Title
CA01	2004	National insurance contributions for employees
CA02	2004	National insurance contributions for self-employed people with small earnings
CA04	2004	Class 2 and Class 3: direct debit – the easier way to pay
CA07	2004	Unpaid and late-paid contributions
CA08	2004	Voluntary national insurance contributions
CA09	2003	National insurance contributions for widows or widowers
CA10	2003	National insurance contributions for divorcees
CA11	2003	National insurance contributions for share fishermen
CA12	2003	Training for further employment and your National Insurance record
CA13	2004	National insurance contributions for married women with reduced elections
CA14*	2002	Termination of contracted-out employment: manual for salary related pension schemes and salary related parts of mixed benefits schemes
CA14A*	2002	Termination of contracted-out employment: manual for money purchase pension schemes and money purchase parts of mixed benefits schemes
CA14F*	2003	Technical guidance on contracted-out decision making and appeals
CA15*	2003	Cessation of contracted-out pension schemes manual
CA16*	2004	Appropriate personal pension scheme manual
CA17‡	2005	Employees' guide to minimum contributions
CA19*	2003	Using the accrued GMP liability service
CA20*	2003	Using the contracted-out contributions/earnings information service
CA21*	2004	Using the National Insurance number/date of birth checking service
CA22*	2002	Contracted-out data transactions using magnetic media
CA23	2001	National insurance contributions for mariners
CA24	2001	National insurance contributions for masters and employers of mariners
CA25	2004	National insurance for agencies and people finding work through agencies
CA26	2003	National insurance contributions for examiners, moderators and invigilators, lecturers, teachers and instructors
CA33†	2005	Employer's manual on Class 1A NICs on cars and fuel
CA37*	2004	Simplified Deductions Scheme for employers
CA42*	2004	Foreign going mariner's and deep-sea fisherman's contributions for employers
CA44†	2005	National insurance for company directors
CA50*	1999	Making your year end return on tape or disk
CA51/52*	2004	Submitting year end returns on magnetic media – Technical guide
CA65	2003	NIC for people working for embassies, consulates and overseas employers
CA72	2004	National insurance contributions – deferring payment
CA75*	2001	Resolving benefit involved cases
CA76*	2001	National insurance abroad – a guide for employers of employees from abroad
CA82	2001	If you think our decision is wrong
CA84	2002	Stakeholder pension scheme manual
CA85*	2003	Contracted-out stakeholder pension scheme manual
CA86	2004	Employees' guide to statutory sick pay
CA87	2003	National insurance contributions and the Welsh language
CA89*	2003	Payroll cleansing. A free service offered by the Inland Revenue
CA90*	2003	Convention on social security between the UK and the Republic of Korea
CA91*	2003	Agreement between the UK and Japan on social security
CA92*	2004	Services to the pension industry – an information guide
CA93	2004	Shortfall in your NICs. To pay or not to pay?
CA1437*	2001	Employer's guide to centralised payments of national insurance contributions
CWG2†	2005	Employer's further guide to PAYE and NICs
CWG5†	2005	Class 1A NICs and benefits in kind – a guide for employers
P/SE/1	2004	Starting your own business
CWL2	2003	NIC for self-employed people, Class 2 and Class 4
IR 56	1999	Employed or self-employed? A guide for tax and national insurance
IR 148	2001	Are your workers employed or self-employed? – construction workers
NI38	2004	Social security abroad
NI132	2002	National insurance for employers of people working abroad
OCSS1	2003	NICO. Our customer service standards

Stamp taxes

Rates of tax
(FA 1963 s 55; FA 1999 s 111, Sch 13; FA 2000 ss 114, 116; FA 2003 ss 55, 56, 125, Schs 4, 5, 20; SI 2003/2914; FA 2005 s 95)

Stamp duty land tax
Applies to contracts entered into, or varied, after 10 July 2003 and completed, or leases granted, on or after 1 December 2003.

On land transactions[1]

	From 17 March 2005		30 November 2003 to 16 March 2005	
Rate	Residential property[3]	Non-residential or mixed property	Residential property[3]	Non-residential or mixed property
Nil	Up to £120,000	Up to £150,000	Up to £60,000	Up to £150,000
1%	£120,001–£250,000	£150,001–£250,000	£60,001–£250,000	£150,001–£250,000
3%	£250,001–£500,000	£250,001–£500,000	£250,001–£500,000	£250,001–£500,000
4%	£500,001 or more	£500,001 or more	£500,001 or more	£500,001 or more

Lease granted for a premium
The same duty is payable as above for land transactions except that special rules apply to a premium where the rent exceeds £600 p.a.).

Lease rentals[2]
On net present value of rent over term of lease (applying a discount rate of 3.5%)

	From 17 March 2005		30 November 2003 to 16 March 2005	
Rate	Residential property[3]	Non-residential or mixed property	Residential property[3]	Non-residential or mixed property
Nil	Up to £120,000	Up to £150,000	Up to £60,000	Up to £150,000
1%	Excess over £120,000	Excess over £150,000	Excess over £60,000	Excess over £150,000

Notes
[1] These rates apply to the full consideration, not only to that in excess of the previous band.
[2] The 1% rate applies only to the consideration in excess of the nil-rate band.
[3] Applies to residential property outside disadvantaged areas (see page 97).

Stamp duty
For contracts entered into, or varied, after 10 July 2003 and completed, or leases granted, on or after 1 December 2003, stamp duty is abolished for all transfers other than stocks and marketable securities, and interests in partnerships. From 22 July 2004 stamp duty is also abolished for certain partnership transactions involving an interest in land and is replaced by stamp duty land tax. From those dates, transfers of land are subject to stamp duty land tax (see above).

Transfers of stock and marketable securities   0·5%

Other transfers (including land and buildings)
Contracts entered into before 11 July 2003 or completed, or leases granted, before 1 December 2003.

	16.3.99– 27.3.00	28.3.00– 30.11.03
On transfer made pursuant to contract after	9.3.99	21.3.00
Conveyance or transfer on sale with certificate of value[1]		
Not exceeding £60,000	Nil	Nil
£60,001–£250,000	1%	1%
£250,001–£500,000	2·5%	3%
£500,001 or more	3·5%	4%
Conveyance or transfer on sale without certificate of value	3·5%	4%

Lease granted for a premium
The same duty is payable as above for a conveyance or transfer on sale. The nil rate, however, only applies where the rent under the lease does not exceed £600 p.a.

Lease rentals

Furnished residential accommodation for definite term of less than 1 year	£5
Leases not exceeding 7 years, or for an indefinite term:	
—Up to £5,000 (£500 before 28.3.00) p.a.	Nil
—Over £5,000 (£500 before 28.3.00) p.a.	1%
Leases over 7 years and up to 35 years	2%
Leases over 35 years and up to 100 years	12%
Leases over 100 years	24%

[1] These rates apply to the full consideration, not only to that in excess of the previous band.

Rounding

From 1 October 1999, stamp duty is rounded up to the next multiple of £5 in all cases other than for SDRT. (FA 1999 s 112, Sch 14). This does not apply for Stamp Duty Land Tax from 1 December 2003.

Fixed duties

(Stamp Act 1891 Sch 1; FA 1999 Sch 13; FA 2003 s 125, Sch 20)

The fixed stamp duties below are abolished for contracts entered into, or varied, after 10 July 2003 and completed, or leases granted, on or after 1 December 2003.

Leases other than above	£5
Declaration of trust; duplicate or counterpart; exchange or partition; release or renunciation; surrender	£5

Exemptions and reliefs

(FA 2000 ss 129, 130; FA 2001 s 92; FA 2002 ss 110, 116; FA 2003 ss 57–75, 125–130, Schs 3, 6–8, 20; SI 2003/ 2816; FA 2004 ss 296, 302, Sch 39)

(See stamp duty above regarding the general abolition for completions from 1 December 2003.)

(1) transfers to charities for use for charitable purposes
(2) transfers to bodies established for national purposes
(3) gifts inter vivos
(4) land transfers with groups of companies
(5) land transferred in exchange for shares on company reconstruction and acquisitions
(6) transfers of intellectual property (after 27.3.00)
(7) certain transfers to registered social lanclords (after 28.7.00)
(8) certain leases granted by registered social landlords
(9) transfers of goodwill (after 21 April 2002)
(10) property transactions in disadvantaged parts of the UK designated for this purpose (see below)
(11) sale and leaseback arrangements involving commercial property (after 30.11.03) (extended with effect from 22 July 2004 to residential property and lease and leaseback transactions)
(12) certain acquisitions of residential property by house building companies or property traders when people move into a new dwelling or a chain of transactions break down, or by employers involving employee relocations (after 31.11.03) (extended with effect from 22 July 2004 for people buying a new home and unable to move into it immediately)
(13) initial acquisition of assets by trustees of a unit trust scheme (after 30.11.03)
(14) transfers of property to beneficiaries under a will or an intestacy (after 30.11.03)

Disadvantaged areas

(FA 2001 s 92, Sch 30; FA 2002 s 110; FA 2003 s 57, Sch 6; SI 2001/3746; SI 2001/3747; SI 2003/1056; FA 2005 s 96, Sch 9)

Residential property: from 30 November 2001 exemption applies to transfers on sale up to £150,000 and to lease premiums up to £150,000 (except that special rules apply to a premium where the annual rent exceeds £600).

Non-residential property: as above for residential property except that the £150,000 cap was removed from 10 April 2003 to 16 March 2005 and the exemption applied absolutely to transfers on sale, grants of a lease for a premium and lease rentals.

Areas designated as disadvantaged for this purpose are set out in SI 2001/3747.

Stamp Duty Reserve Tax (SDRT)

Agreements to transfer chargeable securities for money or money's worth (eg renounceable letters of allotment)[1]	0.5%
Chargeable securities issued or transferred to an operator of a clearance service[2] or converted into depositary receipts	1.5%
Dealings in units of authorised and unauthorised unit trusts (from 6.2.2000)[3,5]	0.5%
Dealings in shares in open-ended investment companies[4,5]	0.5%
Transfers of foreign currency bearer shares and of sterling or foreign currency convertible or equity-related loan stock issued by UK companies	0.5%

[1] If the transaction is completed by a duly stamped instrument within 6 years from the date on which the charge is imposed, the SDRT will be cancelled or repaid.
[2] Where the operator of a clearance service elects to collect and account for SDRT on the normal rate of 0.5% on dealing within the system the higher SDRT charge of 1.5% does not apply.
[3] Charged on transfers of units, and redemptions on a two-week rolling basis. Where the number of units surrendered in the charge period exceed the number of units issued, the total liability is reduced by the fraction of the total issues over the total surrenders.
[4] The SDRT regime for unit trusts applies to open-ended investment companies with appropriate modifications.
[5] From 6 April 2001 transfers of units in a unit trust and surrenders of shares in open-ended investment trusts are exempt when held within individual pension accounts.

Interest on unpaid tax

Stamp duty (Stamp Act 1891 ss 15, 15A; FA 1999 s 109)
For instruments executed from 1 October 1999: Interest runs from the end of 30 days after the date the instrument is executed until the tax is paid. Amounts less than £25 are not charged.

Stamp duty land tax (FA 2003 s 87)
For contracts completed after 30 November 2003: Interest runs from the end of 30 days after the effective date of transaction (normally completion), or the date of a disqualifying event, until the tax is paid. In the case of a deferred payment, interest runs from the date the payment is due until the tax is paid. A penalty carries interest from the date determined until the date of payment (FA 2003 s 88).

Stamp duty reserve tax (SI 1986/1711)
Interest is charged from 14 days after the transaction date for exchange transactions and otherwise from seven days after the end of the month of the transaction. Amounts less than £25 are not charged.

Rates: see page 13.

Repayment supplement

Stamp duty (FA 1999 s 110)
For instruments executed from 1 October 1999: Interest is added to repayments of overpaid stamp duty and runs from 30 days after the date the instrument is executed or the date of payment if later. Amounts less than £25 are not paid.

Stamp duty land tax (FA 2003 s 89)
Interest is added to repayments of overpaid stamp duty land tax and runs from the date tax was paid or an amount was lodged with the Inland Revenue, or the date a penalty was made, to the date the order for repayment is issued.

Stamp duty reserve tax (SI 1986/1711)
Interest is paid from 14 days after the transaction date for exchange transactions and otherwise from seven days after the end of the month of the transaction.

Rates: see page 15.

Penalties

Offence	Penalty
Stamp duty – for instruments executed from 1 October 1999:	
Failure to present instrument for stamping within 30 days after execution (or the day in which it is first received in the UK if executed outside the UK) (Stamp Act 1891 s 15B; SI 1999/2537). (Extended to instruments executed from 24 July 2002 for transfers of UK land and buildings, wherever executed (FA 2002 s 114)).	If presented within one year after the end of the 30 day period: the lower of £300 or the amount of the unpaid duty.
	If presented more than one year after the end of the 30 day period: the greater of £300 or the amount of unpaid duty.
Stamp duty land tax – contracts completed after 30 November 2003:	
Failure to deliver a land transaction return by the filing date (FA 2003 Sch 10 paras 3, 4).	£100 if return delivered within 3 months of filing date, otherwise £200. If not delivered within 12 months of the filing date, penalty not exceeding the amount of tax chargeable.
Failure to comply with notice to deliver return within specified period (FA 2003 Sch 10 para 5).	A penalty not exceeding £60 (on an order from the General or Special Commissioners) for each day on which the failure continues after notification.
Fraudulently or negligently delivering an incorrect return or failing to remedy an error without unreasonable delay (FA 2003 Sch 10 para 8).	A penalty not exceeding the difference between the amount payable in respect of the transaction and the amount that would have been chargeable on the basis of the return delivered.
Fraudulently or negligently giving a self-certificate for a chargeable transaction or failing to remedy an error in respect of such certificate without unreasonable delay (FA 2003 Sch 11 para 3).	A penalty not exceeding the amount of tax chargeable.
Failure to keep and preserve records under FA 2003 Sch 10 para 9 or Sch 11 para 4 (FA 2003 Sch 10 para 11, Sch 11 para 6).	A penalty not exceeding £3,000 unless the information is provided by other documentary evidence.
Failure to comply with notice to produce documents etc under FA 2003 Sch 10 para 14 or Sch 11 para 9 (FA 2003 Sch 10 para 16, Sch 11 para 11).	(a) Initial penalty of £50; (b) further penalty for each day the failure continues not exceeding £30 if penalty determined by an Officer of the Board, or £150 if determined by the court.

Value added tax

Annual accounting scheme

From 10 April 2003 taxable persons with a turnover above £150,000 (from 25 April 2002 to 9 April 2003, £100,000 and before 25 April 2002 all taxable persons) must be registered for at least one year at the date of application for authorisation (SI 1995/2518 Pt VII as amended).

	Can join if taxable supplies in next year not expected to exceed:	Must leave at end of accounting year if taxable supplies exceed:
1.4.04 onwards	£660,000	£825,000
1.4.01–31.3.04	£600,000	£750,000
Before 31.3.01	£300,000	£375,000

Cash accounting scheme

A business may, subject to conditions, account for and pay VAT on the basis of cash paid and received. It can join the scheme at any time (SI 1995/2518, Regs 57, 59 as amended).

	Can join if taxable supplies in next year not expected to exceed:	Must leave at end of accounting year if taxable supplies exceed:	Unless turnover for next year not expected to exceed:
1.4.04 onwards	£660,000	£825,000	£660,000
1.4.01–31.3.04	£600,000	£750,000	£600,000
Before 31.3.01	£350,000	£437,500	£350,000

Registration limits
UK taxable supplies

	Past turnover[1]		Future turnover[1]
	1 year	Unless turnover for next year not expected to exceed:	30 days[2]
1.4.05 onwards	£60,000	£58,000	£60,000
1.4.04–31.3.05	£58,000	£56,000	£58,000
10.4.03–31.3.04	£56,000	£54,000	£56,000
25.4.02–9.4.03	£55,000	£53,000	£55,000
1.4.01–24.4.02	£54,000	£52,000	£54,000
1.4.00–31.3.01	£52,000	£50,000	£52,000
1.4.99–31.3.00	£51,000	£49,000	£51,000

[1] Value of taxable supplies (at zero and positive rates).
[2] Where there are reasonable grounds for believing that limit will be exceeded in this period.

Supplies from other EC countries

	Cumulative total[1] from beginning of calendar year
1.1.93 onwards	£70,000

[1] Value of supplies made by persons in other EC member states to non-taxable persons in the UK.

Acquisitions from other EC countries
VATA 1994 Sch 3

	Past acquisitions[1]	Future acquisitions[1]
	Cumulative total from 1 January	30 days[2]
1.4.05 onwards	£60,000	£60,000
1.4.04–31.3.05	£58,000	£58,000
10.4.03–31.3.04	£56,000	£56,000
25.4.02–9.4.03	£55,000	£55,000
1.4.01–24.4.02	£54,000	£54,000
1.4.00–31.3.01	£52,000	£52,000
1.4.99–31.3.00	£51,000	£51,000

[1] Value of acquisitions of taxable goods from suppliers in other EC member states.
[2] Where there are reasonable grounds for believing that limit will be exceeded in this period.

Deregistration limits

UK taxable supplies

Future turnover	Annual limit
1.4.05 onwards	£58,000
1.4.04–31.3.05	£56,000
10.4.03–31.3.04	£54,000
25.4.02–9.4.03	£53,000
1.4.01–24.4.02	£52,000
1.4.00–31.3.01	£50,000
1.4.99–31.3.00	£49,000

Unless during the year, the person will cease making taxable supplies (or suspend making taxable supplies for 30 days or more).

Supplies from other EC countries

	Past supplies[1]	Future supplies[1]
	Supplies in preceding calendar year	Supplies in following calendar year
1.1.93 onwards	£70,000	£70,000

[1] Value of supplies made by persons in other EC member states to non-taxable persons in the UK.
[2] Where C & E are satisfied that limit will not be exceeded in this period.

Acquisitions from other EC countries

VATA 1994 Sch 3

	Past acquisitions[1]	Future acquisitions[1]
	Acquisitions in preceding calendar year	Acquisitions in following calendar year[2]
1.4.05 onwards	£60,000	£60,000
1.4.04–31.3.05	£58,000	£58,000
10.4.03–31.3.04	£56,000	£56,000
25.4.02–9.4.03	£55,000	£55,000
1.4.01–24.4.02	£54,000	£54,000
1.4.00–31.3.01	£52,000	£52,000
1.4.99–31.3.00	£51,000	£51,000

[1] Value of acquisitions of taxable goods from suppliers in other EC member states.
[2] Where C & E E are satisfied that limit will not be exceeded in this period.

Rate of tax

	Standard rate	VAT fraction	Reduced rate	VAT fraction
1.9.97 onwards	17.5%	7/47	5%	1/21
1.4.94–31.8.97	17.5%	7/47	8%	2/27

Flat rate scheme for farmers: 4% flat rate addition to sale price.

Optional flat rate scheme

Flat rate percentage (determined by trade sector of business) applied to tax-inclusive turnover (VATA s 26B; FA 2002 s 23; SI 1995/2518 Regs 55A–55V).

	Maximum annual taxable turnover[1]	Maximum annual taxable turnover[1] plus exempt/non-taxable income
10.4.03 onwards	£150,000	£187,500
25.4.02–9.4.03	£100,000	£125,000

[1] VAT-exclusive

Flat rate scheme – table of percentages

Trade sector	Flat Rate Percentage	
	before 1.1.04	From 1.1.04
Accountancy or book-keeping	13·5	13
Advertising	11	9·5
Agricultural services	9	7·5
Animal husbandry	11	N/A
Any other activity not listed elsewhere	11	10
Architect	13·5	12·5
Boarding or care of animals	N/A	10·5
Business services that are not listed elsewhere	12·5	11
Catering services, including restaurants and takeaways	13	12
Civil and structural engineer or surveyor	N/A	12·5
Computer and IT consultancy or data processing	14·5	13
Computer repair services	13·5	11
Dealing in waste or scrap	11	9·5
Entertainment or journalism	12	11
Estate agency and property management services	11·5	11
Farming or agriculture that is not listed elsewhere	6·5	6
Film, radio, television or video production	N/A	10·5
Financial services	12	11·5
Forestry or fishing	10	9
General building or construction services*	9	8·5
Hairdressing or other beauty treatment services	13	12
Hiring or renting goods	9·5	8·5
Hotel or accommodation	10·5	9·5
Investigation or security	11	10
Labour-only building or construction services*	14·5	13·5
Laundry or dry-cleaning services	12	11
Lawyer or legal services	13·5	13
Library, archive, museum or other cultural activity	8·5	7·5
Management consultancy	13·5	12·5
Manufacturing fabricated metal products	11	10
Manufacturing food	8·5	7·5
Manufacturing that is not listed elsewhere	10	8·5
Manufacturing yarn, textiles or clothing	9·5	8·5
Membership organisation	7	5·5
Mining or quarrying	10	9
Packaging	9	8·5
Photography	10	9·5
Post offices** (from 1 April 2004)	N/A	2
Postal and courier services*** (before 1 April 2004)	6	5·5
Printing	8·5	7·5
Publishing	10	9·5
Pubs	6	5·5
Real estate activity not listed elsewhere	13	12
Repairing personal or household goods	10	8·5
Repairing vehicles	8·5	7·5
Retailing food, confectionery, tobacco, newspapers or children's clothing	5	2
Retailing pharmaceuticals, medical goods, cosmetics or toiletries	8	7
Retailing that is not listed elsewhere	7	6
Retailing vehicles or fuel	8	7
Secretarial services	11·5	11
Social work	9	8·5
Sport or recreation	8	7
Transport or storage, couriers, freight, removals and taxis***	10	9
Travel agency	10	9
Veterinary medicine	11	9·5
Wholesaling agricultural products	7	6
Wholesaling food	7	5·5
Wholesaling that is not listed elsewhere	8	7

* 'Labour-only building or construction services' means services where the value of materials supplied is less than 10% of turnover of such services; any other building or construction services are 'general building or construction services'.
** From 1 April 2004 a special rate of 2% applies to Post Offices. Previously they fell within the category for postal and courier services.
*** From 1 April 2004 (1 July 2004 for courier businesses that applied to join the scheme before 3 March 2004) couriers must apply the rate for transport (SI 2004/767).

Penalties and surcharges

Offence	Penalty
Failure to submit return or pay tax due within time limit (where a return is late but the tax is paid on time or no tax is due, a default is recorded but no surcharge arises) (VATA 1994 s 59). Failure to pay tax due under the payment on account scheme on time (VATA 1994 s 59A).	The greater of £30 and a specified percentage of outstanding VAT for period, depending on number of defaults in surcharge period: 1st default in period 2%, 2nd default 5%, 3rd default 10%, 4th and further defaults 15%. (Surcharge assessments are not issued for sums of less than £200 unless the rate of the surcharge is 10% or more.)
Evasion of VAT: conduct involving dishonesty (VATA 1994 s 60).	Amount of tax evaded or sought to be evaded (subject to mitigation).
Issuing incorrect certificate as to zero-rating (or, from 27 July 1999, as to eligibility to receive reduced-rate fuel and power) (VATA 1994 s 62; FA 1999 s 17).	Difference between tax actually charged and tax which should have been charged.
Misdeclaration or neglect (VATA 1994 s 63).	15% of VAT which would have been lost if inaccuracy had not been discovered.
Repeated misdeclarations (VATA 1994 s 64).	15% of VAT which would have been lost if second and subsequent inaccuracies within penalty period had not been discovered.
Material inaccuracy in EC sales statement (VATA 1994 s 65).	£100 for each material inaccuracy in 2-year penalty period (which commences following notice of second material inaccuracy).
Failure to submit an EC sales statement (VATA 1994 s 66).	Greater of £50 and a daily penalty (for no more than 100 days) depending on number of failures in default period: 1st failure £5, 2nd failure £10, 3rd and further failures £15.
Failure to notify liability for registration, liability for registration of the transfer of a going concern, or a change in nature of supplies by person exempted from registration (VATA 1994 s 67).	Greater of £50 and a specified percentage of the tax for which the person would have been liable, depending on the period of failure: 9 months or less 5%; over 9 and up to 18 months 10%; over 18 months 15%.
Unauthorised issue of invoices (VATA 1994 s 67).	Greater of £50 and 15% of amount shown as or representing VAT.
Breach of walking possession agreement (VATA 1994 s 68).	50% of VAT due or amount recoverable.
Failure to preserve records for prescribed period (VATA 1994 s 69).	£500
Breaches of regulatory provisions, including failure to notify cessation of liability or entitlement to be registered, failure to keep records and non-compliance with any regulations made under VATA 1994 (VATA 1994 s 69).	Greater of £50 and a daily penalty (for no more than 100 days) of a specified amount depending on number of failures in preceding two years: £5 per day if no previous failures; £10 per day if 1 previous failure; £15 per day if 2 or more previous failures.
Breaches of regulatory provisions involving failure to pay VAT or submit return by due date (VATA 1994 s 69).	Greater of £50 and a daily penalty (for no more than 100 days) of a specified amount depending on number of failures in preceding two years: greater of £5 and ⅙% of VAT due if no previous failures; greater of £10 and ⅓% of VAT due if 1 previous failure; greater of £15 and ½% of VAT due if 2 or more previous failures.
Failure to comply with statutory responsibility to pay correct amount of tax on time (VATA 1994 s 69A).	Distress (diligence, ie poinding and sale and arrestment, in Scotland).
Failure to comply with VAT tribunal directions or summons (VATA 1994 Sch 12 para 10).	Up to £1,000
Failure to comply with the accounting, invoicing, record-keeping and notification requirements for supplies involving investment gold (FA 2000 s 137).	(From 28 July 2000) 17.5% of the value of transactions concerned.
Import of goods from non-EU countries: —failures relating to non-compliance —evasion (FA 2003 ss 24–41).	From 27 November 2003: maximum penalty of £2,500 maximum penalty equal to VAT sought to be evaded.
Failure to notify the use of a designated avoidance scheme within 30 days of the due date of the first return affected by the scheme (VATA 1994 Sch 11A paras 10, 11).	15% of the tax avoided (applies to businesses with supplies of £600,000 or more from 1 August 2004).
Failure to disclose certain other notifiable avoidance schemes within 30 days of the due date of the first return affected by the scheme (VATA 1994 Sch 11A paras 10, 11).	Flat rate penalty of £5,000 (applies to businesses with supplies exceeding £10 million from 1 August 2004).

Default interest

The prescribed rate of interest for the purposes of VATA 1994 s 74 (the provisions of which were operative from 1 April 1990) has varied as follows:

	Rate
From 6 December 2003	6.5%
6 September 2003–5 December 2003	5.5%
6 November 2001–5 September 2003	6.5%
6 May 2001–5 November 2001	7.5%
6 February 2000–5 May 2001	8.5%
6 March 1999–5 February 2000	7.5%
6 January 1999–5 March 1999	8.5%
6 July 1998–5 January 1999	9.5%
6 February 1996–5 July 1998	6.25%
6 March 1995–5 February 1996	7%
6 October 1994–5 March 1995	6.25%
6 January 1994–5 October 1994	5.5%
6 March 1993–5 January 1994	6.25%
6 December 1992–5 March 1993	7%
6 November 1992–5 December 1992	7.75%
6 October 1991–5 November 1992	9.25%

Interest on VAT overpaid in cases of official error
(VATA 1994 s 78)

	Rate		Rate
From 6 December 2003	3%	1 April 1991–15 October 1991	12%
6 September 2003–5 December 2003	2%	1 November 1989–31 March 1991	14.25%
6 November 2001–5 September 2003	3%	1 January 1989–31 October 1989	13%
6 May 2001–5 November 2001	4%	1 November 1988–31 December 1988	12.25%
6 February 2000–5 May 2001	5%	1 August 1988–31 October 1988	11%
6 March 1999–5 February 2000	4%	1 May 1988–31 July 1988	9.5%
6 January 1999–5 March 1999	5%	1 December 1987–30 April 1988	11%
1 April 1997–5 January 1999	6%	1 November 1987–30 November 1987	11.25%
6 February 1993–31 March 1997	8%	1 April 1987–31 October 1987	11.75%
16 October 1991–5 February 1993	10.25%	1 January 1987–31 March 1987	12.25%

Zero-rated supplies

A zero-rated supply is a taxable supply, but the rate of tax is nil.
(References are to VATA 1994 Sch 8)

Group 1—Food
Group 2—Sewerage services and water
Group 3—Books etc
Group 4—Talking books for the blind and handicapped and wireless sets for the blind
Group 5—Construction of buildings etc
Group 6—Protected buildings
Group 7—International services
Group 8—Transport
Group 9—Caravans and houseboats
Group 10—Gold
Group 11—Bank notes
Group 12—Drugs, medicines, aids for the handicapped etc
Group 13—Imports, exports etc
Group 15—Charities etc
Group 16—Clothing and footwear

Reduced rate supplies

(References are to VATA 1994 Sch 7A)

Group 1—Domestic fuel and power
Group 2—Installation of energy-saving materials
Group 3—Grant-funded installation of heating equipment or security goods or connection of a gas supply
Group 4—Women's sanitary products
Group 5—Children's car seats
Group 6—Residential conversions
Group 7—Residential renovations and alterations

Exempt supplies

No tax is chargeable on an exempt supply, and input tax cannot be recovered except as allowed under the partial exemption provisions (SI 1995/2518 Pt XIV; VAT Notice 706).
(References are to VATA 1994 Sch 9)

Group 1—Land
Group 2—Insurance
Group 3—Postal services
Group 4—Betting, gaming and lotteries
Group 5—Finance
Group 6—Education
Group 7—Health and welfare
Group 8—Burial and cremation
Group 9—Subscriptions to trade unions, professional and other public interest bodies
Group 10—Sport, sports competitions and physical education
Group 11—Works of art etc
Group 12—Fund-raising events by charities and other qualifying bodies
Group 13—Cultural services etc
Group 14—Supplies of goods where input tax cannot be recovered
Group 15—Investment gold

Partial exemption

De minimis limit for application of partial exemption rules
SI 1995/2518 reg 106

	Exempt input tax not exceeding
Tax years beginning after 30.11.94	(a) £625 per month on average; and (b) 50% of total input tax for prescribed accounting period
Periods beginning between 1.4.92 and 30.11.94	£600 per month on average

Capital goods scheme

Input tax adjustment following change in taxable use of capital goods
VATA 1994 s 34, SI 1995/2518 regs 112–116 (77/388/EEC art 20), SI 1999/599 reg 6.

From 1 April 1990

Item	*Value*	*Adjustment period*
Computer equipment	£50,000 or more	5 years
Land and buildings	£250,000 or more	10 years (5 years where interest had less than 10 years to run on acquisition)

Adjustment formula

$$\frac{\text{Total input tax on item}}{\text{Length of adjustment period}} \times \text{adjustment percentage}$$

The adjustment percentage is the percentage change in the extent to which the item is used (or treated as used) in making taxable supplies between the first interval in the adjustment period and a subsequent interval. (The first interval generally ends on the last day of the tax year in which the input tax was incurred.)

Car fuel

VAT-inclusive scale figures are used to assess VAT due on petrol provided at below cost price for private journeys by registered traders or their employees, where the petrol has been provided from business resources. The figures relate to return periods beginning on the dates shown.

	12 months £	VAT due per car £	3 months £	VAT due per car £	1 month £	VAT due per car £
From 1 May 2005						
Diesel engine						
Cylinder capacity: 2,000cc or less	945	140·74	236	35·15	78	11·62
Over 2,000cc	1,200	178·72	300	44·68	100	14·89
Any other type of engine						
Cylinder capacity: 1,400cc or less	985	146·70	246	36·64	82	12·21
Over 1,400cc up to 2,000cc	1,245	185·43	311	46·32	103	15·34
Over 2,000cc	1,830	272·55	457	68·06	152	22·64
1 May 2004–30 April 2005						
Diesel engine						
Cylinder capacity: 2,000cc or less	865	128·82	216	32·17	72	10·72
Over 2,000cc	1,095	163·08	273	40·65	91	13·55
Any other type of engine						
Cylinder capacity: 1,400cc or less	930	138·51	232	34·55	77	11·46
Over 1,400cc up to 2,000cc	1,175	175·00	293	43·63	97	14·44
Over 2,000cc	1,730	257·65	432	64·34	144	21·44
1 May 2003–30 April 2004						
Diesel engine						
Cylinder capacity: 2,000cc or less	900	134·04	225	33·51	75	11·17
Over 2,000cc	1,135	169·04	283	42·14	94	14·00
Any other type of engine						
Cylinder capacity: 1,400cc or less	950	141·48	237	35·29	79	11·76
Over 1,400cc up to 2,000cc	1,200	178·72	300	44·68	100	14·89
Over 2,000cc	1,770	263·61	442	65·82	147	21·89
1 May 2002–30 April 2003						
Diesel engine						
Cylinder capacity: 2,000cc or less	850	126·59	212	31·57	70	10·42
Over 2,000cc	1,075	160·10	268	39·91	89	13·25
Any other type of engine						
Cylinder capacity: 1,400cc or less	905	134·78	226	33·65	75	11·17
Over 1,400cc up to 2,000cc	1,145	170·53	286	42·59	95	14·14
Over 2,000cc	1,690	251·70	422	62·85	140	20·85

HM Customs and Excise: VAT notices

New notices no longer carry a designation of the year of issue or revision, but this is retained here as a guide to the year of publication of the latest version. Several leaflets and notices contain Update inserts, published from time to time. The notices can be obtained from the Customs and Excise website at www.hmce.gov.uk/forms/catalogue/catalogue.htm.

(Cancelled leaflets have been deleted from the list.)

Notice		Date	Title
48		2002	**Extra-statutory concessions** (with updates 1 to 3)
60		2004	**The Intrastat general guide**
101		2004	**Deferring duty, VAT and other charges**
400		2002	**HM Customs and Excise Charter**
431		2003	**Visiting forces**
700		2002†	**The VAT guide** (with updates 1 and 2)
	700/1	2002	Should I be registered for VAT? (with supplement including update 2)
	700/2	2005	Group and divisional registration
	700/6	2003	Rulings
	700/7	2002	Business promotion schemes (with update 1)
	700/8	2005	Disclosure of VAT avoidance schemes
	700/9*	2002	Transfer of a business as a going concern (with update 1)
	700/11	2002	Cancelling your registration (with supplement and update 1)
	700/12*	2002	Filling in your VAT return (with update 1)
	700/14	2004	Video cassette films: rental and part-exchange
	700/15	2002	The ins and outs of VAT
	700/17	2002	Funded pension schemes
	700/18*	2002	Relief from VAT on bad debts
	700/21*	2002	Keeping records and accounts (with update 1)
	700/24	2003	Postage and delivery charges
	700/25	2002	Taxis and hire cars
	700/34	1994	Staff (with update 1)
	700/35	1997	Business gifts and samples
	700/41*	2002	Late registration penalty
	700/42*	2002	Misdeclaration penalty and repeated misdeclaration penalty
	700/43	2003	Default interest
	700/44	2002	Barristers and advocates
	700/45*	2002	How to correct VAT errors and make adjustments or claims (with update 1)
	700/46	2002	Agricultural flat rate scheme
	700/47	1993	Confidentiality in VAT matters (Tax advisers) – Statement of practice
	700/50*	2004	Default surcharge
	700/52*	2003	Notice of requirement to give security to Customs and Excise
	700/56	2002	Insolvency
	700/57	2004	Administrative agreements entered into with trade bodies
	700/58	2002	Treatment of VAT repayment returns and VAT repayment supplements (with update 1)
	700/60	2003	Payments on account
	700/62	2003	Self billing
	700/63	2003	Electronic invoicing
	700/64*	2002	Motoring expenses (with updates 1 and 2)
	700/65	2002	Business entertainment
	700/67	2002	Registration scheme for racehorse owners
701	701/1	2004	Charities (with update 1)
	701/2	2004	Welfare
	701/5	2002	Clubs and associations (with update 1)
	701/6	2003	Charity-funded equipment for medical, veterinary etc. uses (with supplement)
	701/7	2002	VAT reliefs for disabled people
	701/8	2003	Postage stamps and philatelic supplies
	701/9	2002	Derivatives and terminal markets
	701/10	2003	Zero-rating of books etc
	701/12*	2002	Disposals of antiques, works of art etc from historic houses
	701/13	2004	Gaming and amusement machines
	701/14	2002	Food
	701/15	2002	Animals and animal food
	701/16	2002	Water and sewage services (with update 1)
	701/18	2002	Women's sanitary protection products
	701/19*	2002	Fuel and power (with update 1)
	701/20	2004	Caravans and houseboats
	701/21*	2002	Gold
	701/21A	2004	Investment gold coins
	701/22	2002	Tools for the manufacture of goods for export
	701/23	2002	Protective equipment
	701/26	2004	Betting and gaming
	701/27*	2002	Bingo
	701/28	2003	Lotteries
	701/30	2002	Education and vocational training (with updates 1 and 2)
	701/31	2002	Health and care institutions
	701/32	2003	Burial, cremation and the commemoration of the dead
	701/35	2004	Youth clubs
	701/36	2002	Insurance (with update 1)
	701/38	2003	Seeds and plants

	701/39	2004	VAT liability law
	701/40	2002	Food processing services
	701/41*	2002	Sponsorship
	701/45	2002	Sport
	701/47	2003	Culture (with update 1)
	701/48	2002†	Corporate purchasing cards (with update 1)
	701/49	2002	Finance and securities
	701/57	2002	Health professionals
	701/58	2002	Charity advertising and goods connected with collecting donations (with update 1)
	701/59	2002	Motor vehicles for disabled people
702		2004	**Imports** (with update 1)
	702/7	2004	Import VAT relief for goods supplied onward to another country in the EC
703		1996†	**Exports and removal of goods from the UK** (with updates 1 and 2)
	703/1	2004†	Supply of freight containers for export or removal from the UK (with updates 1 and 2)
	703/2	2002†	Sailaway boats supplied for export outside the EC (with update 1)
704		2004†	**Retail exports**
	704/1	2003†	VAT refunds for travellers departing from the European Community
705		2004†	**Personal exports of new motor vehicles to destinations outside the EC**
705A		2004†	**Supplies of vehicles under the personal export scheme for removal from the EC**
706		2004	**Partial exemption**
	706/2	2002	Capital goods scheme
708		2002†	**Buildings and construction**
	708/6	2002	Energy-saving materials
709	709/1	2002†	Catering and take-away food
	709/3	2002	Hotels and holiday accommodation (with update 1)
	709/5	2004†	Tour operators' margin scheme
	709/6	2002	Travel agents and tour operators
714		2002	**Zero rating young children's clothing and footwear**
718		2003†	**Margin schemes for secondhand goods, works of art, antiques and collectors' items** (with updates 1 and 2)
719		2002	**VAT refunds for DIY builders and converters** (with update 1)
723		2003	**Refunds of VAT in the European Community for EC and non-EC businesses**
725		2002†	**The Single Market**
726		2003	**Joint and several liability in the supply of specified goods**
727		2002†	**Retail schemes**
	727/2	2002	Bespoke retail schemes
	727/3	2002†	How to work the point of sale scheme (with update 1)
	727/4	2002†	How to work the apportionment schemes (with update 1)
	727/5	2002†	How to work the direct calculation schemes (with update 1)
728		2003†	**New means of transport** (with update 1)
730		2004	**Civil evasion penalty investigations: Statement of practice**
731*		2004†	**Cash accounting**
732*		2003	**Annual accounting** (with update 1)
733*		2004	**VAT flat rate scheme for small businesses** (with update 1)
741		2002	**Place of supply of services** (with update 1)
742		2002†	**Land and property** (with updates 1 and 2)
	742/3	2002	Scottish land law terms
742A		2002	**Opting to tax land and buildings** (with updates 1 to 3)
744A		2002	**Passenger transport**
744B		2002	**Freight transport and associated services**
744C		1997	**Ships, aircraft and associated services**
744D		2002	**International services – zero-rating**
747		2003	**VAT notices having the force of law**
749		2002	**Local authorities and similar bodies**
915*		2002	**Assessments and time limits: statement of practice**
920		1999	**The single currency**
930		2002	**What if I don't pay?**
950		2003	Open Government: Requesting access to information held by Customs and Excise
989*		2002	**Visits by Customs and Excise officers**
990		2003	**Excise and Customs Appeals**
998		2003	**VAT refund scheme for national museums and galleries**
999		2005	**Catalogue of publications**
1000*		2002	**Complaints and putting things right**
CWL4		2001	Fund-raising events: exemption for charities and other qualifying bodies
MISC*	02/CD/26	2003	The Joint Shadow Economy teams – tackling the shadow economy
MISC	02/CD/018	2003	Getting things VAT FREE if you have a disability
MSB1		2002	Money laundering regulation – registration (with updates 1 and 2)
MSB2		2003	Anti-money laundering guide
	04/SB/001	2004	Simplifying VAT for small businesses
	04/SB/002	2004	Simplifying VAT for small businesses – flat rate scheme
	04/SB/003	2004	Simplifying VAT for small businesses – cash accounting
	04/SB/004	2004	Simplifying VAT for small businesses – annual accounting

Information sheets: available also at http://www.hmce.gov.uk

5/95	VAT – changes to tour operators' margin scheme from 1 January 1996
6/95	VAT – NHS dispensing doctors
1/96	VAT – filling in your EC sales list (Form VAT 101)
3/96	Tour operators' margin scheme – practical implementation of the airline charter option following the changes which came into effect on 1 January 1996
4/96	Tour operators' margin scheme – practical implementation of the agency option following the changes which came into effect on 1 January 1996
1/97	Tour operators' margin scheme – practical implementation of the 'trader to trader (wholesale) option' following the changes which came into effect on 1 January 1996
6/97	Drugs, medicine and aids for the handicapped – liability with effect from 1 January 1998
3/98	Local authorities and NHS joint stores depots
5/98	Local authorities: supplies to new unitary authorities under local government reorganisation (transitional arrangements)
6/98	Local authority pension funds VAT treatment and administrative concession
8/98	Charities – supply, repair and maintenance of relevant goods (including adapted motor vehicles) (with correction September 1998)
2/99	Local Authorities: agreement of section 33 recovery methods
3/99	VAT: new deal programme
6/99	Charities: liabilities of routine domestic tasks
8/99	Opticians: Apportionment of charges for supplies of spectacles and dispensing
9/99	Imported works of art, antiques and collectors' pieces: changes to the reduced rate of VAT
12/99	VAT on business cars – changes to take effect on 1 December 1999
2/00	Exports and removals: Conditions for zero-rating
3/00	Supplies through undisclosed agents: revised VAT treatment
2/01	Single or multiple supplies – how to decide
6/01	Changes to the VAT second-hand margin scheme
1/02	VAT civil evasion cases: a new approach to investigations – statement of practice
4/02	Budget 2002: partial exemption – standard method over-ride
1/03	Electronically supplied services and broadcasting services: new EU place of supply rules
2/03	Clarification of VAT treatment of services by financial advisers
3/03	Modernisation of face value vouchers
4/03	Electronically supplied services: a guide to interpretation
5/03	Electronically supplied services: evidence of customer location and status
6/03	Tribunal decision on VAT treatment of repossessed and voluntarily returned cars
7/03	Electronically supplied services: special scheme for non-EU businesses
10/03	Electronically supplied services: supplementary information on the special scheme for non-EU businesses
11/03	Electronic point of sales (EPOS) systems
12/03	Face value vouchers
14/03	New time of supply rules for on-going supplies
15/03	VAT treatment of share registration services
16/03	VAT invoicing changes
17/03	Changes to VAT flat rate scheme (FRS)
03/04	Electronically supplied services: EU enlargement
05/04	Claims made in the light of GMAC High Court decision: VAT treatment of returned cars and other goods
07/04	Eligibility rules for VAT grouping
09/04	Partial exemption: fair recovery of VAT on costs of financial supplies
10/04	Changes to place of supply of natural gas and electricity, and other related changes, which take effect from 1 January 2005

† Publications having legal or quasi-legal force.

* Also published in a Welsh language edition.

Internal guidance manuals

1	Disclosure of confidential taxpayer information
3	Supply and consideration
4	Place of supply
5	Taxable person
6	Business/non-business
7	VAT liability
8	Land and property
8A	Construction
9	Charities
10	Transfer of a going concern
11	Time of supply
12	Valuation
13	Input tax
14	Government and public bodies
15	Partial exemption
16	Single market
17	New means of transport
18	Import reliefs
19	Warehousing and free zones
20	Exports and removals of goods from the UK
21A	Personal exports – retail exports
21B	Personal exports – tax free sales of new motor vehicles for use before export
21C	Sailaway boat scheme
22	Bad debt relief
23	Schemes
24A	Traders' records
24B	Officers' powers
27	Civil penalties
28	Registration
28A	VAT trade classification
29	Reconsiderations and appeals
30	Isle of Man
31	Refunds to overseas business persons
32	Tax avoidance
33	VAT refunds: unjust enrichment, statutory interest, ex gratia payments
37	Control notes
38	Sanitary protection guidance

17.5% VAT (tax included in amount) – VAT fraction ⁷⁄₄₇

Am't	VAT incl. in Am't	Am't	VAT incl. in Am't	Am't	VAT incl. in Am't	Am't	VAT incl. in Am't	Am't	VAT incl. in Am't	Am't	VAT incl. in Am't
£ or p	£ or p	£ or p	£ or p	£ or p	£ or p	£ or p	£ or p	£ or p	£ or p	£ or p	£ or p
1	0·15	71	10·57	141	21·00	211	31·43	281	41·85	810	120·64
2	0·30	72	10·72	142	21·15	212	31·57	282	42·00	820	122·13
3	0·45	73	10·87	143	21·30	213	31·72	283	42·15	830	123·62
4	0·60	74	11·02	144	21·45	214	31·87	284	42·30	840	125·11
5	0·74	75	11·17	145	21·60	215	32·02	285	42·45	850	126·60
6	0·89	76	11·32	146	21·74	216	32·17	286	42·60	860	128·09
7	1·04	77	11·47	147	21·89	217	32·32	287	42·74	870	129·57
8	1·19	78	11·62	148	22·04	218	32·47	288	42·89	880	131·06
9	1·34	79	11·77	149	22·19	219	32·62	289	43·04	890	132·55
10	1·49	80	11·91	150	22·34	220	32·77	290	43·19	900	134·04
11	1·64	81	12·06	151	22·49	221	32·91	291	43·35	910	135·53
12	1·79	82	12·21	152	22·64	222	33·06	292	43·49	920	137·02
13	1·94	83	12·36	153	22·79	223	33·21	293	43·64	930	138·51
14	2·09	84	12·51	154	22·94	224	33·36	294	43·79	940	140·00
15	2·23	85	12·66	155	23·09	225	33·51	295	43·94	950	141·49
16	2·38	86	12·81	156	23·23	226	33·66	296	44·09	960	142·98
17	2·53	87	12·96	157	23·38	227	33·81	297	44·23	970	144·47
18	2·68	88	13·11	158	23·53	228	33·96	298	44·38	980	145·96
19	2·83	89	13·26	159	23·68	229	34·11	299	44·53	990	147·45
20	2·98	90	13·40	160	23·83	230	34·26	300	44·68	1,000	148·94
21	3·13	91	13·55	161	23·98	231	34·40	310	46·17	1,100	163·83
22	3·28	92	13·70	162	24·13	232	34·55	320	47·66	1,200	178·72
23	3·43	93	13·85	163	24·28	233	34·70	330	49·15	1,300	193·62
24	3·57	94	14·00	164	24·43	234	34·85	340	50·64	1,400	208·51
25	3·72	95	14·15	165	24·57	235	35·00	350	52·13	1,500	223·40
26	3·87	96	14·30	166	24·72	236	35·15	360	53·62	1,600	238·30
27	4·02	97	14·45	167	24·87	237	35·30	370	55·11	1,700	253·19
28	4·17	98	14·60	168	25·02	238	35·45	380	56·60	1,800	268·08
29	4·32	99	14·74	169	25·17	239	35·60	390	58·09	1,900	282·98
30	4·47	100	14·89	170	25·32	240	35·74	400	59·57	2,000	297·87
31	4·62	101	15·04	171	25·47	241	35·89	410	61·06	2,100	312·77
32	4·77	102	15·19	172	25·62	242	36·04	420	62·55	2,200	327·66
33	4·91	103	15·34	173	25·77	243	36·19	430	64·04	2,300	342·55
34	5·06	104	15·49	174	25·91	244	36·34	440	65·53	2,400	357·45
35	5·21	105	15·64	175	26·06	245	36·49	450	67·02	2,500	372·34
36	5·36	106	15·79	176	26·21	246	36·64	460	68·51	2,600	387·23
37	5·51	107	15·94	177	26·36	247	36·79	470	70·00	2,700	402·13
38	5·66	108	16·09	178	26·51	248	36·94	480	71·49	2,800	417·02
39	5·81	109	16·23	179	26·66	249	37·09	490	72·98	2,900	431·91
40	5·96	110	16·38	180	26·81	250	37·23	500	74·47	3,000	446·81
41	6·11	111	16·53	181	26·96	251	37·38	510	75·96	3,100	461·70
42	6·26	112	16·68	182	27·11	252	37·53	520	77·45	3,200	476·60
43	6·40	113	16·83	183	27·26	253	37·68	530	78·94	3,300	491·49
44	6·55	114	16·98	184	27·40	254	37·83	540	80·43	3,400	506·38
45	6·70	115	17·13	185	27·55	255	37·98	550	81·91	3,500	521·28
46	6·85	116	17·28	186	27·70	256	38·13	560	83·40	3,600	536·17
47	7·00	117	17·43	187	27·85	257	38·28	570	84·89	3,700	551·06
48	7·15	118	17·57	188	28·00	258	38·43	580	86·38	3,800	565·96
49	7·30	119	17·72	189	28·15	259	38·57	590	87·87	3,900	580·85
50	7·45	120	17·87	190	28·30	260	38·72	600	89·36	4,000	595·74
51	7·60	121	18·02	191	28·45	261	38·87	610	90·85	4,100	610·64
52	7·74	122	18·17	192	28·60	262	39·02	620	92·34	4,200	625·53
53	7·89	123	18·32	193	28·74	263	39·17	630	93·83	4,300	640·43
54	8·04	124	18·47	194	28·89	264	39·32	640	95·32	4,400	655·32
55	8·19	125	18·62	195	29·04	265	39·47	650	96·81	4,500	670·21
56	8·34	126	18·77	196	29·19	266	39·62	660	98·30	4,600	685·11
57	8·49	127	18·91	197	29·34	267	39·77	670	99·79	4,700	700·00
58	8·64	128	19·06	198	29·49	268	39·91	680	101·28	4,800	714·89
59	8·79	129	19·21	199	29·64	269	40·06	690	102·77	4,900	729·79
60	8·94	130	19·36	200	29·79	270	40·21	700	104·26	5,000	744·68
61	9·09	131	19·51	201	29·94	271	40·36	710	105·74	6,000	893·62
62	9·23	132	19·66	202	30·09	272	40·51	720	107·23	7,000	1,042·55
63	9·38	133	19·81	203	30·23	273	40·66	730	108·72	8,000	1,191·49
64	9·53	134	19·96	204	30·38	274	40·81	740	110·21	9,000	1,340·42
65	9·68	135	20·11	205	30·53	275	40·96	750	111·70	10,000	1,489·36
66	9·83	136	20·26	206	30·68	276	41·11	760	113·19	11,000	1,638·30
67	9·98	137	20·40	207	30·83	277	41·26	770	114·68	12,000	1,787·23
68	10·13	138	20·55	208	30·98	278	41·40	780	116·17	13,000	1,936·17
69	10·28	139	20·70	209	31·13	279	41·55	790	117·66	14,000	2,085·11
70	10·43	140	20·85	210	31·28	280	41·70	800	119·15	15,000	2,234·04

Other taxes

Aggregates Levy

(FA 2001 ss 16–49, Schs 4–10; SI 2004/1959)

Levy on commercial exploitation of aggregates including rock, gravel or sand together with any other substance incorporated or naturally occurring with it. Applies to all aggregate (not recycled) extracted in the UK or territorial waters unless exempt. It does not apply to quarried or mined products such as clay, shale, slate, metal and metal ores, gemstones, semi-precious gemstones and industrial minerals. It is charged at 20% of the full rate for aggregate processed in Northern Ireland until 31.3.2011.

From 1 April 2002	£1.60 per tonne

Climate change levy

(FA 2000 s 30, Sch 6)

Levy on supply for industrial or commercial purposes of energy, from 1 April 2001, in the form of electricity, gas, petroleum and hydrocarbon gas supplied in a liquid state, coal and lignite, coke and semi-coke of coal or lignite and petroleum coke.

Taxable commodity supplied	Rate[1]
Electricity	0.43p per kilowatt hour
Gas supplied by a gas utility or any gas supplied in a gaseous state that is of a kind supplied by a gas utility	0.15p per kilowatt hour
Any petroleum gas, or other gaseous hydrocarbon supplied in a liquid state	0.96p per kilogram
Any other taxable commodity	1.17p per kilogram

[1] Rate at which payable if supply is neither a half-rate supply nor a reduced-rate supply. The levy is charged at half the full rate for horticultural producers and at 20% of the full rate for energy intensive users.

Insurance premium tax

(FA 1994 ss 48–74, Schs 6A, 7, 7A)

Insurance Premium Tax (IPT) is a tax on premiums received under insurance contracts other than those which are specifically exempt.

	Standard rate	Higher rate[1]
From 1.7.99	5%	17.5%
1.4.97 – 30.6.99	4%	17.5%
1.10.94 – 30.3.97	2.5%	–

[1] The higher rate applies to sales of motor cars, light vans and motorcycles, electrical or mechanical domestic appliances, and travel insurance.

Landfill tax

(FA 1996 ss 39–71, 197, Sch 5; SI 1996/1527; SI 1996/1528)

Tax on disposal of waste imposed on operators of landfill sites calculated by reference to the weight and type of waste deposited in the site. Exemption applies to mining and quarrying waste, dredging waste, pet cemeteries, waste from reclamation of contaminated land and inert waste used to restore licensed landfill sites.

Period	Active waste per tonne	Inert waste per tonne	Maximum credit[1]
1.4.05–31.3.06	£18	£2	6%
1.4.04–31.3.05	£15	£2	6.8%
1.4.03–31.3.04	£14	£2	6.5%
1.4.02–31.3.03	£13	£2	20%
1.4.01–31.3.02	£12	£2	20%
1.4.2000–31.3.01	£11	£2	20%

[1] Tax credits are available to operators who make donations to environmental trusts of 90% of the donation to the maximum percentage above of the tax payable in a 12-month period.

INDEX

A

Accounts, inheritance tax
    due dates   86
    excepted estates   86
Additional relief for children   64
Addresses, approval and clearance applications   32
Advance corporation tax
    due date   12
    interest on overdue tax   13
    rates   59
Age allowance   64
Aggregates levy   109
Agricultural buildings allowances   60
Agricultural property relief   88
Annual accounting scheme, VAT   99
Annual exemption
    capital gains tax   37
    inheritance tax   88
Approval applications, addresses   32
Attendance allowance   89, 90
Average exchange rates   3
Advisory fuel rates   69
Authorised mileage rates   69

B

Basic rate   63
Basis of assessment
    employment income   85
    other income   9
Beneficial loans to employees   76
Benefits, social security   89
Bereavement benefits   90
Blind person's allowance   64
Bus services   67
Business expansion scheme   74
Business property relief   88

C

Capital allowances
    agricultural buildings   60
    claims, time limits   26
    conversions into flats over shops, etc   60
    dredging   60
    elections, time limits   26
    films   60
    flat conversions   60
    industrial buildings   60
    know-how   60
    machinery and plant   61
    mines and oil wells   62
    patent rights   62
    rates   60
    research and development   62
    scientific research   62
Capital gains tax
    annual exemption   37, 42
    chattel exemption   37, 42
    claims, time limits   28
    due date   11
    elections, time limits   28
    exemptions   42
    gilt-edged securities   41
    hold-over relief for gifts   42
    indexation allowance   38, 44
    interest on overdue tax   12, 13
    leases   40
    offences, penalties   18
    personal representatives   43
    rates   37
    reliefs   42
    retail price index   58
    retirement relief   37
    roll-over relief   43
    returns, penalties   18
    share indentification rules   38
    taper relief   39
    trustees   43
Capital goods scheme, VAT   104
Carer's allowance   89, 90
Cars
    capital allowances   62, 69
    capital gains exemption   42
    fuel for private use
        taxable benefit   68
        VAT   104
    hired, Schedule D deduction   69
    private use   66
Cash accounting scheme, VAT   99
Certificates of tax deposit   10
Charities
    capital gains exemption   42

    covenanted donations to   70
    gift aid   70
    gifts in kind   70
    gifts to, inheritance tax relief   89
    payroll giving scheme   70
    tax return giving   70
Chattels, capital gains exemption   37
Child benefit   89, 90
Child tax credit   84, 89
Claims, time limits
    capital allowances   26
    capital gains tax   28
    corporation tax only   25
    income tax only   23
    Income tax and corporation tax   26
    Inheritance tax   29
Clearance applications, addresses   32
Climate change levy   109
Community investment tax credit   75
Company share option plans   83
Compensation, capital gains exemption   42
Computer equipment   76
Corporation tax
    claims, time limits   25
    corporate venturing scheme   59
    due date   11
    elections, time limits   25
    interest on overdue tax   12, 13
    interest on overpaid tax   16, 17
    marginal relief   59
    offences, penalties   18
    rates   59
    research and development expenditure   59
    returns, penalties   18
Corporate venturing scheme   59
Covenanted payments to charity   70
Customs & Excise publications   105
Cycles and cycle safety equipment   67

D

Deed of covenant, payments under   70
Default interest
    direct taxes   12, 13
    VAT   103
Default surcharge   102
Department of Social Security publications   95
Deregistration limits, VAT   100
Disability living allowance   89, 90
Disabled employees, equipment   76
Dividends   63
Double taxation agreements
    air transport profits   9
    capital taxes   9
    income and capital gains   7
    shipping profits   9
Dredging allowances   60
Due dates of tax   11

E

Elections, time limits
    capital allowances   26
    capital gains tax   28
    corporation tax only   25
    income tax only   23
    Income tax and corporation tax   26
    Inheritance tax   29
Employees
    beneficial loans to   76
    bus services for   67
    business travel, tax-free allowances   67, 69
    car benefits   66
    cycles and cycle safety equipment   67, 76
    disabled, equipment   76
    expenses, fixed rate allowances   71
    fuel benefits   68
    loan of computer equipment   76
    loan benefits   76
    mileage rates   69
    mobile phone benefit   76
    parking facilities for   67
    relocation benefits   77
    share schemes   81
    van benefits   67
Employment income
    basis of assessment   85
    due dates of tax   11
Enterprise investment scheme
    capital gains exemption   42
    income tax relief   73
Enterprise management incentives   81

Enterprise zones
    designated areas 62
    industrial buildings allowances 60
Excepted estates, inheritance tax 86
Excepted transfers 86
Exchange rates
    average 3
    year end 6
Executive share option schemes 83
Exempt supplies, VAT 103
Expensive cars: restricted allowances 69
Explanatory pamphlets
    Customs & Excise 105
    Inland Revenue 33
    National Insurance 95

F

Fixed rate expenses 71
Flat rate schemes, VAT 100
Foreign exchange rates
    average 3
    year end 6
Foreign income
    Basis of assessment 9
    Employment income 85
Foreign service
    Employment income relief 85
    termination payment for 85
FOTRA securities 9
Fuel for private use
    national insurance contributions 94
    taxable charge 68
    VAT 103
Futures exchanges, recognised 31

G

Gilt-edged securities 41
Gift aid 70
Gifts in kind 70
Grossing up table: 17.5% 108
Guardian's allowance 90

H

Higher rate tax 63
    interest on overdue tax 12, 13
    table of rates 63
Hired cars, Schedule D deduction 69
Hold-over relief for gifts 42
Hotels, capital allowances 60

I

Incapacity benefit 89, 90
Income tax
    calendar, 2004–05 inside front cover
    claims, time limits 23
    due dates 11
    elections, time limits 23
    interest on overdue tax 12, 13
    lease premiums 40
    offences, penalties 18
    personal allowances 64
    rates 63
    returns, penalties 18
    table of reliefs 64
Indexation allowance 33, 44
Individual savings accounts 75
Industrial buildings allowances
    enterprise zones 62
    rates 60
Industrial death benefit 89, 90
Inheritance tax
    agricultural property relief 88
    annual exemption 88
    business property relief 88
    charitable gifts, exemption 88
    claims, time limits 29
    due dates for accounts 86
    due dates for tax 12
    elections, time limits 29
    excepted transfers estates and settlements 86
    interest on overdue tax 12, 14
    marriage gifts, exemption 88
    penalties 20
    political parties, gifts exemption 88
    quick succession relief 88
    rates 87
    small gifts exemption 88
    tapering relief 88
Inland Revenue publications 33
Insurance premium tax 109
Insurance premiums, life 64

Interest rates
    certificates of tax deposit 10
    default, VAT 102
    direct taxes 13, 15
    official, beneficial loans 76
    overpaid tax 15, 103
    reckonable dates 12
    repayment supplement 15
    stamp duties 13, 15, 98
    unpaid tax 13, 103
    VAT 103
Invalid care allowance 89, 90
Invalidity allowance 89, 90
Investment reliefs
    business expansion scheme 74
    community investment tax credit 75
    enterprise investment scheme 73
    individual savings accounts 75
    personal equity plans 75
    tax-exempt special savings accounts 75
    urban regeneration companies 73
    venture capital trusts 74

K

Know-how, capital allowances 60

L

Landfill tax 109
Leaflets
    Customs & Excise 105
    Inland Revenue 33
    National Insurance 96
Leases
    depreciation table 40
    premiums
        capital gains tax 40
        income tax 40
        stamp duties 96, 97
Life assurance premium relief 64
Loan to employee, beneficial interest 76
Lower rate of tax 63

M

Machinery and plant allowances 61
    cars 69
    rates 61
Maintenance payments 76
Marginal relief, corporation tax 59
Marriage gifts, inheritance tax relief 88
Married couple's allowance 64
Maternity allowance 89, 90
Maternity pay, statutory 89
Mileage rates 69
Mines and oil wells, capital allowances 62
Misdeclarations, VAT 102
Mobile telephone, employee benefit 76
Mortgage interest relief 64
Motorcycles 69

N

National insurance and State benefits 89
National insurance contributions
    benefits subject to Class 1 and 1A 94
    employers' contributions on benefits 94
    interest on overdue contributions 12, 13
    leaflets 95
    rates
        Class 1, 2, 3, 4 91
        Class 1A 95
        Class 4 64, 91
    weekly and monthly thresholds 77
National Savings Bank interest 77
Nazi persecution, pensions to victims 9
Non-domiciled individuals
    employment income 85
    other income 9
    spouses, inheritance tax 88
Non-residents
    employment income 85
    other income 9

O

Offences
    income and capital gains tax 18
    corporation tax 18
Official rate of interest, employee loans 76
One parent benefit 89
Overseas income, basis of assessment
    employment income 85
    other income 9
Overseas service
    employment income relief 85
    termination payment 85

P

Parking facilities	67
Partial exemption, VAT	103
Patent rights, capital allowances	62
PAYE	
codes	77
interest on overdue tax	12, 13
penalties	19
weekly and monthly thresholds	77
Pay and file	
due date of tax	11
interest on overpaid tax	16
interest on unpaid tax	12, 13
penalties connected with returns	18
Payroll giving scheme	70
Penalties	
corporation tax returns	18
inheritance tax	20
offences under the Tax Acts	19
PAYE returns	19
personal tax returns	18
special information returns	20
stamp taxes	98
standard scale	22
statutory maximum	22
VAT	101
Pension provision	
from 6 April 2006	78
personal pension schemes	79
retirement annuities	80
to 5 April 2005	79, 80
Personal allowances	64
Personal equity plans	75
Personal pension schemes	79
contributions limit	79
earnings cap	79
permitted retirement age	80
Personal representatives	43
Plant and machinery allowances	
cars	61, 69
rates	61
Political parties, gifts to	88
Premiums on leases	
capital gains tax	40
income tax	40
stamp taxes	96, 97
Profit sharing schemes, approved	83
Property income lease premiums	40

Q

Qualifying corporate bonds	42
Quick succession relief	88

R

Rates of tax	
advance corporation tax	59
capital gains tax	37
corporation tax	59
income tax	63
inheritance tax	86
other taxes	109
stamp taxes	96
VAT	100
Reckonable dates, interest	12
Recognised clearing houses	31
Recognised futures exchanges	31
Recognised investment exchanges	31
Recognised stock exchanges	30
Reduced rate supplies, VAT	103
Registration limits, VAT	99
Reliefs (capital gains)	42
Relocation benefits and expenses	77
Remission of tax	14
Rent-a-room scheme	77
Rent, stamp duties	96, 97
Repayment supplement	15
Research and development	59, 62
Retail prices index	58
Retirement annuities contracts	80
permitted retirement age	80
premiums limit	80
Retirement pensions	90
Retirement relief	37
Roll-over relief	43

S

Save as you earn (SAYE) share option schemes	82
Scientific research allowances	62
Securities	
gilt-edged	41
tax-free for non-residents	9
Share incentive plans	81

Share identification rules	38
Share schemes	81
Sick pay, statutory	89
Small companies' rate	59
Small gifts relief	88
Social security benefits	
non-taxable	89, 90
taxable	89, 90
Stamp taxes	
conveyances or transfers	96
disadvantaged areas	97
exemptions	97
fixed	97
interest	98
land transactions	96
leases	96, 97
penalties	98
premiums	96, 97
rates	96
reliefs	97
rent	96, 97
repayment supplement	98
rounding	96
stamp duty land tax	96
stamp duty reserve tax	97
stock transfers	96
Stakeholder pensions	79
Standard scale of penalties	22
Statutory adoption pay	89
Statutory maternity pay	89
Statutory maximum penalty	22
Statutory paternity pay	89
Statutory sick pay	89
Stock exchanges, recognised	30

T

Taper relief, capital gains tax	39
Tapering relief, inheritance tax	88
Tax credits	84
Tax-exempt special savings accounts	75
Tax year 2004–05, calendar	inside front cover
Telephone, mobile	76
Termination payments, exemptions	85
Toll roads, capital allowances	60
Trustees	
capital gains annual exempt amount	37
expenses allowable for CGT	43
Trusts	
dividend rate	63
rate applicable for	63

U

Urban regeneration companies	73

V

Van, employee benefit	67
VAT	
17·5% grossing-up table	108
annual accounting scheme	99
capital goods scheme	104
car fuel for private use	104
cash accounting scheme	99
default interest	103
default surcharge	102
deregistration limits	100
evasion	102
exempt supplies	103
failure to notify liability	102
flat rate schemes	100
interest on overpaid tax	103
internal guidance manuals	107
misdeclarations	102
notices and leaflets	105
partial exemption	104
penalties	102
rates	100
reduced rate supplies	103
registration limits	99
zero-rated supplies	103
Venture capital trusts	
capital gains exemptions	42
income tax reliefs	74

W

Widowed parent's allowance	90
Widow's payment	90
Working tax credit	84, 89
Workshops, capital allowances	60

Z

Zero-rated supplies	103